Stanley Gibbons Cat

COMMONWEALTH

PLATE AND CYLINDER
VARIETIES
1952–1980

For use with the Elizabethan Specialised
Stamp Catalogue

STANLEY GIBBONS PUBLICATIONS LTD
391 STRAND LONDON WC2R 0LX

Retail Price in UK £6·50

By Appointment to H.M. the Queen
Stanley Gibbons Ltd., London
Philatelists

© Stanley Gibbons Publications Ltd., 1981

ISSN 0260–6283   ISBN 0 85259 326 0

1st edition—April 1981

Item No. 2826

**Typeset by CCC, printed and bound in Great Britain by
William Clowes (Beccles) Limited, Beccles and London**

PREFACE

We take pleasure in presenting the First Edition of this *Commonwealth Varieties Catalogue*. Following our announcement in the 1980 edition of the *Elizabethan* that this volume was in preparation we have had many enquiries for it, and we know from our correspondence that the varieties we list are of considerable interest to numerous collectors. We have taken the opportunity of carrying forward from the (1979) *Elizabethan* all those varieties designated with "V" numbers, adding to them the discoveries made since that book went to press.

We believe the broad separation of major and minor varieties into the new scheme of two companion volumes will provide the collecting public with much more convenient lists. No set schedule for the new editions of the *Commonwealth Varieties Catalogue* has yet been fixed because of the nature of the items covered, but the *Elizabethan* parent volume will continue to appear annually as hitherto.

Acknowledgements. We wish to give particular thanks to the following for their help with this edition: A. N. Cartmell (for Falkland Is.); D. Gronbeck-Jones (Canada); Dr. S. P. Gupta (India); Hong Kong Study Circle; David Hume (Pitcairn Is.); T. C. Masters (Malaysia); Michael Milos (Canada); W. Suart (G.B. commemoratives); and D. E. Tichborne (Australia).

J.N.
R.H.O.

PRICES

Prices quoted in this Catalogue are the selling prices of Stanley Gibbons Ltd. at the time the book went to press. All prices are subject to change without prior notice and no guarantee is given to supply all stamps priced.

Prices are for unmounted mint single stamps, unless otherwise stated. Prices are not quoted for used stamps, since varieties tend not to be collected in this condition.

When ordered in pairs or positional blocks the extra stamps are charged at the prices of normals, as shown in the *Elizabethan Catalogue*. Exceptionally, booklet panes and coil strips which contain varieties are priced here as complete items containing the variety mentioned.

ILLUSTRATIONS

We make the enlarged illustrations of varieties from the stamps themselves, as we believe this gives greater accuracy than artists' drawings. It is unlikely that we should list a variety that does not show up well in photographic enlargement, as we consider it will likewise be difficult to perceive in its original, unenlarged state.

UNLISTED ITEMS

The editor is always interested in examining unlisted varieties with a view to adding them to future editions. As a general rule he must see the actual stamps before they can be considered for listing: photographs or photocopies are insufficient evidence. Please give as much information as known about the history of the variety—where it was acquired, etc.—and the position in the sheet if this is available.

Submissions should be in writing to the Catalogue Editor, Stanley Gibbons Publications Ltd., 391 Strand, London WC2R 0LX. Correspondents are asked to include the cost of postage for return of stamps, plus registration fee if required. Where information is solicited purely for the benefit of the enquirer, the editor regrets he cannot reply if postage (or reply coupons) are not enclosed.

CURRENT EDITIONS

Elizabethan Specialised Stamp Catalogue 1981. 17th edition, published 21 November 1980. 1360 pages. ISBN 0 85259 276 0. Item No. 287. Price £11·95.

Philatelic Terms Illustrated, by Russell Bennett and James Watson. 2nd edition, reprinted 1979. 192 pages. ISBN 0 85259 895 5. Item No. 2740. Price £2·50.

Stamp Varieties Explained, by James Watson. Published 1978. 32 pages. ISBN 0 85259 041 5. Item No. 2758. Price 95p.

Postage and packing extra if ordered direct from Stanley Gibbons.

SCOPE OF CATALOGUES

The *Elizabethan Specialised Stamp Catalogue*—and hence the present *Commonwealth Varieties Catalogue*—covers postage stamps issued since the accession (on 6 February 1952) of Her Majesty Queen Elizabeth II. It includes Great Britain, the British Commonwealth and post-independence issues of Ireland, Pakistan and South Africa.

In more detail, the allocation of errors, varieties and flaws to the above two Catalogues is best explained by a list of main categories:

Elizabethan Catalogue

Error or Variety	*Cat. No. of example*
Major changes in perforation	Sierra Leone 214a
Imperforates (as pairs)	Hong Kong 178a
Imperf. betweens (as pairs)	Malayan Postal Union D15ba
Prominent shades	British Honduras 181Ec
Inverted centres/vignettes	K.U.T. 167a
Transposed frames/vignettes	Falkland Is. 216a
Inverted surcharges/overprints	Basutoland 60a
Missing surcharges/overprints	Guyana 393Aa
Errors of surcharge/overprint	Pakistan 124a
Double etc. surcharge/overprint	Cyprus 193a
Surcharge double, one inverted	St. Vincent 380c
Changes in paper	Canada 579Ew
Errors of colour	Jersey 28a
Missing colours	Mauritius 317Ea
Missing denominations, etc.	Northern Rhodesia 78Ea
Missing heads	Pitcairn Is. 102a
Inverted watermarks	Barbados 327Ei
Sideways watermarks	Pakistan 208Ea
Sideways inverted watermarks	South Africa 202Ei
Wrong watermarks	Antigua 381a
Missing embossing	G.B. 895Ee
Printed on the gummed side	Pakistan 131Ea
Changes in gum	Rhodesia 399Ea
Blanket offsets	St. Vincent 479Eb
Changes in printing process	Antigua 373a
Changes in photogravure screen	K.U.T. 184Ea
Re-engraved/redrawn designs	K.U.T. 169a

Please note items outside the scope and hence not listed:

Colours partially omitted—we confine the listing to stamps which have colours completely omitted.

Misplaced or double perforations—do not qualify, nor do issues imperforate only between stamp and margin ("fantails").

Phosphor band varieties—varieties such as double or inverted bands, bands omitted, misplaced or printed on the back are not listed.

Commonwealth Varieties Catalogue

The types of item that we list are: Flaws (marks, spots, dots, blobs, smudges, breaks, nicks, patches, disturbances, malformations, etc.); retouches; re-entries; repairs; weak entries/frames; cracked plates; scratches; significant variations in surcharge/overprint spacings; minor varieties in surcharges/overprints, such as broken letters, thick and thin letters, etc.; damage and deformations in typographic printing.

See also "Quotation of sheet positions", *overleaf*.

Please note items outside the scope and hence not listed:

Doctor-blade flaws. Faulty wiping of the ink on the printing cylinder can cause doctor-blade flaws. These appear as white or coloured lines of varying width, generally extending vertically over several stamps. They are not constant and so are not listable.

Paper creases. Flaws can result from printing on creased paper or from some transient object interposing between cylinder and paper at time of printing. Similarly, if a sheet becomes folded in the press, part of the print will appear on the back. We do not list such varieties.

Colour shifts. Particularly common in modern multicolour issues are shifts in colour caused by faulty registration. Although often quite startling, colour shifts of any magnitude do not qualify for listing.

Litho flaws. In modern litho printing numerous flecks of colour or white (inkless) ring flaws will be found, often arising from dust settling on the plate. They affect only part of a printing and so are regarded as non-constant and unlistable.

Litho shades. Modern litho printing is prone to marked variations in shade, often during the same printing and even in the same sheet. Most of these litho shades are ignored.

CATALOGUE NUMBERS

The numbers and descriptions used in this Catalogue are from the *Elizabethan Catalogue*. At the head of each list will be found a cross-reference printed in square brackets that identifies the inclusive *Elizabethan Catalogue* numbers of the relevant set, e.g. [S.G. 515E/31].

When the *Elizabethan* was launched in 1965 a decision was taken to retain the basic Catalogue numbers as used in the *Part 1 (British Commonwealth) Catalogue*. A suffix "E" (for Elizabethan) was added to those basic numbers wherever a *Part 1* number was further elaborated. Hence in Australia we have:

Part 1	Elizabethan
468*b* 7c.	468*b*E 7c.
c. Green (leaves) omitted	c. Green (leaves) omitted
	Ew. White fluorescent paper

For clarity in the listing, the newly introduced variety (Ew. White fluorescent paper) is also preceded by "E" and the Catalogue number is correctly quoted as 468*b*Ew.

The numbers in the present *Commonwealth Varieties Catalogue* have each of the listed varieties identified with a "V" (for Variety) number and this cross-refers to an accompanying enlarged illustration. Thus, for the Australian stamp mentioned above, the Catalogue listing is:

> 468*b*E 7c. – V97. Broken "DE"
> – V98. Broken "RA"
> Ew. White fluorescent paper
> – V97. Broken "DE"
> – V98. Broken "RA"

showing that the V97 and V98 varieties occur both on the basic stamp and on the stamp on fluorescent paper.

The various items are then quoted as: 468*b*E V97, etc., and 468*b*Ew V97, etc. In each separate country the "V" numbers are allocated in numerical sequence (V1, V2, V3, . . .) according to when they were discovered and added to the listing. For this reason the sequences are not chronological with dates of issue of stamps.

QUOTATION OF SHEET POSITIONS

To qualify for listing any variety or flaw must be *constant* and so occur throughout the entire printing run, although instances can happen where the flaw gradually corrects itself or—having been noticed—it is corrected by the printer. Before constant varieties and flaws can be listed their sheet position must be known.

The notation for position is based on counting the rows downwards and the stamps across the row. Hence in this Catalogue R.10/1 = row 10, stamp 1 (the first stamp in the tenth row down); the alternative designation for this position as used in "Through the Magnifying Glass" (Gibbons *Stamp Monthly*) is R10, S1 = row 10, stamp 1.

The position is quoted in the description of varieties accompanying the illustrations. It is quite usual in philately for flaws to be given a descriptive name, e.g. "butterfly" flaw, "tadpole" flaw.

In listing positions certain other numbers are needed on occasion, as follows.

Booklet numbers. The Catalogue numbers (e.g. E1, E2, . . .) are from the *Elizabethan.*

Roll numbers. The roll number is the number printed on the outer wrapper of the coil which corresponds to the row in the sheet before reeling.

Plate numbers. Plates on a flat-bed press are usually identified by numerals and/or letters in the margins at the foot or sides, termed "plate numbers". This often extends to identifying the individual panes making up the sheet.

Cylinder numbers. These are the numerals and/or letters in the margins identifying the cylinders used in rotary printing, each colour having its own cylinder number/letter. British stamps printed in two panes distinguish the halves by the presence or absence of a dot after the cylinder number.

ADDRESSES

Head Office:	Stanley Gibbons Ltd., 391 Strand, London WC2R 0LX Telephone: 01-836 8444
Shop Department:	391 Strand, London W.C.2 Open Monday–Friday 9 a.m. to 5.30 p.m. and Saturday 9.30 a.m. to 12.30 p.m.
Specialist and Rare Stamp Departments:	Romano House, 399 Strand, London W.C.2 Open Monday–Friday 9 a.m. to 5.30 p.m. and Saturday by appointment only

Cover Illustrations

Front cover: Great Britain 1980 Famous Authoresses. No. 1125 V529: Variety "missing p" (*see* page 40).

Back cover: Malta 1964 Christmas. No. 329 V19: Patch on cloak (*see* page 143).

Great Britain
Definitives

In the case of Great Britain only, we have listed varieties of definitives and special stamps separately.

1952–54. Wmk Tudor Crown.   [S. G. 515E/31]

V176

½d. White dot on foot of "A". Occurs in vertical delivery coils (Roll No. 3).

V177

V32

½d. White spot on "d" of "½d." at right. Occurs in vertical delivery coils (Roll No. 5).

1d. White flaw on top shamrock, later retouched. Occurs on Cyl 2 no dot R. 18/2 and also in 1s. "D" Experimental booklets (Booklets E1/2).

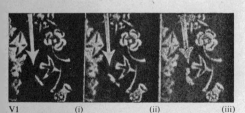

V1   (i)   (ii)   (iii)

1½d. "Butterfly" flaw. This occurs in various stages on R. 19/1 on Cyl 6 dot on No. 517 and on Cyl 14 dot and 15 dot on No. 542, the latter being the clearest example. *Prices are for cylinder blocks of 6.*

V2

1½d. Flaw on end of daffodil stem (Cyl 9 dot)R. 18/1). *Price is for cylinder block of 6.* Also found in 1s. "D" Experimental booklets (Booklets E1/2).

V33

1½d. White flaw over and right of "O" of "POSTAGE". Occurs in sideways delivery coils (Roll No. 2).

V34

1½d. White dot between thistle and rose at right. Occurs in sideways delivery coils (Roll No. 10).

V182

1½d. White flaw joins right lower rose to stem of thistle (Cyl 13 dot R. 19/1).

Normal   V3

V4

2d. Extra leg to "R" of "REVENUE". Occurs on coil with wmk sideways (Roll No. 2).

V185

V102

1½d. Extra white dot below "d" at left (Cyl 13 dot R. 17/10).

V209

1½d. White flaw on daffodil at right. Occurs in sideways delivery coils (Roll No. 8).

2d. Retouched left "2" leaving "d" nearer to "2" and fatter. Occurs on coil with wmk sideways (Roll No. 5).

V184

2d. White flaw on upper left rose appears as an extra petal (Cyl 3 no dot R. 4/8).

V186

2d. V185/6a occur on dot cylinders R. 17/6

V185. White spot on stem of lowest thistle is known as the " Tadpole " flaw (Cyl 4 on Nos. 518, 543 and Cyls 10, 11 on No. 543*b*).

V186. " Tadpole " flaw is now retouched and appears as a dark flaw (Cyl 3 on No. 518; Cyls 3, 6, 7 on No. 543; Cyls 6, 7, 8, 12, 13, 15 on No. 543*b*); and Cyls 15 onwards on No. 573).

V185a. This comprises the " Tadpole " variety and an additional white flaw to left of the adjoining shamrock (Cyl 9 on No. 543 and Cyls 9, 12 on No. 543*b*). On the first printing of Cyl 12 the shamrock flaw is larger but on later printings both flaws appear retouched (V186).

V186a. This is a fourth state which combines the retouched " Tadpole " flaw with the shamrock flaw (Cyl 14, smaller flaw, Cyl 16, larger flaw, on No. 543*b*).

2½d. Broken value circle at right (Cyl 8 no dot R. 20/2).

V62

V188

2½d. White flaw on tail of large "R". Occurs in booklets in position 1 in pane of 6.

V189

2½d. White triangular-shaped flaw in jewels. Occurs in booklets in position 5 in pane of 6.

V211

2½d. Bulge to frame at right. Occurs on sideways delivery coils (Roll No. 7). A second state showing vertical line only is known on Crowns watermark.

V92

4d. Coloured dot below "R" which was later touched out (Cyl 1 no dot R. 10/8).

V193

5d. Dark spot by top of " E " of " POSTAGE " (multi-positive flaw, no dot cyls R. 4/8).

V194

5d. Dark spot on daffodil at lower left (multipositive flaw no dot cyls R. 10/12).

V195

5d. Large retouch on Queen's neck below chin (Cyl 1 dot R. 2/12).

V5

9d. Frame broken at upper right and shading below it missing (Cyl No. 1 no dot R. 8/6). On S.G. 582 it was later retouched. A very similar variety occurs on the same part of the stamp but on a different cylinder (Cyl 2 not dot R. 11/11). Known only on Nos. 582 and 617*c* (see V197).

V200

1s.3d. Triangular-shaped white flaw in Queen's hair (Cyl 1 dot R. 2/9).

V201

1s.6d. White flaw in Queen's hair below diadem (Cyl 1 dot R. 20/1).

V202

1s.6d. White flaw in Queen's hair opposite "N" of "REVENUE" (Cyl 1 dot R. 20/2).

515E	½d. – V176. "A" flaw	...		...	...	3·50
	– V177. Spot on "d"		...	...	...	3·50
516E	1d. – V32. Flaw on shamrock	...		...	...	8·00
517E	1½d. – V1. "Butterfly" flaw (i)		...		...	£120
	– V2. Flaw on daffodil stem		...		...	8·00
	– V102. Extra dot	...		...	...	4·50
	– V182. Rose and thistle joined at right			...		9·00
	a. Wmk sideways					
	– a V33. Flaw over "O"		...	...	...	4·00
	– a V34. Dot over rose		...	...	...	4·00
	– a V209. Daffodil flaw		...	...	...	4·00
518E	2d. – V184. Rose petal flaw		...	...	...	14·00
	– V185. "Tadpole" flaw		...	...	...	15·00
	– V186. Do. Retouched		...	...	...	15·00
	a. Wmk sideways					
	– a V3. Retouched "2"		...	...	...	4·50
	– a V4. Extra leg to "R"		...	...	...	4·50

519E 2½d.(I). – V62. Broken value circle ... ... 6·00
    a. Wmk sideways (I)
      – a V211. Frame retouch ... ... 6·00
    b. Type II
      – b V188. "R" flaw ... ... 4·00
      – b V189. Jewels flaw ... ... 4·00
521 4d. – V92. Dotted "R" ... ... 15·00
522 5d. – V193. Spot by "E" ... ... 5·00
      – V194. Spot on daffodil ... ... 5·00
      – V195. Neck retouch ... ... 5·00
526 9d. – V5. Frame break ... ... 42·00
530 1s.3d. – V200. White flaw in Queen's hair ... 15·00
531 1s.6d. – V201. White flaw in Queen's hair below
      diadem ... ... 40·00
      – V202. White flaw in Queen's hair opposite
      "N" ... ... 40·00

1955–58. *Castles.* Wmk St. Edward's Crown.   [S. G. 536/9]

V206

5s. Major re-entry showing doubling of vertical lines of background above the diadem, and in the diadem along the left edge of the frontal cross, both sides of the side cross and the diagonals R. 8/1).

V8

10s. Weak entry to right of lower pane giving ragged appearance (R. 1/2).

V68

10s. Weak frame at right (R. 4/1). Other weak frames have been found on this stamp in different positions but always on the right-hand side of the stamp.

537 5s. – V206. Major re-entry £130
538 10s. *ultramarine*
    – V8. Weak entry £160
    a. *Dull ultramarine*
    – V68. Weak frame £650

1955–58. Wmk St. Edward's Crown.   [S. G. 540E/56]

V47

½d. White flaw on shamrock at upper right. Occurs in vertical delivery coils (Roll No. 11).

V208

½d. White flaw on "R". Occurs in vertical delivery coils (Roll No. 11).

V10

1d. Horizontal white flaw between right-hand shamrock and diadem (Cyl 7 dot R. 1/6).

V273

1d. White spot on " d ". Occurs in booklets on position 1 or 4 in pane of 6.

V274

1d. White flaw by lower rose. Occurs in booklets on position 2 or 5 in pane of 6.

V9

1½d. White spot between rose and shamrock at lower right (Cyl 15 no dot R. 20/3). Later retouched on Crowns wmk. *Prices are for cylinder blocks of 9.*

V103

1½d. Two white dots extending upwards from shamrock at left appearing as rabbit's ears. Occurs in booklets in position 2 or 5 in pane of 6.

V46

2d. White dot over shamrock at top (Cyl 10 no dot R. 20/1).

V64

2d. White flaw over lower left rose stem (Cyl 14 dot R. 1/1).

V94
2d. White flaw on lower left-hand daffodil. Occurs in booklets in position 3 or 6 in pane of 6. Later retouched.

V104
2d. Damaged " P " in " POST-AGE " appearing as " D ". Occurs in booklets in position 2 or 5 in pane of 6.

V275
2d. Extended stem of left daffodil. Sideways delivery coils (Roll No. 9).

V276
2d. White flaw on lower right shamrock (Cyl 12 dot R. 20/3). Later retouched.

V277
2d. White flaw on Crown (Cyl 11 no dot R. 9/11). Later retouched.

V278
2d. White spot by right thistle (Cyl 14 dot R. 11/10).

V11

2½d. " b " for " D " flaw. White line connecting " D " with circle (Cyl 30 dot R. 19/11).

V12

2½d. " Swan's head " flaw. Top of " 2 " is extended and curled. Occurs in booklets in position 1 or 4 in pane of 6.

V105
2d. White spot between " 2 " and " d " at left. Occurs in booklets in position 2 or 5 in pane of 6.

V106
2d. White spot on top stamen of upper left rose appearing as dew drop. Occurs in booklets in position 2 or 5 in pane of 6. Later retouched.

V109
2½d. White dot between legs of " R " at upper left. Occurs in booklets in position 3 or 6 in pane of 6. Later retouched.

V190
3d. White dot on laurel leaf at left. Occurs in booklets in position 2 or 4 in pane of 6.

V187
2d. White flaw on daffodil at lower left appears as a " double trumpet " (Cyl 10 no dot R. 11/1).

V241
2d. White spot left of daffodil at right (Cyl 9 dot R. 18/8).

V279
3d. White flaw over Queen's eye (Cyl 2 dot R. 13/7).

V199
1s. Pale flaw joins thistl leaves at right Cyl dot R. 4/5).

V107
2d. Large white flaw on lower right shamrock. Occurs in booklets in position 3 or 6 in pane of 6. Later retouched.

V108
2d. White flaw between diadem and upper right rose. Occurs in booklets in position 3 or 6 in pane of 6. Later retouched.

540E	¼d.	– V47.	Flaw on shamrock ...	...	...	3·25
		– V176.	"A" flaw ...	...	...	3·25
		– V177.	Spot on "d"	...	...	3·25
		– V208.	"R" flaw ...	...	...	4·00
541E	1d.	– V32.	Flaw on shamrock ...	...	...	6·00
		– V273.	Spot on "d"	...	...	5·00
		– V274.	White flaw by rose	...	...	5·00
542E	1½d.	– V1.	"Butterfly" flaw (ii)	...	...	18·00
		– V1a.	"Butterfly" flaw (iii)	...	...	6·00
		– V9.	Spot between rose and shamrock	...		5·00
		– V102.	Extra dot	...	...	3·50
		– V103.	"Rabbit's ears"	...	...	3·50
		– V182.	Rose and thistle joined at right	...		3·50
	a.	Wmk sideways				
		– a V33.	Flaw over "o"	...	...	4·00
		– a V34.	Dot over rose	...	...	4·00
		– a V209.	Daffodil flaw	...	...	4·00
543E	2d.	red-brown				
		– V10.	Flaw between shamrock and diadem	...	...	4·00
		– V184.	Rose petal flaw	...	...	3·50
		– V185.	"Tadpole" flaw	...	...	3·50
		– V185a.	Do. with shamrock flaw	...		6·00
		– V186.	"Tadpole" flaw retouched	...		3·50
		– V241.	White spot by daffodil	...		3·50
	a.	Wmk sideways				
		– a V3.	Retouched "2"	...	...	5·00
		– a V4.	Extra leg to "R"	...	...	4·75
		– a V275.	Extended stem on daffodil	...		4·75
543Eb	2d.	light-red-brown				
		– V10.	Flaw between shamrock and diadem	...	...	3·50
		– V46.	Dot on shamrock ...	...	...	4·00
		– V64.	Dot over rose stem	...	...	4·50
		– V94.	Daffodil flaw	...	...	6·00
		– V104.	"D" for "p"	...	...	15·00
		– V105.	Spot after "2"	...	...	15·00
		– V106.	"Dew-drop"	...	...	6·00
		– V107.	Shamrock flaw	...	...	6·00
		– V108.	Diadem flaw	...	...	6·00
		– V185.	"Tadpole" flaw	...	...	3·50
		– V185a.	Do. with shamrock flaw ...			5·50
		V186.	"Tadpole" flaw retouched	...		3·50
		– V186a.	Do. with shamrock flaw ...			5·50
		– V187.	"Double trumpet" flaw	...		4·00
		– V241.	White spot by daffodil	...		3·50
		– V276.	White flaw on shamrock	...		9·00
		– V277.	Flaw on crown	...	...	9·00
		– V278.	Thistle flaw	...	...	9·00
	d.	Wmk sideways				
		– d V3.	Retouched "2"	...	...	8·00
		– d V4.	Extra leg to "R"	...	...	8·00
		– d V275.	Extended stem on daffodil	...		8·00
544E	2½d.(I)	– V11.	"b" for "D" flaw	...	...	6·00
	a.	Wmk sideways (I)				
		– a V211.	Frame retouch	...	...	6·00
	b.	Type II				
		– b V12.	"Swan's head" flaw	...	...	7·00
		– b V109.	Dotted "R"	...	...	7·00
545E	3d.	– V190.	White dot on laurel leaf	...		4·00
		– V279.	White eye ...	...	...	7·00
546	4d.	– V92.	Dotted "R" ...	...	...	12·00
547	5d.	– V193.	Spot by "E"	...	...	14·00
		– V194.	Spot on daffodil	...	...	14·00
		– V195.	Neck retouch	...	...	14·00
551	9d.	– V5.	Frame break	...	...	45·00
554	1s.	– V199.	Thistle flaw	...	...	25·00
555	1s.3d.	– V200.	White flaw in Queen's hair	...		55·00
556	1s.6d.	– V201.	White flaw in Queen's hair below diadem	...	...	60·00
		– V202.	White flaw in Queen's hair opposite "N" ...	...	...	60·00

1957 (19 Nov). *Graphite-lined issue.* Wmk St. Edward's Crown.
[S. G. 561/6]

V28

V29

½d. White flaw at end of middle bar to "E" of "POSTAGE" (Cyl 5 no dot R. 17/9).

Flaw in lower right rose appears as extra stem to thistle (Cyl 5 no dot R. 18/10).

V13

V14

1d. Stop below "d" at left missing. Occurs in sideways delivery coils (Roll No. 3). The dot was added in the Crowns wmk.

Extra stop before "1d." at right. Occurs in sideways delivery coils (Roll No. 2). This was retouched in the Crowns wmk.

V30

V31

Swollen stem to right daffodil appearing as bulb (Cyls 7 and 8 no dot R. 15/2).

Flaw on leaf of shamrock above "1d.". Occurs in sideways delivery coils (Roll No. 8).

1d. Flaw on bulb of thistle at top (Cyls 7 and 8 no dot R. 6/1 and coils).

V242

1½d. Diagonal green stroke below middle "E" of "REVENUE" in bottom margin (Cyl 21 no dot R. 13/8).

V183

561	½d.	– V28.	"E" flaw	...	...	4·75
		– V29.	Extra stem to thistle	...	...	4·75
562	1d.	– V13.	Stop omitted	...	...	4·75
		– V14.	Extra stop ...	...	...	4·75
		– V30.	Bulb on daffodil stem	...	...	4·00
		– V31.	White flaw on shamrock leaf	...	4·75
		– V242.	Thistle flaw	...	...	4·00
563	1½d.	– V183.	Green stroke below "E"	...	...	5·00

1958–65. Wmk Crowns. [S. G. 570E/86]

V48

Booklet pane (½d. × 2, 2½d. × 2). "Comma" after right "½d." on right stamp of pane No. 570E m.

V49

Booklet pane (½d. × 2, 2½d. × 2). Stop right of "d" of left "½d." on left stamp of pane No. 570E m.

½d. "d" at right joined to shamrock by white line. Occurs in vertical delivery coils (Roll No. 11). (Also on violet phosphor, No. 610.)

V69

V95

Booklet pane (½d. × 3, 2½d.). White flaw on right-hand daffodil. Occurs in 2s. Holiday booklet (No. NR1) on bottom left ½d. stamp of pane No. 570E l.

V117

Booklet pane (½d. × 2, 2½d. × 2). White flaw on rose behind neck. (Holiday booklet No. NR2 on upper right ½d. stamp of pane No. 570E m).

V178

½d. Large white flaw by daffodil at right. Occurs in vertical delivery coils (Roll No. 4).

V280

Booklet pane (½d. × 2, 2½d. × 2). Extended stem to lower left rose. Occurs in booklets (Cyl E14 in position 2 in pane of 4 No. 570E m).

V50

Booklet pane (1d. × 2, 3d. × 2). Flaw on "P" (appearing as "R") on bottom right stamp of pane Nos. 571E l and 611E l/m (3d. at left).

V181

1d. Large white spot at bottom of daffodil stem at right (Cyl 5 no dot R. 10/11).

V262

Booklet pane (1d. × 2, 3d. × 2). Large white flaw to right of left thistle (R. 2/2 of pane Nos. 571E l and 611E l/m).

V110

1½d. White flaws in and around thistle at upper left (Cyl 22 dot R. 12/1).

V210

1½d. White spot by upper left daffodil (Cyl 22 dot R. 1/12).

V67

2d. Extension to tip of " 2 " at right (Cyl 24 dot R. 19/10).

V40

Booklet pane (½d. × 3, 2½d.) Screen damage to left of Queen's eyes. Occurs in 2s. Holiday booklet (No. NR1 with black stitching) on the 2½d. stamp in pane No. 570E l.

V263

2½d. Triangular white flaw adjoining left leaf and extra stem to rose (Cyl 50 dot R. 9/4). No. 614 exists with leaf flaw retouched and with both retouched.

V191

3d. White spot on foot of
"T" of "POSTAGE"
(Cyl 37 no dot R. 19/11).

V192

3d. Large white flaw on "E" at top
left (Multipositive flaw, Cyl 69
dot onwards, R. 14/11). Retouched on some cylinders.

6d. Spur to frame (Cyl 10 no dot R. 17/2).

V535

V113

3d. White flaw on diadem
left of "E" (Cyl 4 no
dot R. 18/2).

V196

8d. Flaw by ear shows as an extra
pearl in earring (Cyl 4 dot R.
16/2).

V197

9d. Frame broken at upper right.
Similar to V5 but more pronounced (Cyl 2 no dot R. 11/11).

V111

d. Stem of daffodil is
broken (Cyl 2 no dot
R. 7/2).

V198

White flaw on frame at
lower left opposite " 9d "
(Cyl 2 dot R. 12/5).

570E	½d. – V47. Flaw on shamrock	...	...	...	2·00
	– V69 "d" joined to shamrock		...	...	3·00
	– V176. "A" flaw	...	...	...	2·75
	– V177. Spot on "d"		...	...	2·75
	– V178. Large dot by daffodil		...	...	2·00
	– V208. "R" flaw	...	...	...	2·00
	l. Booklet pane (½d. × 3, 2½d.). Chalky paper				
	– l V40. Screen damage (2½d.)		...	...	20·00
	– l V95. Daffodil flaw (½d.)	...	...	...	20·00
	m. Booklet pane (½d. × 2, 2½d. × 2). Wmk sideways				
	– m V48. Comma flaw (½d.)		...	...	10·00
	– m V49. Spot right of "d" (½d.)		...	...	10·00
	– m V117. Rose flaw (½d.)		...	...	10·00
	– m V280. Rose stem flaw (½d.)		...	...	10·00
571E	1d. – V181. Daffodil flaw		...	...	2·75
	– V242. Thistle flaw		...	...	3·00
	– V273. Spot on "d"		...	...	5·00
	l. Booklet pane (1d. × 2, 3d. × 2). Wmk sideways				
	– l V50. "R" flaw (1d.)	...	...	...	8·00
	– l V262. Thistle flaw (1d.)	...	...	...	24·00
572E	1½d. – V9. Spot between rose and shamrock				3·75
	– V110. Thistle flaws	...	...	...	3·50
	– V210. Daffodil flaw		...	...	3·50
573E	2d. – V67. "Swan's head" flaw		...	...	4·00
	– V104. "D" for "p"	...	...	...	90·00
	– V105. Spot after "2"		...	...	90·00
	– V186. "Tadpole" flaw retouched		...	...	4·00
	a. Wmk sideways				
	– a V3. Retouched "2"		...	...	4·00
	– a V4. Extra leg to "R"	...		...	4·00
	– a V275. Extended stem on daffodil			...	4·00
574E	2½d. (II) – V12. "Swan's head" flaw		...	...	12·00
	– V109. Dotted "R"	...	...	...	7·50
	– V263. Leaf and extra rose stem flaws			...	5·00
	a. Wmk sideways (I)				
	– a V211 Frame retouch		...	...	4·00
575E	3d. – V191. Spot on "T"		...	...	5·00
	– V192. Flaw on "E"		...	...	4·50
578	5d. – V193. Spot by "E"		...	...	6·00
	– V194. Spot on daffodil		...	...	6·00
	– V195. Neck retouch		...	...	6·00
579	6d. – V535. Spur to frame		...	...	6·00
581	8d. – V113. Diadem flaw		...	...	7·00
	– V196. Extra pearl	...		...	7·00
582	9d. – V5. Frame break (Cyl 1 no dot)				14·00
	– V197. Frame break (Cyl 2 no dot)			...	6·00
	– V111. Broken daffodil		...	...	6·00
	– V198. Frame flaw	...		...	...	6·00
584	1s. – V199. Thistle flaw		...	...	6·00
585	1s. 3d. – V200. White flaw in Queen's hair		...		8·00
586	1s. 6d. – V201. White flaw in Queen's hair below diadem	...	...	...	14·00
	– V202. White flaw in Queen's hair opposite "N"	...	...	...	...	18·00

1958–61. Graphite-lined issue. Wmk Crowns. [S. G. 587E/94]

588E	1d. – V242. Thistle flaw	...	...	...	6·00
	– V273. Spot on "d"	...	...	...	9·00

1959–68. Castles. Wmk Crowns. [S. G. 595E/8E]

2s.6d. A series of brown
dots over "battle-
ments" at right (Pl
9A R. 8/4).

V112

V205

2s.6d. Lines of shading weak or omitted at base of collar, on dress and at foot of background (occurs on Pl 5A R. 5/4 and 6/4, the illustration being of the latter).

V68. Weak frame at right (*for illustration see* 538V68).

595E	2s.6d. – V112. Dots on battlements	...	...	...	15·00
	– V205. Weak entry	...	...	...	15·00
	k. Chalky paper				
	– k V112. Dots on battlements	...	...	...	15·00
597E	10s. – V68. Weak frame ...	...	...	...	£100

1959 (18 Nov). *Phosphor-Graphite issue.* [S. G. 599/609]

599	½d. – V28. "E" flaw	...	...	...	10·00
	– V29. Extra stem to thistle	...	...	10·00
600	1d. – V30. Bulb on daffodil stem	...	...	8·00
	– V242. Thistle flaw	...	...	...	8·00
601	1½d. – V183. Green stroke below "E"	...	...	8·00

1960 (22 June)–68. *Phosphor issue.* Two phosphor bands, except where otherwise stated. Wmk Crowns [S. G. 610E/18a]

8d. Petal joined to frame (Cyl 4 dot, R.13/11).

V537

610E	½d. – V47. Flaw on shamrock ...	...	...	2·00
	– V69. "d" joined to shamrock	...	...	2·25
	– V178. Large dot by daffodil	...	...	2·25
	– V208. "R" flaw	...	...	...	2·25
611E	1d. – V181. Daffodil flaw	...	...	3·00
	l. Booklet pane (1d. × 2, 3d. 1 side band × 2). Wmk sideways			
	– l V50. "R" flaw (1d.)	...	...	25·00
	– l V262. Thistle flaw (1d.)	...	...	40·00
	m. Booklet pane (1d. × 2, 3d. × 2). Wmk sideways			
	– m V50. "R" flaw (1d.)	...	...	4·50
	– m V262. Thistle flaw (1d.)	...	...	15·00
612E	1½d. – V9. Spot between rose and shamrock			4·50
	– V110. Thistle flaws	...	...	3·50
	– V210. Daffodil flaw	...	...	3·50
613 a b	2d. Wmk sideways			
	– V3. Retouched "2"	...	...	3·75
	– V4. Extra leg to "R"	...	...	3·75
616c	5d. – V193. Spot by "E"	...	...	5·00
	– V194. Spot on daffodil	...	...	5·00
	– V195. Neck retouch	...	...	4·00
617b	8d. – V113. Diadem flaw	...	...	6·00
	– V196. Extra pearl ...	...	...	6·00
	– V537. Petal joined to frame	...	...	6·00

617c	9d. – V197. Frame break (Cyl 2 no dot)	...	7·00
	– V111. Broken daffodil	...	...	7·00
	– V198. Frame flaw ...	...	...	7·00
618	1s.3d. – V200. White flaw in Queen's hair	...	12·00
618a	1s.6d. – V201. White flaw in Queen's hair below diadem	...	...	...	10·00

1967–70. *Chalky paper.* Two phosphor bands, except where otherwise stated. [S. G. 723/44E]

V118

4d. White patch over eye and hair (Cyl 13 no dot R. 20/12).

V119

4d. White dot on " D " (from 2s. booklet upper right stamp in pane of four).

V212

5d. Scratch severs neck (Cyl 13 dot, R. 19/4).

V540

5d. Scratch through hair (Booklet pane of 6, R. 1/1 or R. 2/1).

V120

6d. Two coloured lines crossing base of crown, one extending in curves through the hair (Cyl 2 no dot R. 18/1).

V121

6d. Large circular retouch above value (Cyl 2 dot R. 11/1).

V213

6d. Two spots in front of neck. Occurs on vertical delivery coils (Roll No. 12).

731Eav	4d.	*deep olive-brown*				
		– V118. White patch	...	...	...	3·00
		– V119. Dot on "D"	...	...	...	3·00
732	4d.	*deep olive-brown* (1 centre band)				
		– V118. White patch	...	...	...	3·00
733Eg	4d.	*bright vermilion* (1 centre band)				
		– V118. White patch	...	...	...	5·00
735Eae	5d.	– V212. Scratch severing neck	...	...	18·00
		– V540. Scratch through hair	...	...	3·00
736	6d.	– V120. Hair flaws	...	...	...	3·50
		– V121. Retouch	...	...	...	3·50
		– V213. Two spots in front of neck	...	3·00

1971 (15 Feb)–80. *Decimal Currency*. Chalk-surfaced paper.

V214

½p. Base of "2" is deformed (Cyl 2 dot, R. 20/9).

V339

½p. Scratch under chin (Cyl 7 dot, R. 16/9).

V375   V375 (retouched state).

½p. Flaw below collar, later retouched as shown, on No. X841E g only (Cyl 2 dot, R 2/9).

V340

Booklet pane (½p. × 2, 2p. × 2) *se-tenant* vert. Heavy lines under chin (Booklet pane, No. X841 E l, R. 2/1). (Later retouched).

V264

Booklet pane (½p. × 2, 2p. × 2) *se-tenant* horiz. Retouch left of Queen's forehead (2p. stamp in booklet pane, No. X841 E la, R. 1/1).

V265

Booklet pane (½p. × 2, 2p. × 2) *se-tenant* horiz. White dot in diadem right of cross (2p. stamp in booklet pane, No.X841 E la, R. 1/1).

V342

Booklet pane (½p. × 2, 2p. × 2) *se-tenant* horiz. Background disturbance left of face (2p. stamp in booklet pane, No. X841E la, R. 1/1).

V343

Booklet pane (½p. × 2, 2p. × 2) *se-tenant* horiz. Dark patch on cheek (2p. stamp in booklet pane, No. X841E la, R. 1/1).

V376

Coil strip (2p., ½p. × 2, 1p. × 2). Line of dots on collar (2nd. ½p. in every 5th., 5p. coil strip No. X841 nEv).

V283

Booklet pane (½p. × 3, 2½p. × 9). Scratch across shoulder (2½p. band at right in Wedgwood pane, No. X841E o, R. 2/1).

V378

Coil strip (6p., 2p., 1p., ½p. × 2). Retouch by dress (first ½p. in every 5th., 10p. coil strip No. X841 Eq, Roll 10).

V380

Coil strip (6p., 2p., 1p., ½p. × 2). Dark scratch in shoulder (1p. stamp in every 5th., 10p. coil strip No. X841 Eq, Roll 1).

V377

Booklet pane (½p. × 2, 1p. × 3, 6p.). Missing necklace shading (½p. stamp in 10p. Booklet pane, No. X841 E, R. 1/2).

V424

Booklet pane (½p. × 2, 1p. × 2, 6½p. × 2, 8½p. × 4). White flaw in cross (8½p. stamp in 50p. Booklet pane No. X841 Es, R. 5/2).

V448

Coil strip (½p. × 2, 7p., 1p. × 2). Red flaw above eye (2nd. ½p. in every 5th. 10p. coil strip No. X843 al, Roll 4).

V410

Booklet pane (½p. × 2, 1p. × 2, 7p.). Flaw by cross (½p. stamp in 10p. Booklet pane, No. X843 am, R. 2/1).

V411

Booklet pane (½p. × 2, 1p. × 2, 7p.). No serif on "P" (1p. stamp in 10p. Booklet pane, No. X843 am, R. 2/2).

V420

Booklet pane (½p. × 2, 1p. × 2, 7p.). Hole below earring (7p. stamp in 10p. Booklet pane, No. X843 am, R. 3/1).

V451

Booklet pane (½p. × 2, 1p. × 2, 7p.). Blue scratch from hair through nose to left margin (7p. stamp in 10p. Booklet pane, No. X843 am, R. 3/1).

V341

Booklet pane (1p. × 2, 1½p. × 2) se-tenant horiz. White patch on collar (1½p. stamp in booklet pane, No. X844E m, R. 1/1).

V422

Booklet pane (1p. × 2, 7p. × 3, 9p. × 3). White scratch across stamp (7p. band at left in 50p. Booklet pane No. X844E na, R. 4/2).

V379

1p. Repair to neck (Vert. coil, Roll No. 9).

V538

Booklet pane (1p. ×,2, 8p.). Large dark area below chin and retouch on chin (1p. stamp in 10p. Booklet pane, No.X845 l, R. 2/2).

V539

Booklet pane (1p. × 2, 8p.). Scratch through dress (1p. stamp in 10p. Booklet pane, No. X845 l, R. 2/2).

V215

1½p. Malformed " 2 " (Cyl. 1 no dot, R. 14/9).

V381

2p. Retouch left of Queen's face (Cyl. 10 no dot, R. 11/7).

V216

2½p. Screen damage (Vert. coil, Roll No. 11).

V243

2½p. Small " 2 " without serif and scratch line through " P " (Cyl 5 no dot, R. 3/5).

V412

2½p. Break in necklace (Cyl. 19 dot, R. 20/10).

V244

Booklet pane (2½p. × 5 and "Tear Off" or "Rushstamps" label). Short curve to large "2" (50p. Booklet pane, No. X850E1, R. 2/2).

V248

3p. Marked scratches extending from hair to crown on stamp below and also retouch on chin (Cyl 9, dot R. 17/2 and 18/2).

V413

3p. Damage by forehead (Cyl. 24 dot, R. 6/2).

V245

Booklet pane (2½p. × 5 and "Stick" or "B. Alan" label). Missing serif to large "2" (25p. Booklet pane, No. X850E1, R. 1/2).

Normal   V249

3p. No serif to " 3 " (50p. Booklet pane of 6, R. 1/2).

V246

Booklet pane (2½p. × 5 and "Tear Off" label). Missing top serif to figure "1" (50p. Booklet pane, No. X850E1, R. 1/2).

V252

Booklet pane (3p. × 5 and "£4,315" label). Large retouch on shoulder and in dress (30p. Booklet pane, No. X853E1, R. 2/1).

V247

Booklet panes (2½p. × 4 and 2 labels) and (3p. × 4, 2½p. × 2). Missing serif to small "2" (25p. Booklet pane "Rushstamps" or "Uniflo" labels pane. No. X850E m, R. 1/1. Also 2½p. band at left in 50p. Booklet pane, No. X851E1, R. 1/3).

V250

Booklet pane (2½p. × 2, 3p. × 4). Short bottom curve to "3" (see normal in V249) (3p. stamp in *se-tenant* 50p. Booklet pane. No. X851E1, R. 1/2).

Booklet pane (3p. × 5 and "£4,315" label). Coloured spot on jaw and large retouch on shoulder (30p. Booklet pane, No. X853E1, R. 2/1).

V251

Booklet panes (2½p. × 2, 3p. × 4) and (3p. × 5 and "£4,315" label). Large retouch in dress (3p. stamp in *se-tenant* 50p. Booklet pane, No. X851E1, R. 1/1 and 30p. Booklet pane, No. X853E1, R. 1/1).

V267

V344

3p. White flaw in hair (Cyl. 31 no dot, R. 1/6).

V345

3p. White flaw in hair, retouched state (Cyl. 31 no dot, R. 1/6).

V346

3p. Indented right hand-margin (Cyl. 31 no dot, R. 2/10). (Later retouched.)

V382

3p. White dot above " P " (Cyl. 31 no dot, R. 11/1).

3½p. White flaw in hair resembling a diamond (35p. Booklet pane of 5, R. 1/1).

V305

V307

3½p. Large retouch under Queen's bust (Cyl 9 no dot, R. 6/3).

V308

3½p. Extra pearl on necklace and three white spots above (50p. Booklet pane of 5, R. 1/1).

V309

3½p. Diagonal white scratch below collar of dress (50p. Booklet pane of 5, R. 1/3).

V310

3½p. Prominent horiz line in top right corner (Booklet pane of 5, R. 1/2).

V414

3½p. White spot on "P" (Booklet pane of 5, R. 2/1).

V415

3½p. White spot on "P" (Booklet pane of 5, R. 1/1).

4½p. Gash on cheek (Cyl 3 dot, R. 6/9).

V311

V312 4½p. Similar variety behind Queen's shoulder on adjoining stamp (Cyl 3 dot, R. 6/8).

4½p Extra " pearls " on necklace (85p. and 45p. Booklet panes, R. 1/2).

V313

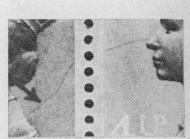

4½p. Long plate scratch (Cyl. 3 no dot, R. 9/9 and 9/10).

V347

5½p. Extra " ear-ring " (Cyl 2 dot, R. 19/1).

V314

V460

5½p. The variety illustrated is from R. 15/10 and shows a scratch through Queen's hair and forehead. The scratch extends across R. 16/1 to 5 and R. 15/6 to 8 as a minor flaw. It is distinct on R. 15/9 and 15/10, (No. X861, Cyl. 2 dot). *Price is for a block of twenty.*

6p. Incomplete "6" (Cyl. 4 dot, R. 12/4).

V449

6½p. Heavy coloured line in band of diadem (Cyl 2 no dot, R. 1/4).

V315

6½p. Retouch above necklace (Horiz coil, Roll No. 8).

V383

V416　　V416a　　V417

6½p. Queen's neck is scratched. Later retouched to give V416a (Cyl. 9 no dot, R. 1/10).

6½p. White flaw on "6" of face-value (65p. booklet pane, R. 2/3).

V418

6½p. Curved frame at top right (Horiz coil, Roll No. 5).

V419

6½p. Dent in top frame (Horiz coil, Roll No. 10).

6½p. Scratch below necklace (11 no dot, R. 8/9).

V532

7p. Missing serif to "7" (Cyls. 3 and 6 dot, R. 5/10 on No. X866; Cyl. 8 dot, R. 5/10 on No. X867).

V348

7p. Scratch down neck (Cyl. 6 dot R. 8/3).

V450

V421

7p. Retouch by forehead (Cyl. 8 dot, R. 10/2).

V452

7p. Scar on lip (Cyl. 14 no dot R. 20/10). (Later retouched.)

V384

8½p. Scar on neck (Cyl. 4 dot, R. 18/1). (Later retouched.)

V423

8½p. Retouch behind head (Cyl. 4 dot, R.14/8).

THE ELIZABETHAN

All other aspects of the stamps of the present reign are fully covered by the *Elizabethan Specialised Stamp Catalogue,* published annually.

V385

8½p. Line under value (Cyl. 6 dot, R. 3/9).

V386

8½p. Retouch left of nose (Cyl. 6 dot, R. 4/1).

V454

9p. As V453 but re-touched as dark patch and a series of white vertical lines below bust.

V425

8½p. Repaired bottom loop to "8" (Horiz. coil, Cyl. R2, Roll 5).

V426

8½p. Deformed bottom loop of "8" (Vert. coil, Cyl. 3 dot, Roll 1, also sheet Cyl. 6 dot, R. 9/1).

V455

9p. As V454 but re-touched as white patch and white lines below bust remain.

V349   Normal

9p. Short tail to " 9 " (Cyls. 3A and 4A dot, R. 1/10).

V456

9½p. Retouch and scratch behind shoulder (Cyl. 13 dot, R. 11/4).

V427

9p. White blob on "9" (90p. Booklet pane, R. 2/4 and Vert. YL coil, Roll 4).

V428

9p. Black scratch through crown (90p. Booklet pane, R. 1/5 and Vert. YL coil, Roll 6).

V457

10p. Vertical scratch through shoulder (Cyl. 3 dot, R. 20/8) (Later retouched).

Cylinder 24 was used to print the 90p. booklet panes and the vertical YL coils.

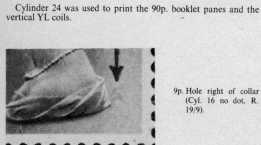

9p. Hole right of collar (Cyl. 16 no dot, R. 19/9).

V453

V541

12p. Two scratches in the background (Cyl. 2 no dot, R. 19/3).

20p. White scar on neck
(Cyl. 4 no dot,
R. 11/5).

V350

V458

50p. White scratch through neck and shoulder (Cyl. 4
no dot, R. 1/4).

V459

50p. Retouches above and below value
(Cyl. 4 no dot, R. 8/2).

(a) Photo. Harrison. With two phosphor bands, except where
stated otherwise.   [S. G. X841E/X913]

X841E	½p. – V214. Deformed "2"	3·00
	– V339. Scratch under chin	2·00
	– V375. Flaw below collar	3·00
l.	Booklet pane (½p. × 2, 2p. × 2 se-tenant vert.)	
	– l V340. Heavy lines under chin (½p.) ...	55·00
la.	Booklet pane (½p. × 2, 2p. × 2 se-tenant horiz.)	
	– la V264. Retouch (2p.)	6·00
	– la V265. Dot in diadem. (2p.)	7·00
	– la V342. Background disturbance (2p.) ...	12·00
	– la V343. Patch on cheek (2p.)	5·00
nEv.	Coil strip (2p., ½p. × 2, 1p. × 2)	
	– nEv V376. Line of dots (½p.)	2·25
o.	Booklet pane (½p. × 3, 2½p. × 3, 2½p. 1 band at left × 3, 2½p. 1 band at right × 3).	
	– o V283. Shoulder scratch (2½p. 1 band at right)	40·00
q.	Coil strip (6p., 2p., 1p., ½p. × 2)	
	– q V378. Retouch (½p.)	2·00
	– q V380. Shoulder scratch (1p.) ...	2·00
r.	Booklet pane (½p. × 2, 1p. × 3, 6p.)	
	– r V377. Missing necklace shading (½p.) ...	2·00
s.	Booklet pane (½p. × 2, 1p. × 2, 6½p. 1 band at right × 2, 8½p. × 4)	
	– s V424. Flaw in cross (8½p.)	12·00
Eg.	Gum arabic	
	– Eg V375. Flaw below collar (retouched state)	3·50

X843	½p.	(1 centre band)	
	al.	Coil strip (½p. × 2, 7p., 1p. × 2 each with centre band)	
		– al V448. Red flaw above eyebrow (½p.) ...	1·50
	am.	Booklet pane (½p. × 2, 1p. × 2, 7p. and label each with centre band)	
		– am V410. Flaw by cross (½p.)	1·25
		– am V411. No serif to "P" (1p.)	1·25
		– am V420. Hole below earring (7p.) ...	1·50
		– am V451. Blue scratch (7p.)	1·25
X844E	1p.	(2 bands)	
	m.	Booklet pane (1p. × 2, 1½p. × 2 se-tenant horiz.)	
		– m V341. White patch on collar (1½p.) ...	3·00
	na.	Booklet pane (1p. × 2, 7p. 1 band at right × 3, 9p. × 3)	
		– na V422. Horizontal white scratch (7p.)	4·50
	Eg.	Gum arabic	
		– Eg V379. Repair to neck	2·00
X845	1p.	(1 centre band)	
	l.	Booklet pane (1p. × 2, 8p. and label each with centre band)	
		– l V538. "Beard" flaw (1p.)	1·25
		– l V539. Scratch through dress (1p.) ...	1·00
X847	1½p.	– V215. Malformed "2"	3·00
X848E	2p.	– V381. Retouch left of face	1·00
X850E	2½p.	(1 centre band)	
		– V216. Screen damage	3·50
		– V243. Small "2" without serif and scratched "P"	3·50
		– V412. Break in necklace	3·50
	l.	Booklet pane (2½p. × 5 and label with centre band)	
		– l V244. Short tip to large "2" (2½p.) ...	7·00
		– l V245. Large "2" without serif (2½p.) ...	7·00
		– l V246. "1" without top serif (2½p.) ...	7·00
	m.	Booklet pane (2½p. × 4 and 2 labels with centre band)	
		– m V247. Small "2" without serif (2½p.) ...	8·00
	Eg.	Gum arabic	
		– Eg V243. Small "2" without serif and scratched "P"	3·50
X851E	2½p.	(1 band at left)	
	l.	Booklet pane (2½p. 1 band at left × 2, 3p. × 4)	
		– l V247. Small "2" without serif (2½p.) ...	9·00
		– l V250. "3" with short bottom curve (3p.) ...	9·00
		– l V251. Retouch in dress (3p.)	10·00
X852	2½p.	– V412. Break in necklace	3·00
X853E	3p.	– V248. Scratches and chin retouch (vert. pair)	5·00
		– V413. Damage by forehead	3·00
	l.	Booklet pane (3p. × 5 and label)	
		– l V249. "3" without serif (3p.)	7·00
		– l V251. Retouch in dress (3p.)	25·00
		– l V252. Retouch on shoulder and in dress (3p.)	10·00
		– l V267. Spot on jaw and shoulder retouch (3p.)	10·00
	Eg.	Gum arabic	
		– Eg V248. Scratches and chin retouch (vert. pair)	5·00
X854E	3p.	(1 centre band)	
		– V344. Flaw in hair	8·00
		– V345. Do. Retouched	3·00
		– V346. Indented margin	20·00
		– V382. Dot above "P"	3·00
	Eg.	Gum arabic	
		– Eg V345. Flaw in hair retouched ...	3·00
		– Eg V382. Dot above "P"	3·00
		– Eg V413. Damage by forehead ...	3·00
X855E	3½p.	bronze green	
		– V305. "Diamond" in hair	3·50
		– V307. Retouch under bust	4·00
		– V308. Extra "pearl", etc.	3·00
		– V309. Scratch under collar	3·50
		– V310. Prominent line	5·00
X856	3½p.	bronze green (1 centre band)	
		– V307. Retouch under bust	4·00
		– V414. White spot to left of "P"	3·00
		– V415. White spot on bottom right of "P"	3·00

X858	4½p. – V311. Gash on cheek	...	...	3·00
	– V312. Gash behind shoulder	...	...	3·00
	– V313. Extra pearls	...	...	3·50
	– V347. Plate scratch (Pair).	...	...	7·00
X860	5½p. – V314. Extra earring	...	...	3·50
X861	5½p. (1 centre band)			
	– V314. Extra earring	...	...	3·00
	– V460. Long scratch (Block of 20)		...	18·00
X862E	6p. – V449. Incomplete "6"	...	...	30·00
	Eg. Gum arabic			
	– Eg V449. Incomplete "6"	...	...	4·00
X863	6½p. – V315. Line in band	...	...	5·00
X864	6½p. (1 centre band)			
	– V315. Line in band	...	...	5·00
	– V383. Retouch above necklace	...	...	1·75
	– V416. Neck scratch	...	...	4·00
	– V416a. Do. Retouched	...	...	4·00
	– V417. White flaw on "6"	...	...	2·50
	– V418. Curved frame at top right	...	2·75
	– V419. Dent in top frame	...	...	2·75
	– V532. Scratch below necklace	...	...	2·75
X866	7p. – V348. Missing serif	...	...	3·00
	– V450. Neck scratch	...	...	2·75
X867	7p. (1 centre band)			
	– V348. Missing serif	...	...	2·00
	– V421. Retouch by forehead	...	...	1·75
	– V452. Lip scar	...	...	2·00
X873E	8½p. light yellowish green			
	– V384. Scar on neck	...	...	2·00
	– V423. Retouch behind head	...	...	2·50
	Eb. Yellowish green			
	– Eb V385. Line under value	...	...	1·75
	– Eb V386. Retouch left of nose	...	...	2·50
	– Eb V425. Repaired bottom loop to "8"	...	1·75
	– Eb V426. Deformed bottom loop to "8"		2·00
X874	9p. yellow-orange and black			
	– V349. Short tail to "9"	...	...	4·50
X875	9p. deep violet			
	– V427. White blob on "9"	...	...	1·75
	– V428. Black scratch through crown	...	1·75
	– V453. Hole right of collar	...	...	2·50
	– V454. Do. Retouched with dark patch etc.		2·50
	– V455. Do. Third retouch with white patch		1·75
X876	9½p. – V456. Retouch and scratch	...	...	2·00
X878	10p. – V457. Vertical scratch	...	...	2·50
X886	20p. – V350. White scar	...	...	2·00
X887	50p. – V458. Neck scratch	...	...	3·00
	– V459. Value retouches	...	...	3·00

(b) Photo. Harrison. On phosphorised paper

X894	8½p. yellowish green			
	– V385. Line under value	...	...	2·50
	– V386. Retouch left of nose	...	...	3·00
X897	12p. – V541. Background scratches	...	...	1·50

£1 Scratch across Queen's face (Cyl. 2A–1B dot, R. 5/6).

V430

£5 Blue streak on the bottom left-hand corner of the " £ " sign (Cyl. 1A–1B no dot, R. 8/1).

V388

1026	£1 – V387. Mark below Crown	...	...	...	5·00
	– V430. Scratch across face	...	...	...	6·00
1028	£5 – V388. Blue streak	...	...	...	...	12·00

1977 (2 Feb).   [S. G. 1026/8]

£1 Dark mark below Crown (Cyl. 2A–1B dot, R. 9/8).

V387

THE ELIZABETHAN

Uniform with this volume, the *Elizabethan Specialised Stamp Catalogue* covers all other aspects of the stamps of the present reign, from both Great Britain and the British Commonwealth, in considerable detail. See the preliminary pages of this Catalogue for details of this annual publication.

Great Britain

Commemoratives and Special Issues

1953 (3 June). *Coronation.*   [S. G. 532/5]

V6 2½d. Missing pearl   V7 Pearls
    on orb. (Cyl   retouched
    3 dot R. 1/4).

V137
4d. Flaw on leaf by
    daffodil (Cyl 1
    no dot R. 19/1).

Normal   V138

1s.3d. Flaw on right-hand side of lower clover leaf
    (Cyl 2 no dot R. 20/1).

1s.6d. White flaw on daffodil
    and right shamrock leaf
    notched (Cyl 1 dot
    R. 1/6).

V63

1s.6d. White flaw between thistle
    and main stem (Cyl 1 dot
    R. 16/5).

V93

532	2½d. – V6.	Missing pearl	…	…	…	35·00
	– V7.	Pearls retouched	…	…	…	18·00
533	4d. – V137.	Daffodil leaf flaw	…	…	…	8·00
534	1s.3d. – V138.	Clover leaf flaw	…	…		15·00
535	1s.6d. – V63.	Mis-shaped emblems	…	…	…	20·00
	– V93.	Thistle flaw	…	…	…	20·00

1957 (1 Aug). *World Scout Jubilee Jamboree.*   [S. G. 557/9]

V139
2½d. Lack of shading gives
    appearance of broken
    rope strand (Cyl 4 dot
    R. 1/1).

V147
2½d. The retouch is on the
    Queen's left shoulder ex-
    tending across the collar of
    dress (Cyl 5 no dot R. 11/5).

V35
4d. Ninth circle from top on
    right almost solid (Cyl 1
    no dot R. 14/5).

V36
1s.3d. Large retouched area in
    background by cardinal
    point left of Globe (Cyl
    1 dot R. 2/4).

557	2½d. – V147.	Retouch	…	…	…	6·50
	– V139.	Broken rope strand		…	…	6·50
558	4d. – V35.	Solid pearl at right		…	…	8·00
559	1s.3d. – V36.	Large retouch	…	…	…	20·00

1957 (12 Sept). *46th Inter-Parliamentary Union Conference*
[S. G. 560]

4d. Broken wreath at
    upper left (Cyl 2 no
    dot R. 2/6).

V37

V65
Partial double frame at top
(Cyl 2 no dot R. 17/3, 17/6
and 18/6).

V140
Break in frame-line at left
opposite second " AR " of
" PARLIAMENTARY " (Cyl 2
no dot R. 12/5).

560	4d. – V37.	Broken wreath	10·00
	– V65.	Partial double frame line at top ...	7·00
	– V140.	Broken frame	7·00

1958 (18 July). *Sixth British Empire and Commonwealth Games, Cardiff.*
[S. G. 567/9]

Normal   V15

3d. Part of shading missing on scale near "M" of "EMPIRE" (Cyl 2 dot R. 1/1).

V38 Flaw   V39 Retouched

White flaw on shading of dragon's body above shoulder, later retouched with irregular pattern of dots (Cyl 2 dot R. 12/2).

V51

3d. White flaw crossing line behind dragon's left foreleg showing as letter "H" (Cyl 7 dot R. 11/2). This was unsuccessfully retouched with light vertical lines across flaw. (V51a)

V141 State II   V141a State III

Flaw on body above second "E" of "EMPIRE". This is a progressive flaw. Initially normal, the first stage showed the faintest outline of a flaw. State II shows the flaw solid and state III with a dark outline and pale centre (Cyl 2 dot R. 20/3).

The retouches across the Queen's cheek and below the chin are quite marked on Cyl 7 dot R. 10/6 but there are other minor retouches in this position in stamp No. 6 in rows 2 to 13.

V142

567	3d. – V15.	Short scale	4·00
	– V38.	Shoulder flaw	6·00
	– V39.	Shoulder flaw retouched	4·00
	– V51.	"H" flaw	12·00
	– V51a.	Retouched	3·00
	– V141.	Body flaw. State II	6·50
	– V141a.	Do. State III	4·50
	– V142.	Retouched face	3·50

1960 (7 July). *Tercentenary of Establishment of "General Letter Office".*
[S. G. 619/20]

3d. Break in horse's mane behind ears (Cyl 1 no dot R. 17/2).

Normal

V16

| 619 | 3d. – V16. Broken mane | ... ... | 4·50 |

1960 (19 Sept). *First Anniv. of European Postal and Telecommunications Conference.*
[S. G. 621/2]

The blurred first "E" in "EUROPEAN" variety occurs on R. 13/5.

V143

Broken diadem. Top left portions of centre cross of diadem broken (R. 1/2).

Normal

V17

621	6d. – V143.	Blurred "E"	... ...	6·00
	– V17.	Broken diadem	... ...	6·00
622	1s.6d. – V143.	Blurred "E"	... ...	22·00
	– V17.	Broken diadem	... ...	22·00

1961 (28 Aug). *Post Office Savings Bank Centenary.* [S. G. 623I/5]

V41   V70

3d. Nick in " s " of " SAVINGS " (Cyl 3D–3E no dot R. 9/3). Later retouched with nick filled in but leaving centre of " s " narrower.

V148

Coloured spot on right-hand side of flower at left (Cyls 3C–3B no dot R. 7/1).

V149

Coloured spot on leaf on lower left-hand branch (Cyls 3C–3B no dot R. 14/4).

I. "TIMSON" Machine

624I	3d. – V41. Nick in "s"	20·00
	– V70. Retouched	5·00

II. "THRISSELL" Machine

624II	3d. – V148. Notch in flower	3·50
	– V149. Notch in leaf	3·50

1961 (18 Sept). *European Postal and Telecommunications (C.E.P.T.) Conference, Torquay.* [S. G. 626/8]

2d. Shading of Queen's ear missing leaving it white (Cyl 1A–1B–1C dot R. 11/2).

V71

626   2d. – V71. White ear   ...   .   3·00

1962 (14 Nov). *National Productivity Year.* [S. G. 631E/3]

2½d. (i) " N " and arrow head of emblem strongly shaded with diagonal cuts and dashes, also three arrows on right (Cyl 1B no dot R. 3/3).

(ii) Arrow head retouched with diagonal lines (Cyl 1B no dot R. 4/4) or retouched with irregular dots (Cyl 1B dot R. 19/6).

V18

Arrows on white of two upper left cubes retouched with irregular dots (Cyl 1B no dot R. 4/5).

V18a

Large retouch on Queen's neck between chin and necklace (Cyl 1B dot, R. 15/4).

V150

3d. Part of map where Kent lies is missing (Cyl 2C no dot R. 18/2).

V19

V151

Flaw on violet cylinder shows as a "lake" in S.W. Scotland (Cyl 2A dot R. 1/3).

V152

Flaw on violet cylinder shows as a "lake" in Yorkshire (Cyl 2C dot R 19/1).

631E	2½d. *myrtle-green and carmine-red (shades)*			
	– V18. Emblem and arrows retouch (i)		...	4·75
	– V18. Arrow head retouch (ii)	...	...	4·00
	– V18a. Arrows retouch	...	...	3·50
	– V150. Neck retouch	...	...	4·00
Ea.	*Blackish olive and carmine-red*			
	– Ea V18. Emblem and arrows retouch (i) ...			4·75
	– Ea V18. Arrow head retouch (ii) ...			4·00
	– Ea V18a. Arrows retouch		...	3·50
	– Ea V150. Neck retouch	...	...	4·00
p.	One phosphor band. *Blackish olive and carmine-red*			
	– p V18. Emblem and arrows retouch (i)	...		6·50
	– p V18. Arrow head retouch (ii)	...	...	4·50
	– p V18a. Arrows retouch	...	...	4·50
	– p V150. Neck retouch	...	...	4·50
632	3d. – V19. "Kent" omitted	...	...	5·00
	– V151. "Lake" in Scotland	...	...	12·00
	– V152. "Lake" in Yorkshire	...	...	5·00

1963 (21 Mar). *Freedom from Hunger.*   [S. G. 634/5]

V20

2½d. Coloured line through "MPA" of "CAMPAIGN" (Cyl 1D–1H dot R.7/2). An unsuccessful attempt was made to touch this out.

2½d. Broken "R" in "FREEDOM" (Cyl 1D–1H no dot R. 16/2).

V72

634	2½d. – V20. Line through "MPA"	3·50
	– V72. Broken "R"	3·50
	p. One phosphor band	
	– p V20. Line through "MPA"	5·00
	– p V72. Broken "R"	5·00

1963 (7 May). *Paris Postal Conference Centenary.*   [S. G. 636]

White spot on frame line at right (Cyl 2A–1B no dot R. 19/3).

V153

636	6d. – V153. Frame flaw ... ... 7·00
	p. Three phosphor bands
	– p V153. Frame flaw ... ... 10·00

1963 (16 May). *National Nature Week.*   [S. G. 637/8]

3d. "Caterpillar" flaw. Brown flaw on top daisy (Cyls 1A–3B–1C–1D dot R. 3/2). Several states exist and subsequently retouched.

V21

4½d. Strong retouch on Queen's nose (Cyl 2E no dot R. 14/4). Subsequently replaced by Cyl 3E, the others being unchanged.

V22

637   3d. – V21. "Caterpillar" flaw ... ... 5·00
p. Three phosphor bands
– p V21. "Caterpillar" flaw ... ... 8·00
638   4½d. – V22. Queen's nose retouch ... ... 5·00
p. Three phosphor bands
– p V22. Queen's nose retouch ... ... 9·00

1963 (31 May). *Ninth International Lifeboat Conference, Edinburgh.*   [S. G. 639/41]

2½d. Grey-coloured flaw on diadem at right shows as extra shading (Cyl 3B dot R. 20/6).

V154

V155

4d. Spot on boom of rear sail (Cyl 1D no dot R. 6/6).

V156

Coloured spot below first "I" of "INTERNATIONAL" (Cyl 1A no dot R. 13/3).

639   2½d. – V154. Shaded diadem ... ... 3·00
p. One phosphor band
– p V154. Shaded diadem ... ... 3·50
640   4d. – V155. Spot on boom ... ... 3·50
– V156. Spot under "I" ... ... 3·50
p. Three phosphor bands
– p V155. Spot on boom ... ... 3·50
– p V156. Spot under "I" ... ... 3·50

1963 (15 Aug). *Red Cross Centenary Congress.*   [S. G. 642/4]

3d. Vertical retouch down centre of cross caused by repair to cylinder (Cyl 2A–2B no dot R. 5/6).

V73

642   3d. – V73. Repaired cross ... ... 5·00

1964 (23 Apr). *Shakespeare Festival.*   [S. G. 646/50E]

V157

3d. A series of black dots go across Puck's head (Cyl 1A–1B–1C dot R. 7/6).

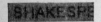

V74

6d. Broken centre bar to " H " and also an oval grey patch on Shakespeare's right cheek (Cyl 1A–1B–1C–1D no dot R. 12/3). Later retouched.

Normal   V114

6d. Missing floorboards at right of stage (Cyl 1A–1B–1C–1D no dot R. 20/1 and 20/2).

V158

1s.3d. White-coloured flaw on necklace appears as large pearl (Cyl 3A–1B (or 2B)–1C–1D dot R. 13/2).

646	3d. – V157. Black dots across Puck's head	...	3·50
	p. Three phosphor bands		
	– p V157. Black dots across Puck's head	...	5·00
647	6d. – V74. Broken "H"		4·00
	– V114. Missing floorboards		4·00
	p. Three phosphor bands		
	– p V74. Broken "H"		10·00
	– p V114. Missing floorboards ...		10·00
648E	1s.3d. – V158. Large pearl		6·00
	p. Three phosphor bands		
	– p V158. Large pearl		10·00

1964 (1 July). *Twentieth International Geographical Congress, London.*   [S. G. 651/4E]

V42

2½d. Short line below " 2½d " (Cyl 3D–1C–1B–1A no dot R. 5/5, R. 9/5 and R. 10/2 and dot R. 3/4, R. 4/5, R. 7/5 (left hand side), R. 19/4 and R. 18/6). Also seen retouched on no dot R. 18/5.

V43

2½d. Horiz line of retouching across lawn after "GEOGRAPHICAL" (Cyl 3D–1C–1B–1A no dot R. 11/1 (*illus.*) and R. 11/6).

V75

4d. Retouches under chin and on throat (Pl 1E–1D–1C–1B–1A no dot R. 20/3).

V115

1s.6d. Line across face and spot on neck (Pl 1D–1C–1B–1A no dot R. 8/4). Later retouched.

651	2½d. – V42. Short line under "2½d."	...	...	2·25
	– V43. Retouches. *From* ...	...	...	2·75
	p. One phosphor band			
	– p V42. Short line under "2½d."	...	...	4·00
	– p V43. Retouches. *From*	...	...	6·50
652E	4d. – V75. Scarred neck ...	...	...	3·00
	p. Three phosphor bands			
	– p V75. Scarred neck ...	...	...	7·00
654E	1s.6d. – V115. Neck flaw ...	...	...	10·00
	p. Three phosphor bands			
	– p V115. Neck flaw ...	...	...	30·00

1964 (5 Aug). *Tenth International Botanical Congress, Edinburgh.*   [S. G. 655/8E]

Normal   V26

3d. Broken right-hand petal of the left-hand flower where the violet overlaps the blue (Cyl 3A–1B–1C dot R. 1/2).

V52

6d. White flaw in rose hip (Cyl 1D–1C–1B–1A no dot R. 2/2).

V23

9d. White line through " INTER " (Cyl 2D–2C–2B–2A no dot R. 1/1).

V159

1s.3d. Coloured flaw on fruit at right (Cyl   1D–1C–1B–1A   no dot R. 14/2).

655	3d. – V26. Broken petal	...	...	...	5·00
	p. Three phosphor bands				
	– p V26. Broken petal	...	...	...	7·50
656E	6d. – V52. Rose hip flaw	...	...	...	3·50
	p. Three phosphor bands				
	– p V52. Rose hip flaw	...	...	...	7·00
657E	9d. – V23. Line through "INTER"	...	...	7·00
	p. Three phosphor bands				
	– p V23. Line through "INTER"	...	...	14·00
658E	1s.3d. – V159. Fruit flaw	...	...	...	7·00
	p. Three phosphor bands				
	– p V159. Fruit flaw	...	...	...	30·00

1964 (4 Sept). *Opening of Forth Road Bridge.*   [S. G. 659/60E]

V76

3d. White dot right of "3" (Cyl 1C–1B–2A dot R. 15/1).

659	3d. V76. Dotted "3"	...	...	...	...	2·75
	p. Three phosphor bands					
	– p V76. Dotted "3"	...	...	...	...	6·50

1965 (8 July). *Churchill Commemoration.*   [S. G. 661E/2E]

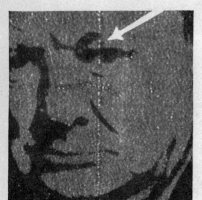

V96

4d. Vertical scratch from chin to top of stamp (Cyls 1A–1B dot R. 20/3).

661E	4d. – V96. Vertical scratch	...	...	...	1·50
	p. Three phosphor bands				
	– p V96. Vertical scratch	...	...	...	3·00

1965 (9 Aug). *Salvation Army Centenary.*   [S. G. 665/6]

V160

3d. White spot at left of diadem (R. 16/6).

V53

1s.6d. Extra pearl in necklace (R. 1 7/1)

665	3d. – V160. Diadem flaw	...	...	...	2·75
	p. One phosphor band				
	– p V160. Diadem flaw	...	...	...	5·00
666	1s.6d. – V53. Extra pearl	...	...	...	6·00
	p. Three phosphor bands				
	– p V53. Extra pearl	...	...	...	12·00

1965 (1 Sept). *Centenary of Joseph Lister's Discovery of Antiseptic Surgery.*   [S. G. 667/8E]

V77

4d. Diagonal white line from handle to top left corner (Cyl 4A–1B–1C no dot R. 17/1).

V116

4d. Large grey retouch outlining Queen's face at left (Cyl 4A–1B–1C no dot R. 18/1).

667	4d. – V77. Corner scratch	...	...	...	...	3·00
	– V116. Face retouch	...	...	...	...	3·00
	p. Three phosphor bands					
	– p V77. Corner scratch	...	...	...	...	5·00
	– p V116. Face retouch	...	...	...	...	5·00

1965 (13 Sept). *25th Anniv. of Battle of Britain.*   [S. G. 671/8E]

4d. T 80. Horizontal line of retouching through wing, cross and roundel (Cyl 2A (or 3A)–1B–1C–3D–1E dot R. 19/3).

V161

4d. T 82 Retouch on body of Stuka (Cyl 3A–1B–1C–3D–1E no dot R. 2/2).

V54

4d. T 83. Horizontal line of retouching through upper part of tailplane (Cyl 2A (or 3A)–1B–1C–3D–1E dot R. 20/3).

V162

673	4d. – V161. Damaged wing ...				2·00
	p. Three phosphor bands				
	– p V161. Damaged wing	...	...	...	2·50
675	4d. – V54. Stuka retouch	...	...	...	2·00
	p. Three phosphor bands				
	– p V54. Stuka retouch	...	...	...	2·50
676	4d. – V162. Damaged tailplane	...	...	...	2·00
	p. Three phosphor bands				
	– p V162. Damaged tailplane	...	...	...	2·50

1965 (8 Oct). *Opening of Post Office Tower.*   [S. G. 679/80E]

3d. White flaw at base of tower resembling extra window (Cyl 1A–1B–1C dot R. 4/18).

V78

679	3d. – V78. Extra window	...	...	...	...	3·50
	p. One phosphor band					
	– p V78. Extra window	...	...	...	...	3·50

1965 (25 Oct). *20th Anniv. of U.N.O. and International Co-operation Year.*   [S. G. 681/2E]

V55   V56

3d. Broken circle in S.E. segment of map (Cyl 1A–1B–1C dot R. 11/4).

3d. Orange flaw in Russia appearing as lake (Cyl 1A–1B–1C dot R. 19/3).

V224   V225 Retouched

3d. Stroke over " s " of " ANNIVERSARY " and large smudge. In retouched state smudge removed but stroke remains (Cyl 1A–1B–1C dot R. 18/3).

681	3d. – V55. Broken circle	...	...	...	...	1·75
	– V56. Lake in Russia	...	...	...	...	1·75
	p. One phosphor band					
	– p V55. Broken circle	...	...	...	...	3·00
	– p V56. Lake in Russia	...	...	...	...	3·00
	– p V224. "Flying saucer" flaw	...				5·00
	– p V225. Retouched	...	...	...	...	2·50

1965 (15 Nov). *I.T.U. Centenary.*   [S. G. 683E/4]

V57

1s.6d. Red pin has projecting arm at right (Pl 2A–1B–1C–1D–2E no dot R. 1/4). This occurs on the phosphor printing but was later retouched leaving faint traces of red on the pink background and it is known only in the retouched state on the ordinary printing.

684	1s.6d. – V57. Retouched	...	...	...	...	3·50
	p. Three phosphor bands					
	– p V57. Red pin with projecting arm	...				20·00
	– p V57. Retouched	...	...	...		25·00

1966 (28 Feb). *900th Anniv. of Westminster Abbey.*   [S. G. 687/8]

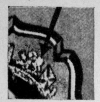

3d. White dot in diadem (Cyl 2A–1B–1C no dot R. 16/2).

V58

687	3d. – V58. Dot in diadem	...	...	...	...	...	1·75
	p. One phosphor band						
	– p V58. Dot in diadem	...	...	...	...	4·50

1966 (2 May). *Landscapes.*   [S. G. 689/92E]

6d. V59 occurs on Cyl 1A–3B–1C no dot R. 10/3. 40,000 sheets were printed before this was discovered and the " D " was added to the cylinder.

V163   V164

4d. Black dash before " E " of " ENGLAND " (Cyl 2A–1B–1C no dot R. 20/5). Later retouched.

1s.3d. Broken " D " of " LTD " at foot of stamp (Cyl 2A–2B–1C no dot R 14/2).

V226

4d. Green flaw in tree trunk (Cyl 2A–1B–1C dot R. 3/4).

689	4d. – V163. Dash before "E"	...	...	...	2·75
	– V226. Green flaw in tree trunk	...	...	4·00
	p. Three phosphor bands				
	– p V226. Green flaw in tree trunk	...	4·00
690E	6d. – V59. "AN" for "AND"	...	...	...	18·00
	p. Three phosphor bands				
	– p V59. "AN" for "AND"	...	...	4·00
691	1s.3d. – V164. Broken "D"	...	...	...	3·00
	p. Three phosphor bands				
	– p V164. Broken "D"	...	...	...	4·00

1966 (1 June). *World Football Cup Competition.*   [S. G. 693/5E]

V165   V79

4d. Coloured flaw shows as a patch on thigh of footballer at right (Cyl 1A–1B–1C–1D–1E no dot R. 3/20).

1s.3d. A strong retouch on footballer's stocking resembles a darn (Cyl 1A–1B–1C–1D–1E (or 2E) no dot R. 19/2).

693	4d. – V165. Patch on thigh	...	...	...	1·75
	p. Two phosphor bands				
	– p V165. Patch on thigh	...	...	2·25
695E	1s.3d. – V79. Darned stocking	...	...	2·50
	p. Three phosphor bands				
	– p V79. Darned stocking	...	...	4·00

1966 (18 Aug). *England's World Cup Football Victory.*   [S. G. 700]

700	4d. – V165. Patch on thigh	...	...	...	2·50

1966 (19 Sept). *British Technology.*   [S. G. 701/4]

V80

4d. Strong retouch consisting of three strong black strokes in the form of an arrow as indicated in illustration (Cyl 1A–1B no dot R. 4/6).

6d. Broken " D " of " LTD " at foot of stamp (Cyl 1A–1B–1C no dot R. 19/6).

V166

701	4d. – V80. Struts flaw	...	...	...	...	1·75
	p. Three phosphor bands					
	– p V80. Struts flaw	...	...	...	...	2·25
702	6d. – V166. Broken "D"	...	...	...	...	2·00
	p. Three phosphor bands					
	– p V166. Broken "D"	...	...	...	...	3·00

1966 (14 Oct). *900th Anniv. of Battle of Hastings.* [S. G. 705E/12E]

V81

712E	1s.3d. – V81. Club flaw	...	...	...	...	3·50
	p. Four phosphor bands					
	– p V81. Club flaw	...	...	...	...	6·00

1966 (1 Dec). *Christmas.* [S. G. 713E/14E]

3d. "T" (designer's initial) is missing (Cyl 1A–2B or 3B (or 4B)–1C–1D–1E no dot R. 6/2).
There are many broken letters in the marginal inscriptions on these stamps but we only list the missing "T" variety.

V82

713E	3d. – V82. Missing "T"	...	...	...	...	1·00
	p. One phosphor band					
	– p V82. Missing "T"	...	...	...	...	1·50

1967 (20 Feb). *European Free Trade Association (EFTA).* [S. G. 715E/16E]

V167
9d. Black protuberance on quay between trucks (R. 8/3).

Normal   V168
1s.6d. Upper ribbon on Queen's hair is broken (R. 11/3).

1s.6d. Strut below wing is broken (R. 13/6).

V83

715E	9d. – V167. Quay flaw	...	...	...	2·50
	p. Three phosphor bands					
	– p V167. Quay flaw	...	...	...	3·25
716E	1s.6d. – V168. Broken ribbon	...	...	...	5·00
	– V83. Broken strut	...	...	...	5·00
	p. Three phosphor bands					
	– p V168. Broken ribbon	...	...	...	5·00
	– p V83. Broken strut	...	...	...	5·00

1967 (24 Apr). *British Wild Flowers.* [S. G. 717E/22]

9d. Notch in small leaf at **right** opposite value (R. 20/2).

V169

721E	9d. – V169. Notch in leaf	...	...	...	3·00
	p. Three phosphor bands					
	– p V169. Notch in leaf	...	...	...	4·00

1967 (10 July). *British Paintings.* [S. G. 748E/50E]

1s.6d. Light patch below "6" appears as extra window (Cyl 2A–1B–1C–1D–1E–1F no dot R. 9/1).

V97

750E	1s.6d. – V97. Extra window	...	...	...	3·00

1967 (24 July). *Sir Francis Chichester's World Voyage.* [S. G. 751]

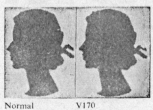

Upper ribbon on Queen's hair is broken (R. 19/3).

Normal   V170

751	1s.9d. – V170. Broken ribbon	...	...	...	2·00

1967 (19 Sept). *British Discovery and Invention.*   [S. G. 752/5E]

4d. Scale broken at 104·6° (Cyls 1A–1B–1C no dot R. 10/2). Other minor breaks occur in various positions on the scale on R. 2/2, 8/5 and 14/5.

V98

1s.6d. Grey flaw on cowling of left-hand engine (Cyls 1A–1B–1C–1D–1E no dot R. 1/2).

V99

| 752 | 4d. – V98. Major scale break | ... | ... | ... | 2·00 |
| 754E | 1s.6d. – V99. Cowling flaw | ... | ... | ... | 2·00 |

1968 (29 Apr). *British Bridges.*   [S. G. 763/6]

4d. No curve at left to central slab (R. 10/6).

V227

V122   V123

9d. "HARRISON" and "RESTALL" are redrawn (R. 18/3 and 18/4 respectively)

1s.6d. White flaw shows as broken corner stones on left side of nearest tower (R. 15/1).

V171

763	4d. – V227. No curve to slab	...	...	...	3·00
764E	9d. – V122. "HARRISON" redrawn	...	...	...	3·00
	– V123. "RESTALL" redrawn	...	...	...	3·00
765E	1s.6d. – V171. Broken stones	...	...	...	4·50

1968 (29 May). *British Anniversaries.*   [S. G. 767/70]

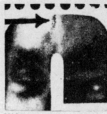

4d. Prominent retouch on large " C " appearing as bruise on forehead (Cyl 1A–1B–1C–1D no dot R. 3/2).

V124

V125

1s.9d. Bulwarks below mast at rear are broken (Cyl 2A–1B–1C R. 8/2).

| 767 | 4d. – V124. Retouch on "c" | ... | ... | ... | 8·00 |
| 770 | 1s.9d. – V125. Broken Bulwarks | ... | ... | ... | 4·00 |

1968 (12 Aug). *British Paintings.*   [S. G. 771E/4]

4d. White patch on Queen's right hand resembling a blister (Cyl 2A–3C–2D–3E–2F no dot R. 2/8).

KNOWN c.157
V126

| 771E | 4d. – V126. Blister on hand ... | ... | ... | ... | 1·50 |

PHILATELIC TERMS ILLUSTRATED

The essential philatelic dictionary. Terms covering printing methods, papers, errors, varieties, watermarks, perforations and much more are explained and illustrated, many in full colour. See the preliminary pages of this Catalogue for details of the current edition.

1968 (25 Nov). *Christmas.*   [S. G. 775E/7E]

Normal   V127

4d. Grey dapples on horse nearest to the boy and extending to the boy's belt and trousers are heavily retouched (Cyl 1A–1B–2C–1D–1E no dot R. 12/4).

775E 4d. – V127. Retouched dapples   ...   .   2·00

1969 (3 Mar). *First Flight of "Concorde".*   [S. G. 784E/6]

4d. Dark flaw in Atlantic Ocean appears as an oil slick (R. 13/2).

V172

V536

4d. Broken line on fuselage (R. 5/1)

784E 4d. – V172. "Oil slick" flaw ...   .   1·75
        – V536. Broken line   ...   .   2·50

1969 (2 Apr). *Anniversaries.*   [S. G. 791/5]

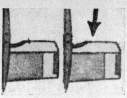

5d. Windshield in front of cockpit is missing (R. 3/4).

Normal   V146

791   5d. – V146. Missing windshield   ...   .   2·50

1969 (13 Aug). *Gandhi Centenary Year.*   [S. G. 807]

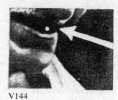

1s.6d. White patch in Gandhi's mouth appears as tooth (R. 20/3). Later retouched to near normal.

V144

807   1s.6d. – V144. Tooth flaw ...   .   3·50

1969 (26 Nov). *Christmas.*   [S. G. 812E/14E]

1s.6d. There is a break in the arch above the crown of the King at right (R. 1/6).

V145

814E 1s.6d. – V145. Broken arch   ...   .   3·00

1970 (11 Feb). *British Rural Architecture.*   [S. G. 815/18E]

V207. 5d. The yellow is omitted from the chimney at left once in every sheet on R. 12/2. Later added to cylinder and appearing normal.

1s.6d. Broken panes in middle window (No dot, R. 3/2).

V228

815   5d. – V207. Yellow omitted from chimney at left   1·75
818E 1s.6d. – V228. Broken window   ...   .   3·00

1970 (1 Apr). *Anniversaries.*   [S. G. 819E/23]

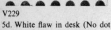

V229

5d. White flaw in desk (No dot and dot R. 2/6).

V230

5d. White spot in hem (No dot and dot, R. 5/5).

V231

5d. Parts of base of desk and front of foot missing (No dot and dot, R. 20/4).

V223

1s.6d. Missing portion of blue in bottom right-hand corner of Union Jack (R. 20/5).

819E	5d. – V229. White flaw in desk	...	...	1·75
	– V230. White spot in hem ...	...	...	1·75
	– V231. Missing portions of desk and foot			1·75
822E	1s.6d. – V223. Flag flaw	...	...	3·50

1970 (3 June). *Literary Anniversaries.*   [S. G. 824/28E]

1s.6d. Retouch consists of diagonal black lines over triangular green patch N.E. of " Grasmere " (R. 1/18).

V232

Normal   V233

1s.6d. Green line gives impression of extra road leading up foot hill (R. 6/8).

828E	1s.6d. – V232. Retouch in slope	...	...	3·50
	– V233. Extra road ...	...	...	3·50

1970 (18 Sept). *"Philympia 70" Stamp Exhibition.*   [S. G. 835/7]

V237

5d. White blob between " os " of " postage " (No dot, R. 5/6). Later retouched.

V238

5d. Weak entry of frame-line in top left corner (Dot, R. 1/2).

V239. 1s.6d. Missing dot over i " of " " printed " (R. 6/12).

835	5d. – V237. White blob ...	...	...	...	3·00
	– V238. Weak entry	...	...	...	1·50
837	1s.6d. – V239. Missing dot over "i"	...	...	3·50

1970 (25 Nov). *Christmas.*   [S. G. 838E/40E]

4d. Gold frame at right by shepherd's arm is thinned and has been strengthened by two parallel chestnut lines (No dot, R. 4/6).

V240

838E	4d. – V240. Thinned frame ...	...	...	...	1·75

1971 (25 Aug). *British Anniversaries.*   [S. G. 887/9]

9p. Spot under " u " of " union " and line to left of boot (R. 3/8).

V351

889	9p. – V351. Spot and line flaw	...	...	...	6·00

STAMP VARIETIES EXPLAINED

In this *Stanley Gibbons Guide* James Watson presents the knowledge essential to every philatelist—the various processes that are used to print stamps. By demonstrating just how varieties occur, he enables collectors to assess their relative importance and shows what contribution, if any, they can make to philatelic study. See the preliminary pages of this Catalogue for details of the current edition.

1971 (13 Oct). *Christmas.*　　　　　　　[S. G. 894/6E]

7½p. Horizontal black line on the mane of the middle horse (Cyl. 1B, R. 2/9).

V352

896E　7½p. – V352. Line on mane　...　...　...　3·75

1972 (21 June). British Architecture (Village Churches).
　　　　　　　　　　　　　　　　　[S. G. 904E/8E]

3p. Break in line of boarding (Cyl. 2A, R. 2/9).

V353

9p. Gap in vertical shading on tower (Cyl 1B, R. 1/6).

V284

904E　3p. – V353. Broken line　...　...　...　...　1·00
908E　9p. – V284. Gap in tower　...　...　...　...　5·00

1972 (18 Oct). *Christmas.*　　　　　　[S. G. 913E/15E]

2½p. Broken ribbon and scratch across Queen's head causing deformed lip (Dot cyl., R. 7/8).

V285

913E　2½p. – V285. Broken ribbon　...　...　...　1·50

1972 (20 Nov). *Royal Silver Wedding.*　　[S. G. 916/18]

V286　　　　　　　　　　V354

3p. White patch by Duke's eyebrow (R. 9/6).　　20p. Scratch under face-value (R. 9/6).

916　3p. – V286. White patch　...　...　...　...　2·00
917　20p. – V354. Scratch under value　...　...　...　6·00

1973 (28 Feb). *Tree Planting Year. British Trees* (1st issue).
　　　　　　　　　　　　　　　　　　[S. G. 922]

9p. Broken left leg of " k " (R. 9/2).

V287

922　9p. – V287. Broken "k"　...　...　...　...　4·00

1973 (18 Apr). *British Explorers.*　　　[S. G. 923E/7E]

3p. Livingstone. Line down left of shirt is missing or very weak (R. 3/7).

V288

923E　3p. – V288. Shirt variety　...　...　...　...　1·75

1973 (16 May). *County Cricket 1873–1973.*　[S. G. 928E/30]

V289　　　　　　　　　　V290

3p. Short " i " in " Cricket" (No dot, R. 1/3).　　3p. Broken " c " in " Cricket " (No dot, R. 10/7).

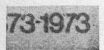

V291

All values. Break in " 7 " of
" 1973 " (No dot, R. 4/9).

V292

7½p. Black spot on shirt above
belt (Dot and no dot.
R. 9/1).

7½p. Break in hat
outline and
streak of white
behind eye (No
dot, R. 5/10).

V316

928E	3p. – V289. Short "i" in "Cricket"	...	...	2·50
	– V290. Broken "c" in "Cricket"	...	...	2·50
	– V291. Broken "7" in "1973"		...	2·25
929E	7½p. – V291. Broken "7" in "1973"	...	...	3·50
	– V292. Spot on shirt ...	...	...	4·00
	– V316. Break in hat and streak behind eye			4·00
930	9p. – V291. Broken "7" in "1973"	...	...	3·50

1973 (15 Aug). *400th Birth Anniv. of Inigo Jones.*   [S. G. 935E/8]

5p. Newmarket. Missing right serif to left leg of
" n " in " designer " (R. 9/1).

V293

937	5p. – V293. Missing serif	...	...	...	...	2·25

1973 (28 Nov). *Christmas.*   [S. G. 943E/8E]

3p. Strong retouch under " 3 " (Cyl 1B dot,
R. 8/7).

V294

944E	3p. – V294. Retouch under "3"	...	...	...	3·00

GIBBONS STAMP MONTHLY

Finest and most informative magazine for all collectors.
Obtainable either from your newsagent or by postal
subscription—details on request.

1974 (24 Apr). *Bicentenary of the Fire Prevention (Metropolis)
Act.*   [S. G. 950/3]

V317

3½p. Broken connecting rod
to right of chain-drive
wheel. (No dot, R. 4/10).

V318

5½p. Broken handrail (No
dot, R. 5/10).

950	3½p. – V317. Broken connecting rod	...	...	2·25
951	5½p. – V318. Broken handrail	...	...	2·75

1974 (12 June). *U.P.U. Centenary.*   [S. G. 954/7]

V319

3½p. Staff of pennant on
bow is almost missing
(No dot, R. 8/1).

V320

5½p. " Bomb-burst " damage
to wheels at left (No dot,
R. 6/4).

954	3½p. – V319. Pennant staff flaw	...	...	...	2·2.
955	5½p. – V320. "Bomb-burst" on wheels	...	...	3·5(

1974 (10 July). *Medieval Warriors.*   [S. G. 958/6] |

V355

4½p. Break in
" u " of
" Bruce "
(Dot Cyl.
R. 10/6).

V321

5½p. Serif to left
of " 4 of
"1416" (No
dot, R. 4/1).

V322

10p. Brown cuved line
joins " a " of
" Black " to
horse's tail (Dot,
R. 7/2).

958	4½p. – V355. Broken "u" of "Bruce"	...	...	2·0
959	5½p. – V321. Serif to "4" of "1416" ...	...	...	2·5
961	10p. – V322. Line below "a" of "Black"	...	...	5·(

1974 (9 Oct). *Birth Centenary of Sir Winston Churchill.*

[S. G. 962/5]

V323
4½p. Vertical cut severing ear (Dot, R. 1/6).

V356
5½p. White spot above face-value (Dot Cyl., R. 4/2).

8p. Cut below Churchill's left eye (Dot, R. 2/3).

V324

962	4½p. – V323. Severed ear	...	...	...	...	2·50
963	5½p. – V356. White spot flaw	...	...	...	3·00
964	8p. – V324. Cut below left eye	...	...	...	3·50

1974 (27 Nov). *Christmas.*

[S.G. 966/9]

4½p. Reversed " Q " for " O " in date (Cyl 1B–1C 1D 1E 1F –1G dot, R.1/8).

/325

967 4½p. – V325. Reversed "Q" for "O" ...   .   1·50

1975 (19 Feb). *Birth Bicentenary of J. M. W. Turner.*   [S. G. 971/4]

Turner

/326
5½p. Break in second " r " (No dot, R. 1/3).

1775-1851

V327
Apostrophe before " 1851 " (No dot, R. 6/5).

1775-18,51

'328
top between " 18 " and " 51 " (No dot, R. 8/5).

Turner

V329
10p. Break in second " r " (No dot, R 6/8).

972	5½p. – V326. Break in 2nd "r"	...	...	...	2·00
	– V327. Apostrophe before "1851"	...	...	2·00
	– V328. "18.51" ...	...	...	...	2·00
974	10p. – V329. Break in 2nd "r"	...	...	...	4·00

1975 (23 Apr). *European Architectural Heritage Year.* [S. G. 975/9]

7p. Edinburgh Outlines to both chimneys almost missing (Dot, R. 8/1).

V330

V357
7p. Edinburgh. Outline of left chimney missing (No dot, R. 1/1).

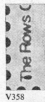

V358
7p. Chester. " T " of " The " is thickened at base (No dot, R. 4/6).

975	7p. – V330. Missing chimney outlines	...	...	2·50
	– V357. Missing left chimney	...	...	2·00
976	7p. – V358. Thick "T"	...	...	...	2·00

1975 (11 June). *Sailing.*

[S. G. 980/3]

7p. Grey moon-shaped flaw at top of red sail at left (No dot, R. 9/1).

V359

980 7p. – V359. Grey moon flaw   ...   .   2·25

1975 (13 Aug). *150th Anniv. of Public Railways.*   [S. G. 984/7]

10p. Top serif omitted from " 1 " of " Class " (Dot, R. 1/10).

V360

V361
10p. Orange glow in
driver's cab (No
dot, R. 6/4).

V362
12p. Grey " obstruction " on
line in front of engine
(No dot, R. 5/9).

V429

12p. "n" in "Train" has bottom serif
missing (Dot, R. 5/8).

986	10p. – V360. Missing serif	...	...	...	...	2·50
	– V361. Orange glow in cab	...	...	...	2·75
987	12p. – V362. Obstruction on line	...	...	...	3·50
	– V429. Missing serif to "n"	...	...	...	2·50

1975 (22 Oct). *Birth Bicentenary of Jane Austen.*   [S. G. 989/92]

8½p. Break in top frame (No dot,
R. 9/10).

V363

13p. Break in
bottom frame
(No dot, R. 3/2).

V364

989	8½p. – V363. Break in top frame	...	...	...	2·00
992	13p. – V364. Break in bottom frame	...	...	3·50

THE ELIZABETHAN

Uniform with this volume, the *Elizabethan Specialised Stamp Catalogue* covers all other aspects of the stamps of the present reign, from both Great Britain and the British Commonwealth, in considerable detail. See the preliminary pages of this Catalogue for details of this annual publication.

1976 (10 Mar). *Telephone Centenary.*   [S. G. 997/1000]

V365
8½p. Blue spot in Queen's
head appearing as
an eye (No dot,
R. 5/3).

V366
13p. Large Bump at back of
Queen's head (No dot,
R. 7/5).

997	8½p. – V365. Blue eye	...	...	...	1·50
1000	13p. – V366. Bump on Queen's head	...	...	3·00

1976 (4 Aug). *British Cultural Traditions.*   [S. G. 1010/13]

V389
10p. Brown mark on
handkerchief (No
dot, R. 1/5).

V390
Brown line between handkerchief and ribbon (No dot,
R. 3/5). The same stamp show
a yellow and red line on the
dancer's right arm.

V391

13p. Short serif to first "1"
(Dot Cyl., R. 3/1).

V392
13p. Broken harp-string
(Dot Cyl., R. 3/3).

V393
Broken harp-string
(No dot, R. 6/1).

1011	10p. – V389. Brown mark on handkerchief	...	2·
	– V390. Brown line	...	...	...	2·
1013	12p. – V391. Short serif	...	...	...	3·
	– V392. Broken harp-string	...	...	3·
	– V393. Broken harp-string	...	...	3·(

1976 (29 Sept). *500th Anniv. of British Printing.*   [S. G. 1014/17]

V394

8½p. Rider's pointed shoe
is broken at the tip
(Dot R. 9/5).

V395

Gap in shading by the
horse's hind leg
(Dot cyl., R. 3/6).

| 1014 | 8½p. – V394. Break in shoe | ... | ... | ... | 1·50 |
| | – V395. Gap in shading | ... | ... | ... | 1·50 |

1976 (24 Nov). *Christmas.*   [S. G. 1018/21]

11p. The " 3 " in the date has a purple
hook at the bottom (No dot, R. 3/2).

V396

| 1020 | 11p. – V396. Hook on "3" | ... | ... | ... | 2·75 |

1977 (12 Jan). *Racket Sports.*   [S. G. 1022/5]

V397

8½p. The white centre-line
extends through the
serving-line and off the
edge of the stamp
(No dot, R. 2/10).

V398

Black patch above player's
hand (No dot, R. 7/6).

V399

3p. Screening dots are missing at the bottom of the stamp, by
the player's foot (Dot Cyl., R. 10/1).

1022	8½p. – V397. Extended line	...	...	...	2·25
	– V398. Patch above hand	...	...	...	1·75
1025	13p. – V399. Missing screening dots	...	...	3·00

1977 (2 Mar). *Royal Institute of Chemistry Centenary.*   [S. G. 1029/32]

8½p. Dot by pipette
(No dot, R. 6/3).

V431

8½p. Dot over "a" of "Barton"
(Dot pane, R. 2/8).

V432

| 1029 | 8½p. – V431. Dot by pipette | ... | ... | ... | 1·50 |
| | – V432. Dot over "A" | ... | ... | ... | 1·50 |

1977 (5 Oct). *British Wildlife.*   [S. G. 1039/43]

V433

No. 1042. Shortened whiskers
(Dot cyl., R. 7/9.)

V434

No. 1042. Broken "e"
in "Otter" (No dot,
R. 8/9).

| 1042 | 9p. – V433. Shortened whiskers | ... | ... | 2·00 |
| | – V434. Broken "e" in "Otter" | ... | ... | 2·00 |

1978 (1 Mar). *British Architecture (Historic Buildings).*   [S. G. 1054/8E]

V435

9p. Bite from "9" (No
dot, R. 2/9).

V436

11p. Joined "fo" in
"Caernarfon" (No
dot, R. 5/2).

| 1054 | 9p. – V435. Bite from "9" | ... | ... | ... | 1·40 |
| 1056 | 11p. – V436. Joined "fo" | ... | ... | ... | 1·60 |

1978 (31 May). *25th Anniversary of Coronation.*   [S. G. 1059/62]

V461

9p. Cluster of white dots over "at" (Dot, R. 1/1).

11p. White retouch under "the Cor" (No dot, R. 4/5).

V462

11p. Chunk missing from cross (No dot, R. 3/5).

V463

11p. Extra pearl in band of orb (No dot, R. 3/6).

V464

THE ELIZABETHAN

All other aspects of the stamps of the present reign are fully covered by the *Elizabethan Specialised Stamp Catalogue,* published annually.

13p. White spot on back of neck (Dot, R. 5/10).

V465

V466

13p. Damaged "a" in "Coronation" (Dot, R. 6/8).

1059	9p. – V461. White dots	...	...	...	...	1·40
1061	11p. – V462. White retouch	...	...	...	1·60
	– V463. Damaged cross	...	...	...	1·60
	– V464. Extra pearl	...	...	...	1·60
1062	13p. – V465. Spot on neck	...	...	...	1·75
	– V466. Damaged "a"	...	...	...	1·75

1978 (5 July) *Horses.*   [S. G. 1063/6]

9p. Black line under plough on horse (No dot, R. 8/1)

V467

V468

9p. Extra dot over "i" (No dot, R. 6/9).

V469

V470

10½p. Weak figures (Dot, R. 3/5).

11p. Blob on hoof (No dot, R. 9/2)

1063	9p – V467. Black line	...	...	...	...	1·40
	– V468. Extra dot	...	...	...	...	1·40
1064	10½p. – V469. Weak figures	...	...	...	1·40
1065	11p – V470. Blob on hoof	...	...	...	1·60

1978 (2 Aug). *Centenaries of Cyclists Touring Club and the British Cycling Federation.* [S. G. 1067/70]

V471

9p. "Valve" on lady's rear wheel (No dots, R. 7/7).

V472

9p. Black line in spokes of lady's front wheel (Dot, R. 10/1).

V473

10½p. Broken stay to mudguard (No dot, R. 5/3).

V474

10½p. Chunk out of chain guard (Dot, R. 9/2).

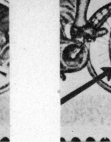

V475

10½p. Broken wheel (Dot, R. 10/9).

V476

10½p. Broken cross-bar (Dot, R. 10/2).

V477

13p. Damaged "p" (No dot, R. 2/5).

V478

13p. Broken "g" and white spot on shirt (No dot, R. 5/5).

V479

13p. Broken "y" (No dot, R. 5/10).

V480

13p. Break in tyre tread (No dot, R. 6/4).

PHILATELIC TERMS ILLUSTRATED

The essential philatelic dictionary. Terms covering printing methods, papers, errors, varieties, watermarks, perforations and much more are explained and illustrated, many in full colour. See the preliminary pages of this Catalogue for details of the current edition.

V481

13p. Short leg to "n" (No dot, R. 1/1).

V482

13p. Broken "g" (No dot, R. 10/5).

1067	9p. – V471. "Valve" on wheel	...	...	...	1·50
	– V472. Black line in spokes	...	...	1·40
1008	10½p – V473. Broken stay	...	...	...	1·40
	– V474. Chunk out of chain guard	...	1·50
	– V475. Broken wheel	...	...	...	1·75
	– V476. Broken cross-bar	...	...	1·75
1070	13p. – V477. Damaged "p"	...	...	...	1·75
	– V478. Broken "g" and spot on shirt	...	2·00
	– V479. Broken "y"	...	...	...	1·60
	– V480. Break in tyre tread	...	...	1·60
	– V481. Short leg to "n"	...	...	1·60
	– V482. Broken "g"	...	...	...	1·60

1978 (22 Nov). *Christmas.*   [S. G. 1071/4]

V483

7p. Long diagonal scratch (Dot, R. 1/10 only with 1F gold cyl).

V484

7p. Plate scratch (No dot, R. 8/4).

V485

7p. "Bubble" flaw by man's mouth (No dot, R. 3/1).

V486

9p. Bottom side of collecting box missing (Dot, R. 1/7 and R. 2/4).

V487

9p. Damaged foot to "p" (Dot, R. 7/1).

V488

13p. Damaged top to "1" (Dot, R. 6/4).

V489

13p. Part of magenta garter missing from right leg (Dot, R. 10/5).

1071	7p. – V483. Long scratch	...	...	...	2·00
	– V484. Plate scratch	...	...	...	2·00
	– V485. "Bubble" flaw	...	...	...	2·00
1072	9p. – V486. Collecting box flaw	...	...	1·50
	– V487. Damaged "p"	...	...	...	1·50
1074	13p. – V488. Damaged "1"	...	...	...	1·60
	– V489. Part of garter missing	...	...	1·60

1979 (7 Feb). *Dogs.*   [S. G. 1075/8]

V490

10½p. Short serif to figure "1" (Dot, R. 1/3).

V491

10½p. Sliced corner to "p" (Dot, R. 8/5).

| 1076 | 10½p. – V490. Short serif | ... | ... | ... | 1·6 |
| | – V491. Sliced "p" | ... | ... | ... | 1·6 |

1979 (21 Mar). *Spring Wild Flowers.*   [S. G. 1079/82]

10½p. Pale yellow petal falling away to the right central daffodil (Dot, R. 1/8).

V492

V493

11p. Vertical dark scratch through blue-bell leaves (Dot, R. 10/8)

| 1080 | 10½p. – V492. Yellow petal falling away | ... | ... | 1·50 |
| 1081 | 11p. – V493. Scratch through leaves | ... | ... | 1·75 |

1979 (9 May). *First Direct Elections to European Assembly.*
[S.G. 1083/6]

V494

9p. Bottom right ballot box damaged at left (No dot, R. 9/3).

V495

V496

10½p. Part of stripe of bottom right flag missing (No dot, R. 7/3).

13p. Break in Queen's ribbon (Dot, R. 6/9).

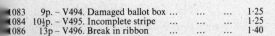

1083	9p. – V494. Damaged ballot box	...	...	...	1·25
1084	10½p. – V495. Incomplete stripe	...	...	...	1·25
1086	13p – V496. Break in ribbon	...	...	...	1·40

1979 (6 June). *Horse Racing Paintings and Bicentenary of the Derby.*
[S. G. 1087/90]

V497

V498

10½p. Semi-circle of brown dots appearing as leaves over left hand tree (Dot, R. 6/1).

11p. Short serif to first figure "1" (No dot, R. 4/5).

V499

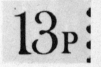

V500

11p. Large yellow spot on rear horse (No dot, R. 8/2).

13p. Bottom left serif of "1" missing (No dot R. 9/9).

1088	10½p. – V497. Brown dots	...	...	...	...	1·25
1089	11p. – V498. Short serif	...	...	...	...	1·40
	– V499. Yellow spot	...	...	...	...	1·40
1090	13p – V500. Serif missing	...	...	...	...	1·40

1979 (11 July). *International Year of the Child.*   [S. G. 1091/4]

V501

V502

9p. Outline of duck's bill broken (No dot, R. 8/8).

9p. Patch of white on roof of shed at right (No dot, R. 9/2).

V503

V504

9p. Large yellow patch above Rabbit's right paw (No dot, R. 5/1).

10½p. Large white tear in Toad's coat between its legs (No dot, R. 2/5).

1091	9p. – V501. Duck's bill broken	...	...	...	1·10
	– V502. White patch	...	...	...	1·10
	– V503. Yellow patch	...	...	...	1·10
1092	10½p. – V504. Torn coat tail	...	...	...	1·25

1979 (22 Aug–24 Oct). *Death Centenary of Sir Rowland Hill.*
[S. G. 1092/9]

11½p. Large dot on breeches (Dot, R. 2/2).

V505

11½p. White chimney at extreme right (Dot, R. 10/8).

V506

15p. Envelope incomplete (No dot, R. 8/7).

V507

1096	11½p. – V505. Dot on breeches	...	...	...	1·40
	– V506. White chimney	...	...	...	1·40
1098	15p. – V507. Envelope incomplete	...	...	1·75

1979 (26 Sept). *150th Anniv. of Metropolitan Police.* [S. G. 1100/3]

V508   V509

10p. Loss of deep green above wall. (Dot, R. 2/1)   10p. "Bird" on Policeman's helmet (No dot, R. 3/1).

V510   V511

10p Extra cloud under Queen's head (No dot, R. 1/7).   10p. Large bird under Queen's head (No dot, R. 10/5).

V512   V513

13p. White patch on trousers (No dot, R. 9/7).   13p. Railings are faint (No dot, R. 7/5).

1100	10p. – V508. Pale patch	...	...	...	...	1·10
	– V509. "Bird" on helmet	...	...	...	1·50
	– V510. Extra cloud	...	...	...	1·40
	– V511. Large bird	...	...	...	1·50
1102	13p. – V512. White patch	...	...	...	1·40
	– V513. Faint railings	...	...	...	1·40

1979 (21 Nov). *Christmas.* [S. G. 1104/8]

V514   V515

8p. Black dot over tassels of blanket (No dot, R. 4/1)   8p. White patch at bottom of king's cloak (Dot, R. 2/9).

V516

10p. Break in fold of angel's robe
(No dot, R. 2/1).

V517

11½p. White blob over Joseph's
left eye (Dot, R. 1/2).

V518

13p. Large white patch on left hind-leg
(No dot, R. 7/7).

1104	8p. – V514. Black dot over tassels	...	...	1·25
	– V515. White patch on cloak	...	...	1·00
1105	10p. – V516. Break in fold of robe	...	...	1·40
1106	11½p. – V517. White blob over eye	...	...	1·40
1107	13p. – V518. White patch on hind-leg	...	...	1·75

1980 (16 Jan). *Centenary of Wild Bird Protection Act.*
[S. G. 1109/12]

519

0. White nick in thin wavy line at
left (No dot, R. 1/9).

V520

10p. Nick out of grey wavy line
near top (Dot, R. 1/3).

521

0p. Break in blue wavy line left of
tail (Dot, R. 4/1).

V522

10p. Break in blue line to the right
of bird's tail (No dot, R. 4/7).

V523

11½p. Top left thin blue line cut
short at left (Dot, R. 1/2).

V524

13p. Break in blue line under bird's
left leg (No dot, R. 6/2).

15p. Claws of left Wagtail
filled by unsuccessful
retouch and dark
scratches added on
branch (No dot, R. 1/3).

V525

1109	10p. – V519. White nick from line at left ...	...	1·25
	– V520. Wavy line flaw ...	...	1·25
	– V521. Broken line left of tail	...	1·25
	– V522. Broken line right of tail	...	1·25
1110	11½p. – V523. Short line	...	1·40
1111	13p. – V524. Broken line beneath leg	...	1·50
1112	15p. – V525. Claw and branch retouch	...	1·75

1980 (12 Mar). *150th Anniv. of Liverpool and Manchester Railway.*
[S. G. 1113/17]

V526

12p. Centre step filled in with grey
dots (No dot, R. 8/4).

V527

12p. Broken rail (No dot, R. 1/5).

1116	12p. – V526. Grey step	...	...	...	...	1·50
1117	12p. – V527. Broken rail	...	...	...	...	1·50

1980 (7 May). *London Landmarks.*   [S. G. 1120/4]

V528

15p. "H" partially re-engraved (Dot, R, 1/10).

1125   15p. – V528. Re-engraved "н"   ...   .   1·50

1980 (9 July). *Famous Authoresses.*   [S. G. 1125/8]

V529

12p. Missing "p" in value (No dot, R. 4/6).

V533

13½p. Broken line in "CEPT" emblem (Dot, R. 1/3).

V534

15p. Nick in eyebrow (No dot, R. 8/7).

1125   12p. – V529. Missing "p"   ...   .   12·00
1126   13½p. – V533. Line break   ...   .   1·25
1127   15p. – V534. Eyebrow flaw   ...   .   1·75

Great Britain
Regional Issues

I. NORTHERN IRELAND

1958–67 [S. G. NI1/6]

4d White spot on top flower (Cyl 1 no dot R 7/7). This was retouched on the phosphor issue leaving two deep ultramarine spots.

V61

4d. White dot under "s" (Cyl 1 dot R. 2/4). Retouched on the phosphor issue.

V86

4d. White dot on leaf of plant (Cyl 1 no dot R. 3/12). Retouched on 4d. vermilion.

V87

NI2   4d. – V61. Flower flaw ... ... 2·50
       – V86. Dot under "s" ... ... 4·00
       – V87. Dot on leaf ... ... 2·50
       p. Two phosphor bands
       – p V61. Flower flaw retouched ... ... 2·50
       – p V87. Dot on leaf ... ... 2·50

1968–70. Chalky paper. Two phosphor bands, except where otherwise stated. [S. G. NI 7E/11]

5d. White flaw near junction of flax plant stalks appears as an extra leaf (Cyl 1 no dot R. 13/2).

V203

NI7E   4d. – V61. Flower flaw retouched ... ... 2·00
       – V87. Dot on leaf ... ... 2·00
       Ev. PVA gum
       – Ev V61. Flower flaw retouched ... ... 20·00
       – Ev V87. Dot on leaf ... ... 20·00

NI8   4d. (1 centre band)
       – V61. Flower flaw retouch ... ... 3·00
       – V87. Dot on leaf ... ... 3·00
NI10   5d. – V203. "Extra leaf" ... ... 3·00

1971 (7 July)–78. Decimal Currency. Chalky paper. Two phosphor bands, except where otherwise stated. [S. G. NI12/26]

3½p. Rectangle of white dots below chin (Cyl 1 no dot, R. 4/10).

V331

(R. 1/6)   V295   (R. 20/7)

5½p. Cylinder scratch extends diagonally from R. 1/6 to R. 20/7 in no dot cyl 1. Supplied in blocks of 40.

V296   V367

5½p. Missing top to cross on crown (Cyl. 1 no dot, R. 11/10).

6½p. White spot over small crown (Cyl. 1 dot, R. 15/3).

V337   V401

6½p. Dark spot in band of crown (Cyl. 1 dot, R. 16/6).

6½p. Spot in hair (Cyl. 1 dot, R. 12/8).

V437   V297

7p. Spot on crown (Cyl. 1 no dot, R. 6/3).

8p. Dark spot over Queen's upper lip (Cyl 1 no dot, R.3/7).

V438

9p. Sliced " 9 " (Cyl. 1
dot, R. 9/10).

V439

9p. Curved flaw over crown
(Cyl. 1 no dot, R. 16/10).

10p. Cross-shaped jewel on crown
has its left-side missing
(Cyl. 1 dot, R. 8/3).

V400

V440

10½p. Missing cross
(Cyl. 3 no dot,
R. 4/3).

V441

10½p. Heavy line under
bust (Cyl. 3 no
dot, R. 18/2).

V442

10½p. White blob over
crown (Cyl. 3 no
dot, R. 20/8).

NI16	3½p.	(1 centre band)			
		– V331. White dots under chin	...	...	2·50
NI19	5½p.	– V295. Cylinder scratch (in block of 40)	...		25·00
		– V296. No top to cross in crown	...	...	2·25
NI20	5½p.	(1 centre band)			
		– V296. No top to cross on crown	...		2·25
NI21	6½p.	(1 centre band)			
		– V337. Spot in band	...	...	1·50
		– V367. Spot over crown	...	...	1·50
		– V401. Spot in hair	...	...	1·75
NI21a	7p.	(1 centre band)			
		– V437. Spot on crown	...	...	1·25
NI23	8p.	– V297. Lip flaw	...	...	2·25
NI24a	9p.	– V438. Sliced "9"	...	...	1·50
		– V439. Curved flaw over crown	...	...	1·50
NI25	10p.	– V400. Cross partly missing	...	...	1·75
NI25a	10½p.	– V440. Missing cross	...	...	2·00
		– V441. Heavy line under bust	...	...	1·25
		– V442. White blob over crown	...	...,	1·25

II. SCOTLAND

1958–67   [S.G. S1/6]

3d. White flaw on lower left of " U "
of " REVENUE " (Cyl 3 dot R. 19/8).

V44

V88

3d. Coloured dot in " d ", later
retouched (Cyl. 3 dot R. 20/12).

V100

3d. White flaw after final " E " of " REVENUE "
(Cyl 5 dot R. 20/2).

V101

4d. White flaw before second
" E " of " REVENUE " (Cyl
2 dot R. 10/9). Retouched
on No. S9.

V253

4d. White spot on " T "
(Cyl 2 dot R. 4/4).

V45

6d. Broken " v " of " REVENUE "
(Cyl 1 no dot R. 11/12).

V89

6d. Curl on point of thistle
leaf, later retouched (Cyl
1 no dot R. 7/7).

6d. Leaf half-way down at right
has V-shaped cut in solid
colour (Cyl 4 no dot R. 2/10).

V204

V90

1s.3d. Broken oblique in value (Cyl 4 no dot
R.15/2).

S1   3d. – V44.   Spot on "U"   ...   .   2·75
       – V88.   Dot in "d" ...   .   2·50
       – V100. Spot after "E"   ...   ...   2·25
     p.   Two phosphor bands
       – p V100. Spot after "E"   ...   ...   14·00
     pa.   One side phosphor band
       – pa V100. Spot after "E"   ...   ...   6·00
S2   4d. – V101. Dot before "E"   ...   ...   2·00
       – V253. White spot in "T"   ...   ...   2·00
     p.   Two phosphor bands
       – p V101. Dot before "E"   ...   ...   2·00
       – p V253. White spot on "T"   ...   ...   2·00
S3   6d. – V45.   Broken "v"   ...   .   3·00
       – V89.   Curled leaf ...   .   2·50
       – V204. Cut leaf   ...   .   2·50
     p.   Two phosphor bands
       – p V204. Cut leaf   ...   .   10·00
S5   1s.3d. – V90.   Broken oblique   ...   ...   3·00
     p.   Two phosphor bands
       – p V90. Broken oblique   ...   ...   3·00

1967–70. Chalky paper. Two phosphor bands, except where otherwise stated   [S.G. S7E/13]

5d.   Large retouch on Queen's shoulder (Cyl 2 dot, R. 16/6).

V235

S7E   3d.   (1 centre band)
       – V100. Spot after "E"   ...   .   2·00
     Ev.   PVA gum
       – Ev V100. Spot after "E"   ...   ...   2·25
S11   5d. – V235. Shoulder retouch   ...   ...   5·50

1971 (7 July)–78. *Decimal Currency.* Chalky paper. Two phosphor bands, except where otherwise stated.   [S.G. S14E/28]

V332
4½p. White spot in S.W. corner of "4" (Cyl 1 no dot, R. 2/7).

V333
4½p. Large white blob joining hind legs of lion (Cyl 1 no dot, R. 3/5).

4½p. Large white stop after "p" (R. 5/1, Cyl 1 no dot). (Believed later retouched).

V368

V298
5½p. Dark squiggle in hair below band (Cyl 1 no dot, R. 2/10).

V299
5½p. Spot in " 5 " (Cyl. 1 no dot, R. 11/10).

V402
6½p. Break in lion's tail (Cyl 1, no dot, R. 1/4).

V403
6½p. Missing claw (Cyl. 1, no dot, R. 2/6).

V404

6½p. Extra claw (Cyl 1 no dot, R. 4/3).

V443

7p. White spot on "p" (Cyl. 1 no dot, R. 8/5).

V405
8½p. Flaw on toes (Cyl 2 dot, R. 8/10).

V406
8½p. White scratch by mane (Cyl 2 dot, R. 11/1).

V530

10½p. White spot on lion's thigh (Cyl. 4 dot, R. 18/3).

S19   4½p. – V332. Spot in "4"   ...   .   2·25
       – V333. Blob joining hind legs   ...   2·50
       – V368. Stop after "P"   ...   .   4·00
S21   5½p. – V298. Hair flaw   ...   .   2·50
       – V299. Spot in "5"   ...   .   2·50
S22   5½p.   (1 centre band)
       – V298. Hair flaw   ...   .   2·50
       – V299. Spot in "5"   ...   .   2·50

S23	6½p.	(1 centre band)				
		– V402. Broken tail	...	...	...	...	1·50
		– V403. Missing claw	...	...	...	...	1·50
		– V404. Extra claw	...	...	...	...	1·50
S23*a*	7p.	(1 centre band)				
		– V443. White spot on "p"	...	...	...	1·00
S26	8½p.	– V405. Flaw on toes	...	...	...	...	1·75
		– V406. Scratch by mane	...	...	...	1·75
S27	10p.	– V530. White spot	...	...	...	...	2·00

III. WALES

1958–67.   [S. G. W1/6]

3d. White flaw joining spine of Dragon's wing to tail (Cyl. 2 no dot R. 16/1).

V27

3d. White flaw on left of right value oval, later retouched (Cyl. 1 no dot R. 6/3).

V91

| W1 | 3d. | – V27. Wing-tail flaw | ... | ... | ... | ... | 2·00 |
| | | – V91. Bulge on oval | ... | ... | ... | ... | 5·50 |

1967–70. Chalky paper. Two phosphor bands, except where otherwise stated.   [S. G. W7/12]

4d. White spot before "E" of "POSTAGE" (Cyl 2 no dot R. 17/12). Later retouched on 4d. sepia.

V134

4d. White spot after "E" of "POSTAGE" (Cyl 2 no dot R. 18/10). Later retouched on 4d. sepia.

V135

4d. White spot above dragon's hindleg (Cyl 2 no dot R. 20/1). Retouched on 4d. bright vermilion.

V136

W8	4d.	– V134. Spot before "E"	...	...	...	2·00
		– V135. Spot after "E"	...	...	...	2·00
		– V136. Spot over hindleg	...	...	...	2·00
W9	4d.	(1 centre band)				
		– V134. Spot before "E"	...	...	...	3·00
		– V135. Spot after "E"	...	...	...	3·00
		– V136. Spot over hindleg	...	...	...	3·00

1971 (7 July)–78. *Decimal Currency.* Chalky paper. Two phosphor bands, except where otherwise stated.   [S. G. W13E/27]

V255

2½p. **Extra curved line from top of dragon's head to bottom of central leg** (Cyl 3 no dot R. 4/6).

V369

2½p. Dragon's snout is **severed** (Dot, R. 3/1). **(Later retouched.)**

V370

2½p. **Extra line in wing** (Dot, R 18/8).

V256

3p. Break in the line down dragon's breast (Cyl 1 no dot R. 2/1).

V268

3p. White "v" shaped flaw appearing as extra claw to hind leg (Cyl 1 no dot, R.1/81).

V300
3p. Forelegs joined by white flaw and broken blue line down dragon's body (Cyl 1 no dot, R. 6/10).

V371
3p. Broken body line near foot (Cyl 1 dot, R. 10/10).

V408
6½p. Dragon's barbed tail is "blunt" (Cyl. 1 dot, R. 4/6).

V531
6½p. Dark blob in diadem (Cyl. 1 no dot, R. 14/9).

V334
3½p. Break in line down dragon's breast, as V256 (Cyl 2 dot, R. 3/7).

V335
3½p. Large white spot between "1" of fraction and "P" (Cyl 2 dot, R. 17/5).

V373
8½p. White spot over crown (Cyl 1 no dot, R. 8/1).

V444
11p. Front wing-tip is missing (Cyl 1 no dot, R. 15/7).

V336
4½p. Vertical scratch below Queen's eye (Cyl 1 dot, R. 5/4).

V337. See V337 of Northern Ireland.

V445
11p. Two wing-tips missing at front (Cyl 1 no dot, R. 16/9).

Normal

5p. Extra claw on dragon's hind foot (Cyl 3 dot, R. 17/2).

V257

V301
5½p. Dark spot on forehead (Cyl 1 no dot, R. 15/9).

V372
6½p. Missing tip to dragon's wing (Cyl 1 dot, R. 20/7).

V407
6½p. Mark on dragon's wing (Cyl 1 dot, R. 4/8).

W13E	2½p.	(1 centre band)			
		– V255. Extra line in dragon	...	...	3·00
		– V369. Severed snout	...	...	4·00
		– V370. Extra line in wing	...	...	2·50
	Eg.	Gum arabic			
		– Eg V370. Extra line in wing	...	...	2·50
W14E	3p.	– V256. Break in line in dragon	...	...	2·50
		– V268. Extra hind claw	...	...	2·50
		– V300. Dragon flaws	...	...	2·50
		– V371. Broken body line	...	...	2·50
	Eg.	Gum arabic			
		– Eg V256. Break in line in dragon	...		6·00
		– Eg V300. Dragon flaws	...	...	6·00
		– Eg V371. Broken body line	...	...	6·00
W15	3p.	(1 centre band)			
		– V371. Broken body line	...	...	2·25
W16	3½p.	– V334. Dragon line break	...	...	2·75
		– V335. Spot in value	...	...	2·75
W17	3½p.	(1 centre band)			
		– V334. Dragon line break	...	...	2·75
		– V335. Spot in value	...	...	2·75
W18	4½p.	– V336. Scratch below eye	...	...	2·50
		– V337. Spot in band	...	...	2·50
W19	5p.	– V257. Extra claw	...	...	4·00
W20	5½p.	– V301. Spot on forehead	...	...	2·50
W21	5½p.	(1 centre band)			
		– V301. Spot on forehead	...	...	2·50
W22	6½p.	(1 centre band)			
		– V372. Missing wing tip	...	...	1·50
		– V407. Mark on wing	...	...	1·50
		– V408. Blunt tail	...	...	1·50
		– V531. Dark blob in diadem	...	...	1·75
W25	8½p.	– V373. White spot over crown	...		1·75
W27	11p.	– V444. Missing wing-tip	...	...	1·25
		– V445. Two missing wing-tips	...	...	1·25

Channel Islands: Guernsey

(a) Regional Issues

1958–67   [S. G. 6/8]

V128

4d. Coloured line across top of stem (Cyl 1 no dot R. 12/8). Retouched on No. 11 (See V179).

8	4d. – V128. Stem flaw	...	...	...	...	3·50
	p. Two phosphor bands					
	– p V128. Stem flaw	...	...	...	...	3·50

1968–69. Chalky paper. Two phosphor bands, except where otherwise stated.   [S. G. 9/12]

V129

V179

4d. Spot over " 4 " has been retouched (Cyl 1 no dot R. 16/10). Corrected on No. 11.

Former flaw is now retouched but still shows as a smudge to right of stem (Cyl 1 no dot R. 12/8).

V130

V234

5d. Large coloured spot over central stamen (Cyl 1 no dot R. 12/1).

5d. Still visible after re-touch on late printing.

9	4d. – V128. Stem flaw	...	...	...	...	3·50
10	4d. *olive-sepia* (1 centre band)					
	– V128. Stem flaw	...	...	...	...	3·50
	– V129. Retouched "4"	...	...	...	...	3·50
11	4d. *bright vermilion* (1 centre band)					
	– V179. Stem flaw retouched	...		...	...	5·00
12	5d – V130. Stamen flaw	...	...	...	...	4·00
	– V234. Retouched	...	...	...	...	6·00

(b) Independent Postal Administration

1969 (1 Oct)–70. *Views*   [S. G. 13E/28]

V270

V271

½d. Nick in white frame at left (Pl. 1A–1A, R. 4/2).

½d. White patch in wall at left (Pl. 1B–1B, R. 3/2).

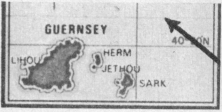

V173

1d. and 1s.6d. Extra line above line of latitude (Pl. 1A–1A, R .1/2).

V174

1d. and 1s.6d. Extra line of latitude partly removed with diagonal line below " 3 " (Pl. 1A–2A, R. 1/2).

V219

V218

1d. (14*b*). Dagger in William's shoulder (Pl. 2B–2B, R. 4/1).

1d. (14*b*) and 1s.6d. (23*b*). Faint circle to the left of compass (Pl. 2A–2A 1d. or 1A–2A 1s.6d., R. 4/3).

V374

4d. White spot by lily (from booklets).

Jersey

Normal   V175   V220

1s.9d. Small patch of white obscures ear-ring so that it seems to be missing (Pl. 1A–1A, R. 1/4).

£1 (28 and 28a). White spot over " A " of " BAILI-WICK " (R. 6/3).

Two types of 1d. and 1s.6d.
  I. Latitude inscr " 40° 30′ N "
  II. Corrected to " 49° 30′ N "

13E	½d. – V270. Nick in frame		...	...	1·75
	– V271. White patch in wall		...	...	1·75
	Ea. Thin paper				
	– Ea V270. Nick in frame		...		3·00
	– Ea V271. White patch in wall		...		3·00
14E	1d.(I) – V173. Extra line of latitude		...		4·00
	Ea. Thin paper				
	– Ea V174. Partly corrected line of latitude		...	...	5·50
14b	1d.(II) – V218. Faint circle		...	...	3·00
	– V219. Dagger in shoulder		...		3·00
18Ea	4d. Booklet stamp with margins				
	– a V374. White spot		...	...	3·50
23E	1s.6d.(I) – V173. Extra line of latitude		...		7·00
	Ea. Thin paper				
	– Ea V174. Partly corrected line of latitude		...	...	7·00
23b	1s.6d.(II) – V218. Faint circle		...		17·00
24E	1s.9d. – V175. Missing ear-ring		...		15·00
28	£1 (perf 12½)				
	– V220. White spot over "A"		...	...	25·00
	a. Perf 13				
	– a V220. White spot over "A"		...		7·00

1970 (11 Nov). Christmas.   [S. G. 40/43]

4d. Large " AS " in " CHRIST-MAS " (Plate A1, R. 6/1).

V217

40	4d. – V217. Large "AS"	...	...	...	1·50

STAMP VARIETIES EXPLAINED

In this *Stanley Gibbons Guide* James Watson presents the knowledge essential to every philatelist—the various processes that are used to print stamps. By demonstrating just how varieties occur, he enables collectors to assess their relative importance and shows what contribution, if any, they can make to philatelic study. See the preliminary pages of this Catalogue for details of the current edition.

(a) Regional Issues

1958–67.   [S. G. 9/11]

Normal V84

2½d. Letters of " POSTAGE " are thinner resulting in more white showing in the " o " and " G " (Cyl 1 no dot R. 18/1).

V24

3d. " Halberd " flaw to left of mace (Cyl 1 no dot R. 20/3). Subsequently retouched.

V85

3d. Tomato on truss at left joined to leaf by white line (Cyl 1 no dot R. 19/9). Later retouched.

V180

3d. Diagonal scratch through Queen's collar at right (Cyl 2 no dot R. 9/8).

V60

4d. White flaw over top leaf at left (Cyl 1 no dot R. 3/6). Later retouched on ordinary and exists only re-touched on the phosphor issue.

9	2½d. – V84. Thin "POSTAGE"	...	...	...	...	6·50
10	3d. – V24. "Halberd" flaw	...	...	...	...	7·00
	– V85. Joined tomato	...	...	...	...	7·00
	– V180. Scratched collar	...	...	...	...	7·00
	p. One centre phosphor band					
	– p V180. Scratched collar	...	...	...		3·00
11	4d. – V60. Leaf flaw	...	...	...	...	3·00

1968–69. [S. G. 12/14]

5d. White dot above lowest leaf at right (Cyl 1 no dot R. 16/6).

V132

5d. Top leaf at right is joined to shield by white line (Cyl 1 no dot R. 19/12).

V133

| 14 | 5d. – V132. Leaf dot ... | ... | ... | ... | ... | 4·00 |
| | – V133. Shield flaw | ... | ... | ... | ... | 4·00 |

(b) Independent Postal Administration

1969 (1 Oct)–70. [S. G. 15E/29]

V258   V221

1d. (16a). Break in trunk of tree over 2nd "E" of "JERSEY" (Booklet stamp).   4d, Black blotch on castle wall (Pl. 1A, R. 4/2).

Normal

V222

4d. (19a). Imprint redrawn, the lettering being heavier and less even.

16Ea	1d.	Booklet stamp with margins			
		– a V258. Break in tree trunk	...	...	...	3·00
19E	4d. – V221.	Blotch on castle wall ...	...	...	3·00
	a.	Booklet stamp with margins			
		– a V222. Redrawn imprint	...	...	...	10·00

1970–74. Decimal Currency. [S. G. 42/56]

V302   V272

½p. Two coloured spots over castle (Pl. 1A, R. 5/5).   7½p. White flaw in Queen's hair by ear appearing as missing lock (Pl. 1A, R. 2/4).

| 42 | ½p. – V302. 2 spots over castle | ... | ... | ... | 1·00 |
| 52 | 7½p. – V272. Missing lock in hair | ... | ... | ... | 1·25 |

1971 (15 June). 50th Anniv. of Royal British Legion. [S. G. 61/64]

V259   V260

7½p. Black spot over soldier's right-hand pocket (Pl. 1B, R. 9/4).   9p. Pale green spot above intersection of flag poles (Pl. 1B, R. 2/5).

| 63 | 7½p. – V259. Spot over pocket | ... | ... | ... | 11·00 |
| 64 | 9p. – V260. Green flaw | ... | ... | ... | 11·00 |

1976–78. [S. G. 137/55]

½p. Black bump on back of Queen's head. Reprint of 31.8.78 (Pl. 1B, R. 10/5).

V303

10p. Broken "H" in "PARISH". Reprint of 31.8.78. (Pl. 1A, R. 2/3).

V304

| 137 | ½p. – V303. Bump on head | ... | ... | ... | 1·25 |
| 144 | 10p. – V304. Broken "H" | ... | ... | ... | 1·40 |

1978 (18 Oct). Bicentenary of England–Jersey Government Mail Packet Service. [S. G. 197/201]

8p. White "ear-ring" on Queen's head (Pl. 1B, R. 10/3).

V305

| 198 | 8p. – V305. "Ear-ring" flaw | ... | ... | ... | 1·50 |

Isle of Man

(a) Regional Issues

1968–69. [S. G. 4/7]

V131
5d. White flaw by frame in upper right corner (Cyl 1 no dot, R. 20/1).

V236
5d. Similar flaw in bottom left corner (Cyl 1 no dot, R. 20/12).

7	5d. – V131. Frame flaw (top right)	...	...	...	5·00
	– V236. Frame flaw (bottom left)	...	...	...	5·00

1971 (7 July). *Decimal Currency.* [S. G. 8/11]

V269
2½p. White projection to ankle of bottom leg (Cyl 3 no dot, R. 15/1).

V254
7½p. White flaw on " 7 " (Cyl 4 dot, R. 12/7).

8	2½p. – V269. Ankle flaw	...	...	...	...	2·50
11	7½p. – V254. Flaw on "7"	...	...	...	...	3·75

(b) Independent Postal Administration

1973 (4 Aug). *Steam Railway Centenary.* [S. G. 35/38]

V338
2½p. Stop before " Y " of " Centenary " (R. 4/5).

V303
7½p. Apostrophe after " NICHOLSON " (R. 8/5).

35	2½p. – V338. Stop before "Y"	...	...	...	1·75
37	7½p. – V303. Apostrophe flaw	...	...	...	5·00

1973 (4 Sept). *Golden Jubilee of the Manx Grand Prix.* [S. G. 39/40]

V304
3p. Black spot behind Queen's neck (R. 10/5).

V375
Double " J " in imprint (Pl. 1C, R. 5/1).

3½p. Green lines in front o motor bikes (Pl. 1D, R. 5/1).

V376

39	3p. – V304. Spot behind neck		...	...	...	2·25
	V375. Double "J"	...	...	...	...	2·25
40	3½p. – V376. Green lines	...	...	...	...	2·25

1977 (1 Mar). *Silver Jubilee.* [S. G. 94/96]

25p. Line on Queen's nose (Pl. 1B, R. 3/5).

V446

96	25p. – V446. Line on Queen's nose	...	...	...	3·50

POSTAGE DUE STAMPS

1975 (8 Jan). [S. G. D9/16]

All values. Red dot in margin, above crown (Pl. 1A, R. 3/1).

V9

D 9	½p. – V9. Red dot	...	...	...	...	...	1·00
D10	1p. – V9. Red dot	...	...	...	...	...	1·00
D11	4p. – V9. Red dot	...	...	...	...	...	1·00
D12	7p. – V9. Red dot	...	...	...	...	...	1·00
D13	9p. – V9. Red dot	...	...	...	...	...	1·50
D14	10p. – V9. Red dot	...	...	...	...	...	1·75
D15	50p. – V9. Red dot	...	...	...	...	...	2·50
D16	£1 – V9. Red dot	...	...	...	...	...	4·00

Abu Dhabi

1966 (1 Oct). *Surcharge.*   [S. G. 15/25]

  V1. Thick bar 1½–2mm long above "D" of "Dinar" (R.7/3).
25 1d. on 10r. – V1. Short bar above "D"   ...   ...   55·00

Aden

79	15c.	– V1. Setting mark	...	2·50
82E	50c. *indigo-blue*	– V3. Re-entry ...	...	2·00
	Ea. Pale indigo-blue	– V3. Re-entry ...	...	2·00

1953 (15 June)–63. *Views.* Wmk Script CA.   [S. G. 48/72E]

15c. Setting mark outside left frame (R. 4/3, Pl. 1).

V1

V2   Normal

25c. Diagonal flaw on wall of building near portrait (R. 1/5). Removed by retouching on Nos. 55E and *Ea.*

V3   V4

50c. Re-entry in Arabic inscription at top centre. Consists of short lines within character (R.7/1).

70c. Setting mark over top frame (R. 5/10, Pl. 1).

52	15c. *blue-green*	– V1. Setting mark	...	2·25
53E	15c. *greenish grey*	– V1. Setting mark	...	2·25
	Ea. Deep greenish grey	– V1. Setting mark	...	2·25
	Eb. Greenish slate	– V1. Setting mark	...	2·25
54	25c.	– V2. Wall flaw	...	20·00
58	50c. *dull blue*	– V3. Re-entry	...	3·00
59E	50c. *deep blue* (perf 12)	– V3. Re-entry	...	3·00
	Ea. Perf 12 × 13½	– V3. Re-entry	...	2·50
60	70c. *brown-grey*	– V4. Setting mark	...	9·00
61	70c. *black* (perf 12)	– V4. Setting mark	...	9·00
	a. Perf 12 × 13½	– V4. Setting mark	...	9·00

1959 (26 Jan). *Revised Constitution*   [S. G. 74/5]

74	15c. – V1. Setting mark	...	...	...	...	3·00

Aitutaki

1972 (20 Nov). *Royal Silver Wedding.*   [S. G. 46/47]

15c. Curved dotted line on right cheek of Princess appears as a scar (R. 2/2 on 50% of sheets).

V1

47   15c. – V1. Scar on cheek   ...   .   6·00

Anguilla

1968 (14 Oct). *35th Anniv. of Anguillan Girl Guides.*   [S. G. 40/43]

40c. White flaw over hyphen in dates (R.5/3).

V1

43   40c. – V1. Flaw over date   ...   .   2·50

1970 (10 Aug). *40th Anniv. of Scouting in Anguilla.*   [S. G. 80/83]

15c. " Footprint " above " PRAC-TICE " (R. 4/4)."Apostrophe" over " C " of " SCOUTING " (all stamps on 4th vertical row).

V2

81   15c. – V2. "Footprint" and "Apostrophe" flaws   ...   1·75

1972 (20 Nov). *Royal Silver Wedding.*   [S. G. 145/6E]

25c. Dot on curtain over Queen's head (Pl. 4A, R. 1/3).

V4

145   25c. – V4. Dot on curtain   ...   .   15·00

1976 (10 Feb–1 July). *New Constitution.*   [S. G. 223/40]

All values. Italic second " o " in " CONSTITUTION " (various positions as listed).

V5

V6

2c. on 1c. Diagonal stroke across " TI " of CONSTITU-TION " (R. 2/5).

V7

20c. and 10 on 20c. Black dot over " H M " (Pl. 1A, R. 1/5).

20c. and 10 on 20c. Red "flame" on library roof (Pl. IA, R.3/4).

V8

223	1c.	– V5. Italic "o" (R.4/5)	...	...	1·50
224	2c. on 1c.	– V5. Italic "o" (R.4/5)	...	...	1·50
		– V6. Diagonal stroke	...	...	2·50
225	2c.	– V5. Italic "o" (R.5/2)	...	...	1·50
226	3c. on 40c.	– V5. Italic "o" (R.2/2)	...	...	1·50
227	4c.	– V5. Italic "o" (R.5/2)	...	...	1·50
228	5c. on 40c.	– V5. Italic "o" (R.2/2)	...	...	1·50
229	6c.	– V5. Italic "o" (R.5/2)	...	...	1·50
230	10c. on 20c.	– V5. Italic "o" (R.3/2)	...	...	1·75
		– V7. Black dot over "HM"	...	...	2·75
		– V8. Flame on roof	...	...	2·75
231	10c.	– V5. Italic "o" (R.3/2)	...	...	2·00
232	15c.	– V5. Italic "o" (R.2/2)	...	...	2·00
233	20c.	– V5. Italic "o" (R.3/2)	...	...	2·00
		– V7. Black dot over "HM"	...	...	2·75
		– V8. Flame on roof	...	...	2·75
234	25c.	– V5. Italic "o" (R.3/2)	...	...	2·25
235	40c.	– V5. Italic "o" (R.2/2)	...	...	2·25
236	60c.	– V5. Italic "o" (R.3/2)	...	...	2·50
237	$1.	– V5. Italic "o" (R.3/2)	...	...	2·50
238	$2·50.	– V5. Italic "o" (R.3/2)	...	...	3·50
239	$5.	– V5. Italic "o" (R.2/2)	...	...	7·00
240	$10.	– V5. Italic "o" (R.4/5)	...	...	14·00

1977 (9 Feb). *Silver Jubilee.*   [S. G. 269/73]

$2.50 Broken 2nd "I" in "COMMISSIONER" (Pl. 1D, R.5/2)

V9

272   $2·50 – V9. Broken "I"   ...   .   4·50

Antigua

1960 (1 Jan). *New Constitution.*   [S. G. 138/9]

CONSTITUTION   12c. Broken " c " in " CONSTITUTION "
V2   (R. 7/9).

139   12c. – V2. Broken "c"   ...   .   2·00

1965 (17 May). *I.T.U. Centenary.*   [S. G. 166/7]

TELECOMMJNICATION   Broken " U " in " TELECOMMUNICA-
V1   TION " appearing as a " J " (R. 5/2).

166   2c. – V1. Broken "U"   ...   .   1·75
167   50c. – V1. Broken "U"   ...   .   5·00

1965 (25 Oct). *International Co-operation Year.*   [S. G. 168/9]

All the issues of this omnibus series were printed in double panes
and divided before issue, with the exception of New Hebrides. The
same plate numbers were used on each pane. It follows, therefore,
that the varieties do not exist on every sheet.

4c. and 15c. Left hand sprig of leaves
broken (R. 6/4 on decimal currency
sheets of 50 and R. 8/4 on sterling
currency sheets of 60).

V6

15c. Broken " Y " in " YEAR " appearing as a
" v " (R. 7/1).

V3

168   4c. – V6. Broken leaves   ...   .   1·75
169   15c. – V3. Broken "Y"   ...   .   6·00
      – V6. Broken leaves   ...   .   2·50

1966 (1 July). *World Football Cup Championships.*   [S. G. 176/7]

ENGLAND   6c. Vertical stroke between " G " and
              " L " of " ENGLAND " (R. 1/1).

V4

176   6c. – V4. "ENGLAND" flaw   ...   .   2·50

1966 (20 Sept). *Inauguration of W.H.O. Headquarters, Geneva.*
                                              [S. G. 178E/9]
V8. Dotted "r" in "Headquarters". See V5 of Dominica.
178E   2c. – V8. Dotted "r"   ...   .   2·25

1967 (18 May). *Attainment of Autonomy by the Methodist
Church.*   [S. G. 203/5]

4c. Line projecting from near corner of
building, stretching two-thirds way
up roof (R. 1/2).

V5

203   4c. – V5. Roof flaw   ...   .   2·00

1968 (31 Oct). *Opening of St. John's Deep Water Harbour.*
                                              [S. G. 221/5]

$1 Dot in front of Queen's nose (Pl. 1, R.2/5)

V7

225   $1. – V7. Spot by nose   ...   .   3·25

1976 (28 Dec). *Special Events, 1976.*   [S. G. 519/25]

50c. Dots beneath bowler's hand and
elbow (PL. 1A, R.10/1).

V9

522   50c. – V9. Dots under hand and elbow   ...   ...   1·75

Ascension

1965 (25 Oct). *International Co-operation Year.*   [S. G. 89/90]

V1. Broken leaves. See V6 of Antigua.

89	1d. – V1. Broken leaves	...	...	...	...	2·50
90	6d. – V1. Broken leaves	...	...	...	...	5·00

1966 (24 Jan). *Churchill Commemoration.*   [S. G. 91/94]

White flaw to right of St. Paul's, below level of dome (Plate 1A, R. 4/5).

V2

91	1d. – V2. Dot by St. Paul's	...	...	...	2·00
92	3d. – V2. Dot by St. Paul's	...	...	...	3·00
93	6d. – V2. Dot by St. Paul's	...	...	...	4·00
94	1s.6d. – V2. Dot by St. Paul's	...	...	...	8·00

1966 (20 Sept). *Inauguration of W.H.O. Headquarters, Geneva.*   [S. G. 97/98]

V3. Dotted "r" in "Headquarters". See V5 of Dominica.

98	1s.6d. – V3. Dotted "r"	...	...	...	...	5·00

1968 (8 July). *Human Rights Year.*   [S. G. 110/12]

V4

All values.
Red scratch on Queen's throat (R. 1/1).

V5

All values.
White spot on Queen's forehead (R. 3/5).

All values. Fine red line through top of first "s" of "ASCENSION" (R. 4/11).

V6

110	6d. – V4. Scratch on throat	...	...	...	1·75
	– V5. Spot on forehead	...	...	...	1·75
	– V6. Scratch on "s"	...	...	...	1·75

111	1s.6d. – V4. Scratch on throat	...	...	...	2·50
	– V5. Spot on forehead	...	...	...	2·50
	– V6. Scratch on "s" ...	...	...	...	2·50
112	2s.6d. – V4. Scratch on throat	...	...	...	3·00
	– V5. Spot on forehead	...	...	...	3·00
	– V6. Scratch on "s"	...	...	...	3·00

1969 (3 Mar). *Fishes.* (2nd. series).   [S. G. 117/20]

1s.6d. Black dot over "s" of "ISLAND" (Pl. 1A, R. 5/5).

V7

119	1s.6d. – V7. Dot on "s"	...	...	...	...	4·00

1972 (20 Nov). *Royal Silver Wedding.*   [S. G. 164/5]

V10. See V4 of Anguilla

164	2p. – V10. Dot on curtain	...	...	...	2·75

1973 (14 Nov). *Royal Wedding.*   [S. G. 178/9]

2p. Flaw on Princess Anne's dress appears as a strand of cotton (Pl.1B R.3/2).

V8

178	2p. – V8. "Cotton" on dress ...	...	...	...	2·50

1976 (26 Apr). *Birds.*   [S. G. 199/214]

3p. Plate damage affects the bird on the left, whose head is green instead of brown; the bird in the centre, which has a green mark on its back; and the bird on the right, which has a green patch on the base of its tail. A red smudge also occurs in the sky (Pl. 1D, R. 2/1).

V9

201	3p. – V9. Plate damage	...	...	...	2·00

1977 (7 Feb). *Silver Jubilee.*   [S. G. 222E/4]

V11   V12

8p. Bump on "p" of face-value 25p. Blue dot before "A" of
     (PL. 1D, R.2/1).   "Ascension" (Pl. 1C, R.3/1).

222   8p. – V11. Bump on "P" ...   .   2·50
224   25p. – V12. Dot before "A" ...   .   3·50

1977 (3 Oct). *Centenary of Visit of Professor Gill (astronomer).*
                                 [S. G. 229/32]

         25p. Horizontal scratch at the foot of the "F" in
             top left map title (Pl. 1C, R. 3/5).

V13

232   25p. – V13. Scratch by "F" ...   .   3·00

Australia

MASTER PLATES. Master plates of recess-printed £.s.d. stamps were of 240, 320, 480 or 640 subjects.

Plates of 240 gave left and right sheets of 120 or four sheets of 60 for the Arms types.

Plates of 320 gave upper and lower sheets of 160 each divided into two panes, or four sheets of 80.

Plates of 480 gave four sheets of 120.

Plates of 640 gave four sheets of 160 each divided into panes of 80.

When listing plate varieties we have given the position of the sheet in the master plate where this is known.

PHOTOGRAVURE CYLINDERS: No. 343 was the first stamp printed in photogravure in Melbourne. All photogravure issues are continuously printed "in the web" using double cylinders giving two post office sheets. These are either left and right or upper and lower, the position being distinguished by the coloured bars and crosses which are centrally placed.

In listing varieties we give the position of the sheet where this is known.

1949–65. *Pictorials.* [S. G. 228/24*d*]

1s. Roller flaw over "O" of "ONE" (upper plate, right pane R. 1 to 6 No. 6). Also occurred on the earlier water-marked issue.

V19

1s. Major retouch consisting of repair to weak entry over a large area at left of bird's feathers (Upper plate left pane R. 9/3).

V26

2s.6d. Fine line through "AUSTRALIA" (R. 12/2).

V49

£2 Roller flaw below "E" of "POS-TAGE" (R. 5/1 and 6/1). Later retouched.

V1

230*d*	1s.	– V19. Roller flaw	...	...	...	15·00
		– V26. "Green Mist" retouch		...	...	25·00
253	2s.6d.	– V49. Line through "AUSTRALIA"	...	...	15·00
224*d*	£2	– V1. Roller flaw	...	...	...	£350

1953 (11 Feb). *Food Production.* [S. G. 255/60]

V29	V39
3d. Beef. Gash in value tablet (Upper panel R. 5/2).	3½d. Beef. Shading line above "B" of "BEEF" broken, giving appearance of an apostrophe (Upper and lower pane R. 1/6).

257	3d. – V29. Gash in value tablet	...	...	...	3·00
260	3½d. – V39. "Apostrophe" before "BEEF"	...	...	3·00

1953–56. *Queen Elizabeth II.* [S. G. 261/263*a*]

3d. Flaw in hair over forehead (lower plate, right pane R. 1/7). Later retouched.

V2

3½d. Re-entry. Doubling of lower left frame line and "AU" (Lower plate, left pane R. 4/7).

V20

262	3d.	– V2. Flaw in hair	...	...	7·00
262a	3½d. (no wmk)	– V20. Re-entry	...	...	5·50
263	3½d. (wmk)	– V20. Re-entry	...	...	5·50

1954 (2 Feb). *Royal Visit.*   [S. G. 272/4]

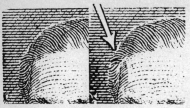

Normal   V3

3½d. Retouch to Duke's forehead (Lower right plate, R. 3/6).

272   3½d. – V3. Retouch £140

1954 (7 Apr). *Telegraph Centenary.*   [S. G. 275]

Weak entry in lower right corner causing loss of detail (R.3/5 and less prominent on R. 4/5).

Normal   V4

275   3½d. – V4. Weak entry   ...   .   4·00

1954 (9 June). *40th Anniv. of Australian Red Cross Society.*
                                                      [S. G. 276]

Short left arm to cross (Left plate R. 10/4).

Normal   V5

276   3½d. – V5. Short left arm to cross   ...   .   7·50

1955 (10 Aug). *World Centenary of Y.M.C.A.*   [S. G. 286]

3½d. Top left corner of triangle broken (R. 8/5).

V30

286   3½d. – V30. Broken triangle   ...   .   3·50

1956 (31 Oct). *Olympic Games, Melbourne.*   [S. G. 290/3]

V21   V94

7½d. Roller flaw. Vertical line under lip of torch (R. 2 to 6 No 5).   7½d. Weak entry (R 9/1, 10/1).

1s. Short "L" in "AUSTRALIA" (R. 5/10).

V14

2s. Cloud under "th" of "XVIth" (R. 4/8).

V6

2s. Flaw on "T" of "AUSTRALIA" (R. 2/4).

V7

291   7½d. – V21. Roller flaw   ...   .   4·50
       – V94. Weak entry   ...   .   9·00
292   1s. – V14. Short "L" ...   .   4·50
293   2s. – V6. Cloud under "th"   ...   .   6·00
       – V7. Flaw on "T"   ...   .   5·50

1957 (21 Aug). *Flying Doctor Service.*   [S. G. 297]

V22

Weak entry below "AUSTRALIA" has been retouched (Upper left plate R. 1/6).

On the same stamp there are four states of the so-called "wandering dot" variety, of which our illustration shows state 4. In state 1 the dot appears below the bottom line of shading, in states 2 and 3 it appears in two different positions between the first and second lines of shading and in state 4 it comes between the second and third lines of shading. *Price, each state* £2 *un.*

297   7d. – V22. Weak entry. *From*   ...   .   2·50

1958 (6 Jan). *Inauguration of Australian "Round the World" Air Service.* [S. G. 301]

Re-entry on final " A " of " AUSTRALIA " (R. 7/6).

V8

301	2s. – V8. Re-entry	...	...	...	...	18·00

1958 (10 Feb). *War Memorial, Canberra.* [S. G. 302/3]

5½d. No. 303. Coloured flaw on pedestal at right (Lower left plate R. 4/8).

V23

303	5½d. – V23. Spot on pedestal ...	...	...	...	5·00

1958 (10 Sept). *75th Anniv. of Founding of Broken Hill.* [S. G. 305]

V24

Horizontal line over " AL " of " AUSTRALIA " (R. 10/7).

Dot in " R " of " AUSTRALIA " (R. 8/2).

V50

305	4d. – V24. Line over "AL"	...	...	...	...	3·50
	– V50. Dot in "R"	...	...	...	...	3·50

1959–62. *Queen Elizabeth.* [S. G. 308E/314]

V25

1d. Re-entry. Line running through base of " RALIA " (Lower right plate, right pane R. 1/8).

Normal   V9

5d. Lines on jaw and neck recut appearing as a swelling on the jaw. Occurs on bottom right stamp of booklet pane of 6. Die B.

308E	1d. – V25. Re-entry at base ...	...	...	...	2·50
314	5d. – V9. Retouch to jaw	...	...	...	15·00

1959–64. *Pictorials.* [S. G. 316/327]

V10

8d. Retouch under " USTRA " (Upper right plate, right pane R. 1/1).

V11

8d. Weak entry. One horizontal line of shading missing and diagonal line retouched (lower plate, left pane R. 7/4).

Normal V123

8d. Retouch to tablet and left frame (Right pane R. 10/2).

8d. Retouch to shading right of head (Lower left plate, right pane R. 9/6). The illustration shows the last of four states of the retouch in this position. Other retouches exist on this value.

V12

V40

8d. Retouch to shading above
animal's left ear (Upper
right plate, left pane
R. 10/3).

V41 2s. " T " of " AUSTRALIA " retouched with vertical lines of
shading.   The letter is lighter in colour and also appears
to have a slight kink (Right plate R. 6/8).

V35

2s.3d. Retouch to first " T " of " WATTLE '
gives appearance of a thin " T '
(R. 4/9).

317E	8d.	*red-brown*			
		– V10. Retouch under "USTRA"	...	...	4·50
		– V11. Weak entry, below top frame line	...		4·50
		– V123. Retouch to tablet	...	...	4·00
	Ea.	*Pale red-brown*			
		– V12. Retouch right of head		...	13·00
		– V40. Retouch over ear	...	...	4·50
323	2s.	– V41. "T" retouched	...	...	8·00
324	2s.3d.	*green/maize*			
		– V35. Thin "T"	...	...	8·00
324a	2s.3d.	*yellow-green*			
		– V35. Thin "T"	...	...	15·00

1959 (22 Apr). *150th Anniv. of the Australian Post Office.* [S. G. 331]

V48. Frame scratch. See V4 of Norfolk Island.
331   4d. – V48. Frame scratch   ...   .   2·00

1960 (21 Sept). *Centenary of Northern Territory Exploration.*
                                                   [S. G. 335E]

V27

Major re-entry below rider's right
arm (Lower left plate R. 4/4).   This
occurs only on Type I.

335E 5d. – V27. Major re-entry   ...   .   12·00

1960 (9 Nov). *Christmas.*   [S. G. 338]

V13

Re-entry. " 19 " of " 1960 "
partially double (Lower left
plate R. 5/2).   On upper left
plate R. 10/10 there is a
similar partial doubling of
" 19 " but to right of " 1 "
and inside " 9 ".   Same price
for either variety.

338   5d. – V13. Re-entry   ...   .   4·00

1961 (8 Nov). *Christmas.*   [S. G. 341]

V31

5d. Thin   frame   line   below
" S "   of   " AUSTRALIA "
(R. 7/8).

341   5d. – V31. Thin frame line   ...   .   2·25

1963–65. *Navigators.*   [S. G. 355/60]

£2 Roller flaw, right-hand frame line
at top (R. 1/3).

V18

360   £2. – V18. Roller flaw £300

1963 (3 Dec). *Opening of COMPAC.*   [S. G. 362]

V28. See No. 820 V11 of New Zealand
362   2s.3d. – V28. Broken cable   ...   .   22·00

1964 (11 Mar).–65. *Birds.*   [S. G. 363/9]

V32

V15

9d. Grey dot on upper branch (R. 5/12).

1s.6d. Horizontal scratch over " ALI " (R. 1/8). A similar scratch occurs across the tail and tree on the next stamp (R. 1/9) (*same price*).

V36

V37

1s.6d. Line over " L " of " AUSTRALIA " (R. 3/7).

2s. Broken upper branch (R. 5/11).

V42

2s.6d. A green line runs under " USTR " of " AUSTRALIA " (Left cylinder R. 11/1).

364	9d.	– V32. Dot on branch	...	...	...	5·50
365	1s.6d.	– V15. Scratch over "ALI"	...	...	...	5·00
		– V36. Line over "L"	...	...	...	5·00
366	2s.	– V37. Broken branch	...	...	...	7·00
368	2s.6d.	– V42. Line under "USTR"	...	...	...	12·00

1965 (14 Apr). *50th Anniv. of Gallipoli Landing.*   [S. G. 373/5]

V33

2s.3d. Pale patch over " I " of " AUSTRALIA " (R. 2/5).

375   2s.3d. – V33. Patch over "I" ...   .   20·00

1965 (24 May). *Churchill Commemoration.*   [S. G. 377]

V51

V52

Retouch appears as diagonal scratches across " LIA " (Lower cylinder R. 1/11).

Retouch below " TR " (Lower cylinder R. 3/4).

| 377 | 5d. | – V51. Retouched "LIA" | ... | ... | ... | 2·25 |
| | | – V52. Retouch below "TR" | ... | ... | ... | 2·25 |

1965 (4 Aug). *50th Death Anniv. of Lawrence Hargrave (aviation pioneer)*   [S. G. 379]

V44

Small nick in port wing of tailplane (R. 3/3).

379   5d. – V44. Nick in wing ...   .   2·00

1966 (14 Feb).–73. *Decimal currency.*   [S. G. 382/403]

V67

V73

3c. Frame-line missing at upper right (R. 4/4). Later retouched twice, but still leaving frame weakness.

4c. White flaw over ear-ring (R. 2/9).

V45

5c. Green dot to right of " c " in value (Left cylinder R. 1/2).

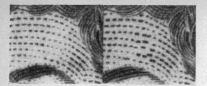

7c. Normal   V81 Forehead retouch (R.1/10).

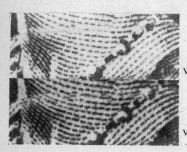

V82. " Cut-throat "
flaw.

V83. " Cut-throat "
retouched.

7c. " Cut-throat " flaw (R. 1/3).

7c. Normal   V89. Shading
shading   is
beneath   re-cut
eye appears   (R. 9/2).
feint.

V90. Frame re-entry (R. 10/5).

V53
10c. White dot to bottom
left of central design
appears as an extra
coral. (Upper pane,
R. 3/3). Subsequently
retouched to a white
smudge.

V46
15c. Black partially omitted,
giving appearance of
damage to claws and
" LI " of " AUSTRALIA "
(R. 2/8). Similar varieties
occur on R. 2/9 and 3/8
(*same price*).

THE ELIZABETHAN

Uniform with this volume, the *Elizabethan Specialised Stamp Catalogue* covers all other aspects of the stamps of the present reign, from both Great Britain and the British Commonwealth, in considerable detail. See the preliminary pages of this Catalogue for details of this annual publication.

Normal

V69

V68   V69

15c. Black spot over   75c. Heavy recutting below
" U " of " AUS-   left-hand cuff and cross-
TRALIA " (Right-   hatching on hand
hand sheet, R. 4/3).   (Right-hand sheet,
                              R. 2/1).

V99   V100   V101   V102

75c. Frame line at bottom left shows progressive wear (R.2/2). This comes in four stages: V99 Nick in frame; V100 Broken frame; V101 Missing frame; V102 Repaired frame.

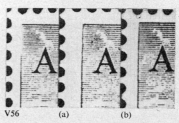

V56   (a)   (b)

$1. Weak frame at top left (Upper plate, R. 10/3). This was first retouched by hand (a) and later by rule (b). The original variety occurs on a reddish purple shade.

Normal   V84

$1. Recut lines over " R " (Lower pane, R. 7/1).

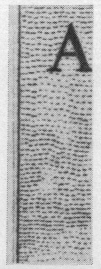

$4. Re-entry on left-hand frame line. Later removed (R. 4/9). A similar re-entry occurs on R. 5/9 which was not removed (*same price*).

V116

384	3c. – V67.	Damaged frame-line	...	...	6·00
385	4c. – V73.	Ear-ring flaw ...	...	...	2·00
386	5c.	*brown, yellow, black and emerald-green*			
	– V45.	Dot to the right of value	...	...	2·50
	b.	*brown, yellow, black and blue-green*			
	– V45.	Dot to the right of value	...	...	2·50
388a	7c. – V81.	Forehead retouch	...	...	2·25
	– V82.	"Cut throat" flaw	...	...	3·50
	– V83.	"Cut throat" flaw retouched	...	...	2·25
	– V89.	Recut beneath eye	...	...	2·25
	– V90.	Frame re-entry	...	...	2·25
391	10c. – V53.	Extra coral	...	...	8·00
393	15c. – V46.	Damaged claw	...	...	12·00
	– V68.	Spot above "U"	...	...	10·00
400	75c. – V69.	Major retouch	...	...	9·00
	– V99.	Nick in frame	...	...	5·00
	– V100.	Broken frame	...	...	5·00
	– V101.	Missing frame	...	...	5·00
	– V102.	Repaired frame	...	...	5·00
401	$1 – V56.	Weak entry ...	...	...	10·00
	– V56a.	Hand retouched	...	...	12·00
	– V56b.	Rule retouched	...	...	12·00
	– V84.	Recut lines over "AR"	...	...	12·00
403	$4 – V116.	Frame line re-entry	...	...	40·00

1966 (14 Feb)–67. *Coil Stamps.*   [S. G. 404/5a]

Varieties (occurring every 14th stamp in one of the fourteen coils):

V34

3c. Dot before "3".

V117

White dot under " L " of " AUSTRALIA ".

V118

White patch beneath chin.

V54

4c. White spot on Queen's throat appears as a wart.

V55

5c. Pearl at front of diadem is missing.

V103

All values. Patchy printing gives the appearance of " white lips ".

V104

All values. Spot by last " A " of " AUSTRALIA " appears as serif.

Printed in the web from cylinders of 196 subjects (14 × 14) and guillotined into 14 rolls of 1,000 stamps. The 4c. was also issued in coils of 250 (113,000 stamps printed thus).

404	3c. – V34.	Dot before "3"	...	...	...	2·75
	– V103.	White lips	...	...	...	2·75
	– V104.	Serif on "A"	...	...	...	2·75
	– V117.	White dot under "L"	...	...	...	2·75
	– V118.	White patch under chin	...	...	...	2·75
405	4c. – V54.	Wart on neck	....	...	...	4·00
	– V103.	White lips	...	...	...	4·00
	– V104.	Serif on "A"	...	...	...	4·50
405a	5c. – V55.	Missing pearl	...	...	...	4·50
	– V103.	White lips	...	...	...	4·00
	– V104.	Serif on "A"	...	...	...	4·50

1966 (24 Oct). *350th Anniv. of Dirk Hartog's Landing in Australia.*   [S. G. 408E]

White flaw in ship's bow appears as a shot-hole (Left cylinder R. 4/10).

V57

408E	4c. – V57.	Shot-hole in bow	...	...	...	2·00

1967 (5 Apr). *150th Anniv. of Australian Banking.*   [S. G. 410]

4c. Broken frame between " R " and " S " of " YEARS " (Left-hand pane, R. 8/1).

V38

410	4c. – V38.	Broken frame	...	...	...	1·75

1967 (7 June). *50th Anniv. of Lions International.*   [S. G. 411]

Small white flaw between " R " and " A " of " AUSTRALIA " gives the appearance that they are joined (R. 2/6).

V47

411	4c. – V47.	"RA" joined	...	...	...	1·75

1968 (10 July). *State Floral Emblems.*   [S. G. 420/5E]

V74

30c. Brown vein runs down upper left leaf (R. 4/6).

V95

30c. Extra bud on flower (R. 4/5).

425E	30c. – V74. Leaf flaw	...	...	... ...	10·00
Eb.	Type II*				
	– V74. Leaf flaw	...	...	... ...	15·00
	– V95. Extra bud	...	...	... ...	12·00

  * A limited reprinting, prior to withdrawal, from new printing cylinders shows colour variations from the original. In the reprint greater areas of white are shown in the pink tones of the petals.

1968 (6 Aug). *International Soil Science Congress and World Medical Association Assembly.*   [S. G. 426/7]

5c. (No. 427) Greenish blue line extends backward from the hypodermic and appears as a needle through the thumb. (Right pane, R. 2/1).

V58

427	5c. – V58. Needle through thumb	...	...	...	2·00

1969 (17 Sept). *Primary Industries.*   [S. G. 440/3]

7c. Two green spots on cane (Lower pane, R. 5/6).

V60

440	7c. – V60. Spots on cane	...	...	...	5·50

1969 (12 Nov). *50th Anniv. of First England–Australia Flight.*   [S. G. 450/2]

Normal   V59

5c. (No. 452). Retouches occur on the pink car in various positions in the sheet; we list those we have seen that appear most marked, but others may also exist (Left-hand pane, R. 1/3, 2/2, 3/1, 10/3; right-hand pane, R. 1/3, 2/5, 3/1).

V61   V121

5c. (No. 452). Broken "R" in "ACROSS" (Right-hand pane, R. 10/3).   5c. (No. 451). Long "N" in "HUDSON" (Left-hand pane, R. 8/1).

451	5c. – V121. Long "N"	...	...	...	...	3·50
452	5c. – V59. Retouches to car	...	...	...		4·00
	– V61. Broken "R"	...	...	...	...	3·50

1970 (16 Mar). *World Fair, Osaka.*   [S. G. 454/5]

20c. Long "R" in "AUSTRALIA" (Left-hand pane, R. 2/5).

V62

455	20c. – V62. Long "R" ...	...	...	...	...	4·50

1970 (13 Apr). *Eleventh International Grasslands Congress.*   [S. G. 458]

White blob on stem by last "A" of "AUSTRALIA" (Right-hand pane R. 7/5).

V63

458	5c. – V63. White blob	...	...	...	...	1·75

1970 (20 Apr). *Bicentenary of Captain Cook's Discovery of Australia's East Coast.* [S. G. 459/65]

5c. (No. 459). Red mark on sail at left (Top pane, R. 5/1).

V64

459	5c. – V64. Red mark on sail ...	...	...	...	1·75

1970–75. *Coil Stamps.* Ordinary paper. [S. G. 465aE/8d]

Varieties (occurring every 14th stamp in one of the fourteen coils):

AU | RALIA

V96 | V105
2c. Break in "A" of | 2c. Green dots over "AL".
"AUSTRALIA".

STURT'S DESERT ROSE 4c

Normal

STURT'S DESERT ROSE 4c

V65

4c. Faint inscription.

DESERT | RA

V97 | V98
7c. Broken "DE" | Broken "RA" in
in "DESERT" | "AUSTRALIA"

465aE	2c. – V96. Break in "A" ...	...	...	...	1·75
	– V105. Green dots ...	...	...	...	1·75
	Ew. White fluorescent paper (1972)				
	– V96. Break in "A" ...	...	...	...	1·75
	– V105. Green dots ...	...	...	...	1·75
466	4c. – V65. Faint inscription ...	...	...	...	3·00
468bE	7c. – V97. Broken "DE" ...	...	...	...	1·50
	– V98. Broken "RA" ...	...	...	...	1·50
	Ew. White fluorescent paper (1973)				
	– V97. Broken "DE" ...	...	...	...	1·50
	– V98. Broken "RA" ...	...	...	...	1·50

1971 (21 Apr). *Centenary of Australian Natives' Association.* [S. G. 486]

BECK | BECK

"K" of imprint redrawn by hand (Right hand pane, R. 2/1).

Normal | V70

486	6c. – V70. "K" of imprint redrawn ...	...	...	...	1·40

1971 (9 June). *50th Anniv. of R.A.A.F.* [S. G. 489]

V71 | V72
Blue spot in cloud be- | Elongated "I" in "AUSTRALIAN"
hind 3rd 'plane up | (Lower pane, R. 3/10). This
(Lower pane, R. 1/3). | was corrected later.

489	6c. – V71. "Hole" in cloud ...	...	...	...	1·75
	– V72. Elongated "I" ...	...	...	...	1·75

1971 (5 July). *Animals.* [S. G. 490/3]

24c. Spot on woman's skirt (Lower pane, R. 4/1).

V85

493	24c. – V85. Spot on skirt ...	...	...	...	5·50

1971 (29 Sept)–74. *Aboriginal Art.* Ordinary paper [S. G. 494E/497E]

V91 | V92 | V93
25c. Dot by "AU" | 25c. Dot re-touched | 30c. Nick at bottom
of "AUSTRALIA" | (R. 5/3, left- | of left-hand
(R. 5/3, left- | hand pane). | figure (R. 1/2,
hand pane). | | upper pane).

495E	25c. – V91. Dot by "AU" of "AUSTRALIA" ...	...	3·00
	Ew. White fluorescent paper (11.71)				
	– V92. Dot retouched ...	...	...	...	3·50
496E	30c. – V93. Nick in figure ...	...	...	...	3·00
	Ew. White fluorescent paper ('73)				
	– V93. Nick in figure ...	...	...	...	3·00

STAMP VARIETIES EXPLAINED

In this *Stanley Gibbons Guide* James Watson presents the knowledge essential to every philatelist—the various processes that are used to print stamps. By demonstrating just how varieties occur, he enables collectors to assess their relative importance and shows what contribution, if any, they can make to philatelic study. See the preliminary pages of this Catalogue for details of the current edition.

1971 (13 Oct). *Christmas.* Ordinary paper   [S. G. 498E/499E]

No. 499. Break in horiz line of first crown (Right-hand pane, R. 5/4 and 10/4). Later retouched.

V66

| 499E | 7c. – V66. Crown with line broken | ... | ... | 9·00 |

Ew. White fluorescent paper
– V66. Crown with line broken   ... ... 10·00

1972 (18 Apr). *50th Anniv. of Country Women's Association.*
[S. G. 509]

V75

7c. Major retouches to background appearing as " green rain ". V75 is at top left (Lower pane R. 5/1) and V76 is at upper left side (Upper pane R. 1/10).

V76

509 7c. – V75. "Green rain" (1) ... ... 2·00
– V76. "Green rain" (2) ... ... 2·00

1972 (2 Aug)–73. *Rehabilitation of the Disabled.* [S. G. 514E/16E]

12c. Break in boy's left foot (Lower pane, R. 2/2).

V77

18c. Acute accent on " B " (Left pane, R. 9/2).

V78

18c. Smudge between " LI " of " REHABILITATION " (Right pane, R. 10/1).

V79

514E	12c. – V77. Broken foot	...	...	...	...	2·00
515	18c. – V78. Accent on "B"	...	...	...	...	5·00
	– V79. Smudge after "L"	...	...	...		4·00

1972 (28 Aug). *Olympic Games, Munich.*   [S. G. 518/21]

35c. Thick " 1 " in " 1972 " and damaged " M " in " Munich " (Upper pane, R. 5/1).

V80   Normal

521 35c. – V80. thick "1" and "1972" ... ... 10·00

1972 (15 Nov)–74. *Pioneer Life.* Ordinary paper   [S. G. 523E/9E]

10c. Puddle above " r '' of " Water '' (R.4/6).

V106

V107 40c. White flaw appears as a break in the verandah's gutter (right pane, R.4/4).

V108 40c. Cylinder scratch (R.10/3, 10/4, 10/5, 10/6) (stamps 3 and 4 shown).

V109 80c. Black spots on ship's side appear as port holes (Right pane, R.5/4).

V110 80c. Retouch behind top deck (Right pane, R.8/5).

80c. Sky retouch (Right pane, R8/3).

V111

524E 10c. – V106. Puddle above "r" ... ... 2·50
Ew. White fluorescent paper (mid '74)
    – V106. Puddle above "r" ... ... 2·50
526E 40c. – V107. Broken gutter ... ... 3·00
    – V108. Cylinder scratch (strip of 4) ... ... 7·00
Ew. White fluorescent paper (mid '74)
    – V107. Broken gutter ... ... 3·00
    – V108. Cylinder scratch (strip of 4) ... ... 7·00
529E 80c. – V109. Extra port holes ... ... 3·50
    – V110. Retouch behind top deck ... ... 3·50
    – V111. Sky retouch ... ... 3·50
Ew. White fluorescent paper (mid '74)
    – V109. Extra port holes ... ... 3·50
    – V110. Retouch behind top deck ... ... 3·50
    – V111. Sky retouch ... ... 3·50

1973 (7 Mar). *Metric Conversion.* [S. G. 532/5]

V86
No. 532. Dot on
"M" (Sheet C,
R 5/1).

V87
No. 534. Extended
" M " (Sheet B,
R. 2/9).

V88
No. 535. Flaw appears
as comma after
" Metric " (Sheet
C, R. 4/3).

532 7c. – V86. Dot on "M" ... ... 3·75
534 7c. – V87. Extended "M" ... ... 4·00
535 7c. – V88. Comma after "Metric" ... ... 3·75

1973 (4 Apr). *25th Anniv. of W.H.O.* [S. G. 536]

Thick "wo" in "WORLD"
(Sheet B, lower pane R. 5/4).

V120

536 7c. – V120. Thick "wo" ... ... 2·00

1973 (6 June). *National Development* (2nd series). [S. G. 541/4]

35c. Vertical green
retouch extending
through contour
lines (upper pane,
R.2/8).

V112

544 35c. – V112. Green retouch ... ... 10·00

1973 (17 Oct). *Architecture.* [S. G. 566/9]

V113
50c. Break in window at left
(upper pane, R.5/1).

V114
50c. Retouch above "50"
(lower pane, R.3/1).

559 50c. – V113. Broken window ... ... 5·50
    – V114. Retouch above "50" ... ... 5·50

1973 (21 Nov). *50th Anniv. of Regular Radio Broadcasting.* [S. G. 560]

7c. Black blob in speaker (Left pane, R. 8/1).

V124

560 7c. – V124. Black blob ... ... 1·75

1974 (13 Feb). *Animals.* [S. G. 561/4]

20c. Black flaw by wombat's ear
appears as an extra tuft of
hair (lower pane, R.2/1).

V115

561 20c. – V115. Extra tuft of hair ... ... 2·00

1974 (24 July). *Non-Olympic Sports.* [S. G. 569/75]

7c. White void below boot (Left pane, R. 3/5).

V125

572 7c. – V125. White void ... ... 2·25

1974 (9 Oct). *150th Anniv. of First Independent Newspaper, "The Australian".* [S. G. 578]

7c. Black flaw appears as a cigar (Right pane, R. 3/5).

V126

578	7c. – V126. Cigar flaw	...	...	...	...	5·50
	a. Perf. 14 × 14½				
	– V126. Cigar flaw	...	...	...	...	3·00

1975 (29 Jan). *Environment Dangers.* [S. G. 586/8]

10c. Extensive weakness behind wheel (Left pane, R. 5/1).

V127

10c. Break in outline of finger (Left pane, R. 6/2).

V128

10c. Break in leftside of match (Left pane, R. 7/2).

V129

586	10c. – V127. Extensive weakness	...	...	...	2·50
588	10c. – V128. Break in finger	...	...	...	2·50
	– V129. Break in match	...	...	...	2·50

1975 (26 Mar). *Famous Australians (6th series).* [S. G. 590/5]

10c. White gash over ear (Right pane, R. 2/9).

V130

595	10c. – V130. Gash by ear	...	...	...	...	2·50

1975 (6 Aug). *Famous Australians (7th series).* [S. G. 602/7]

10c. Full stop after "women" (Right pane, R. 2/1).

V131

607A/B	10c. – V131. Full stop flaw (*same price either perf*)	2·50

1975 (29 Oct). *Christmas.* [S. G. 612/13]

15c. Black flaw on lid of chalice (Left pane, R. 4/5).

V132

15c. Black strap over shoulder (Left pane, R. 5/10).

V133

612	15c. – V132. Flaw on chalice.	...	...	...	2·40
	15c. – V133. Strap over shoulder	...	...	...	2·40

1976 (5 Jan). *75th Anniv. of Nationhood.* [S. G. 14]

18c. Three legged kangaroo (Upper pane R. 2/4).

V134

614E	18c. – V134. Extra leg	...	...	...	...	2·50

PHILATELIC TERMS ILLUSTRATED

The essential philatelic dictionary. Terms covering printing methods, papers, errors, varieties, watermarks, perforations and much more are explained and illustrated, many in full colour. See the preliminary pages of this Catalogue for details of the current edition.

1976 (27 Sept). *National Stamp Week.* [S. G. 633/4]

18c. Island of in Cairns insert stamp (Upper pane R. 3/9).

V135

633   18c. – V135. Dot in insert stamp   ...   .   2·25

1976 (27 Sept). *National Stamp Week.* [S. G. MS634]

Break in top of panel beneath "Australia" (R.1/1, once in every 100 sheets).

V119

MS634 – V119. Break in panel (*complete sheet with variety*)   8·00

1977 (9 Mar). *Australia–England Test Cricket Centenary.* [S. G. 647/52]

45c. Break in vertical line on pad (Lower pane R. 4/4).

V136

652   45c. – V136. Break in line   ...   .   3·00

1978 (15 May). *50th Anniv. of Royal Flying Doctor Service.* [S. G. 663]

18c. Extensive disturbed area between horse's head & nose of plane (Left pane R. 4/3).

V137

663   18c. – V137. Extensive disturbance ...   .   2·00

1978 (3 July). *Birds.* [S. G. 669/79]

20c. Missing outline of jockey's face (Upper pane R. 2/2).

V138

679   20c. – V138. Flaw on jockey's face ...   .   3·00

1979 (26 Jan). *Australia Day.* [S. G. 703]

Break on ship's planks (Right-hand pane, R. 5/6).

V122

703   20c. – V122. Broken planks ...   .   1·75

POSTAGE DUE STAMPS

1946–57 [S. G. D119/28]

1d. Lower left serif of figure " 1 " is broken and shading lines shortened. (Left and right panes, Rows 4 and 5, No. 2 thus occurring four times on each printing sheet).

V16

D120   1d. – V16. Broken serif to "1"   ...   .   2·00

1958–60 [S. G. D132E/141]

1d. Outline omitted in a number of places, notably around dot (R. 4/1 and 10/1). This was later partly corrected.

V17

D133 1d. – V16. Broken serif to "1"   ...   .   4·00
    a.   Type II ('59)*
       – V17. No outline of dot   ...   .   5·00
  * Type II has a clear white line surrounding the numeral, "D" and stop.

Australian Antarctic Territory

1961 (5 July) [S. G. 6]

Weak entry at left (R. 1/5 and 2/5).

Normal   V2

6 5d. – V2. Weak entry ... ... 3·00

1961 (18 Oct). 50th Anniv. of 1911–14 Australian Antarctic Expedition. [S. G. 7]

V1   V3

Weak entry in background at right bottom corner and along bottom to " s " (R. 9/9).   Broken " s " in " AUSTRALIAN " (Left-hand pane, R. 11/1).

7 5d. – V1. Weak entry ... ... 2·75
       – V3. Broken "s" ... ... 2·75

1966 (28 Sept) – 71. Views. [S. G. 8E/18]

2c. Flaw in penguin's tail causes it to appear broken (Upper pane, R. 1/12).

V4

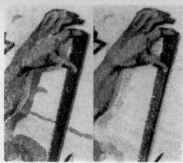

7c. Blue missing from ruler, which appears grey (R. 2/1).

Normal   V5

9E   2c. – V4. Broken tail-feathers ... ... 2·25
12 7c. – V5. Blue missing from ruler ... ... 3·00

1973 (15 Aug). Views. [S. G. 23/34]

V6   V7.

1c. Spot after "s" of "AUSTRALIAN" (Upper pane, R. 4/10).   5c. Damaged "ri" of "Territory" (Lower pane, R. 2/1).

V8

7c. Weakness behind "penguin" (Lower pane, R. 5/10).

V9   V10

25c. Dash by "25c." (Left-hand pane, R. 8/2).   50c. Gap in clouds (Upper pane, R. 2/2).

23 1c. – V6. Spot after "s" ... ... 1·50
24 5c. – V7. Damaged "ri" ... ... 2·50
25 7c. – V8. Screen damage ... ... 1·50
30 25c. – V9. Dash by "25c." ... ... 3·00
33 50c. – V10. Gap in clouds ... ... 2·00

Bahamas

1963 (2 Sept). *Red Cross Centenary.*   [S. G. 226/7]

1d. Triangle in diadem at
   right (Pl. 1–1 and
   1a–1a. R. 11/1–5).

V1

226   1d. – V1. Flaw in diadem   ...   .   4·00

1965 (25 Oct). *International Co-operation Year.*   [S. G. 265/6]

V2. Broken leaves. See V6 of Antigua.

265   ½d. – V2. Broken leaves   ...   .   1·50

1966 (24 Jan). *Churchill Commemoration.*   [S. G. 267E/270]

V3. Dot by St. Paul's. See V2 of Ascension.
V4. Flaw by Queen's ear. See V11 of Solomon Islands.

267E   ½d. – V3. Dot by St. Paul's   ...   .   1·25
268   2d. – V3. Dot by St. Paul's   ...   .   1·75
269   10d. – V3. Dot by St. Paul's   ...   .   2·50
       – V4. Flaw by Queen's ear   ...   .   2·50
270   1s. – V3. Dot by St. Paul's   ...   .   2·50
       – V4. Flaw by Queen's ear   ...   .   2·50

1974 (23 Apr). *Centenary of Universal Postal Union.*   [S. G. 424/7]

13c. Background border is
     chipped (PL. 1A, R. 1/2)

V5

425   13c. – V5. Chipped background   ...   .   2·75

Bahrain

All V numbers are those of Great Britain where the varieties are
illustrated. G.B. numbers in brackets.

1952–54. *Queen Elizabeth II.* Wmk Tudor Crown.   [S. G. 80/89]

81   1a. on 1d. (516) – V32. Flaw in shamrock   ...   ...   4·00
86   4a. on 4d. (521) – V92. Dotted "R"   ...   .   3·00

1955 (23 Sept)–60. *Castles.* Waterlow ptgs.   [S. G. 94I/6I]

96I   10r. on 10s. (538) – V8. Weak entry ...   .   45·00

1956–57. *Queen Elizabeth II.* Wmk St. Edward's Crown
[S. G. 97/101]

98   4a. on 4d. (546)   – V92. Dotted "R"   ...   ...   5·00
101   1r. on 1s.6d. (556)   – V201. White flaw in Queen's
                               hair below diadem   ...   3·50
                           – V202. White flaw in Queen's
                               hair opposite "N"   ...   3·50

1957 (1 Apr)–59. *New Currency.*   [S. G. 102/12]

104   6np. on 1d. (541) – V32. Flaw on shamrock   ...   2·75
109   25np. on 4d. (546) – V92. Dotted "R"   ...   ...   4·00
111   50np. on 9d. (551) – V5.   Frame break at upper right   5·50

1957 (1 Aug). *World Scout Jubilee Jamboree.*   [S. G. 113E/15]

113   15np. on 2½d. (557) – V147. Retouch   ...   ...   4·00
114   25np. on 4d. (558) – V35. Solid pearl at right   ...   6·00

Barbados

1965 (17 May). I.T.U. *Centenary.*   [S. G. 320/1]

V1. Broken "u" in "TELECOMMUNICATIONS". See V1 of Antigua.

320   2c. – V1. Broken "u"   ...   .   2·00
321   48c. – V1. Broken "u"   ...   .   3·00

1968 (27 Feb). *20th Anniv. of the Economic Commission for Latin America.*   [S. G. 371]

"L" in "E.C.L.A." is considerably shorter than the normal (R. 6/2).

V2

371   15c. – V2. Short "L" ...   .   2·25

1968 (4 June). *World Meteorological Day.*   [S. G. 372/4]

50c. White spot on gun barrel (R. 1/9).

V3

374   50c. – V3. Spot on gun barrel   ...   .   2·50

1970 (11 Mar). *Surcharge.*   [S. G. 398]

4 X

Missing top right serif on X (R. 4/5, 4/10, 9/5, 9/10).

V4

398   4c. on 5c. – V4. Missing serif   ...   .   1·25

STAMP VARIETIES EXPLAINED

In this *Stanley Gibbons Guide* James Watson presents the knowledge essential to every philatelist—the various processes that are used to print stamps. By demonstrating just how varieties occur, he enables collectors to assess their relative importance and shows what contribution, if any, they can make to philatelic study. See the preliminary pages of this Catalogue for details of the current edition.

1971 (17 Aug). *Tourism.*   [S. G. 429E/33]

1 c. Boat in the background has a black flaw on its mast, resembling a bolt (Pl. 1A, R. 3/2).

V6

429E   1c. – V6. "Black bolt" flaw   ...   .   1·75

1973 (11 Dec). *25th Anniv. of University of West Indies.*   [S. G. 476E/86]

25c. Broken " R " in " RESIDENCE " (Pl. ?, R. 5/1).

V5

477   25c. – V5. Broken "R"   ...   .   2·00

1977 (7 Feb). *Silver Jubilee.*   [S. G. 574/6]

V7
15c. Black line through pediment of church (Pl. 1B, R. 2/2).

V8
$1 Black "scars" on footman's face (Pl. 1D, R. 2/4).

574   15c. – V7. Line on church   ...   .   2·25
576    $1. – V8. Scarred face   ...   .   4·00

Barbuda

1969 (24 Mar). *Easter Commemoration.* [S. G. 32/34]

All values. Strong white scratch extending from lower left angel over Christ's head to the black frame and a similar parallel scratch passing below Christ's feet (Pl. 1B, R. 1/2).

V1

32	25c. – V1. Plate scratches	...	...	...	...	1·25
33	35c. – V1. Plate scratches	...	...	...	...	1·50
34	75c. – V1. Plate scratches	...	...	...	...	2·00

Basutoland

1961 (14 Feb). *Decimal surcharges.*   [S. G. 58/68]

25c

V1

25c. on 2s.6d. Short curve to " 2 " at
top (Type I) (R. 4/4).

66   25c. on 2s.6d. – V1. Short curve to "2"   ...   ...   8·00

1961–63. *Views.*   [S. G. 69/79E]

V2   Normal

Weak entry in medallion. Weak horiz lines right of Queen's hair
and diagonals missing (Pl. 3B–1, R. 1/3).

72Ea	2½c. – V2. Weak entry	...	...	...	...	4·50
74	5c. – V2. Weak entry	...	...	...	...	3·00
75	10c. – V2. Weak entry	...	...	...	...	4·00
77	25c. – V2. Weak entry	...	...	...	...	5·00

1965 (10 May). *New Constitution.*   [S. G. 94E/97]

3½c. Inside line of pillar to the left
is broken near the top (R. 2/3).

V7

V4   V5

5c Blue line between " GO " of   5c. Red line under " N " of
" GOVERNMENT " (R. 1/1).   " GOVERNMENT " (R. 2/1).

95	3½c. – V7. Broken pillar	...	...	...	...	1·75
96E	5c. – V4. Blue line between "GO"		...	...	1·50
	– V5. Red line under "N"	...	...	...	1·50

1965 (25 Oct). *International Co-operation Year.*   [S. G. 100/1]

V6. Broken leaves. See V6 of Antigua.
V8. Broken "Y" in "YEAR". See V3 of Antigua.

100	½c. – V6. Broken leaves	...	...	...	...	1·90
	– V8. Broken "Y"	...	...	...	...	1·90
101	12½c. – V6. Broken leaves	...	...	...	...	2·50

POSTAGE DUE STAMPS

1951–52.   [S. G. D1*b*/2*a*]

d   **d**

2d. Bolder " d " of " 2d." (R. 9/6 and
10/6).

Normal   V3

D2*a*   2d. – V3. Bolder "D"   ...   .   2·00

1961 (June).   [S. G. D8]

D8   5c. on 2d. – V3. Bolder "D"   ...   .   7·00

Bechuanaland

1955 (3 Jan)–58. *Cattle and Baobab Tree.* . [S. G. 143/53]

1s. 3d. Re-entry appears as a black curved line over left arch of crown (R. 7/6).

V5

150   1s.3d. – V5. Re-entry ...   .   5·00

1960 (21 Jan.). *Seventy-fifth Anniv. of Bechuanaland Protectorate.* [S. G. 154/6]

3d. Flaw on Queen's right eyebrow (Pl. 1A-1A, R. 7/6).

V12

155.   3d. – V12. Eyebrow flaw   ...   .   1·75

1961 (14 Feb–June). *Decimal surcharges.* / [S. G. 157/67]

$2\frac{1}{2}$c $2\frac{1}{2}$c

Normal   V1

Spaced " c " variety. Occurs on the 2½c. on 3d. (R. 10/3).

$2\frac{1}{2}$c

V13

Blunted base to large figure. Occurs on 2½c. on 2d. (R. 9/1 and 10/2).

$3\frac{1}{2}$c $3\frac{1}{2}$c

Normal   V2

Thick " c " variety. Occurs on the 3½c. on 4d, Type II (R. 9/3) and on Type III (R. 7/3).

159E	2½c. on 2d.	– V13. Blunt "2" ...	...	3·00
160	2½c. on 3d.	– V1. Spaced "c" ...	...	20·00
161a	3½c. on 4d. (Type II)	– V2. Thick "c" ...	...	28·00
	d.	Type III		
		– V2. Thick "c" ...	...	10·00
164	12½c. on 1s.3d.	– V5. Re-entry ...	...	10·00

1964 (23 Apr). *400th Anniv. of Birth of William Shakespeare.* [S. G. 185]

Dot under " c " of " 12½c. " (R. 6/2).

V3

185   12½c. – V3. Dot under "c"   ...   .   1·75

1965 (1 Mar). *New Constitution.* [S. G. 186E/9]

V6   V7

White flaw on extreme right of map appearing as a bay (R. 4/1).

White flaw on right hand shore of lake (R. 5/5).

186E	2½c.	– V6. Map flaw	...	...	...	1·75
		– V7. Lake flaw	...	...	...	1·75
187	5c.	– V6. Map flaw	...	...	...	1·75
		– V7. Lake flaw	...	...	...	1·75
188	12½c.	– V6. Map flaw	...	...	...	2·50
		– V7. Lake flaw	...	...	...	2·50
189	25c.	– V6. Map flaw	...	...	...	2·50
		– V7. Lake flaw	...	...	...	2·50

1965 (25 Oct). *International Co-operation Year.* [S. G. 192/3]

V10. Broken "Y" in "YEAR". See V3 of Antigua.
V11. Broken leaves. See V6 of Antigua.

192	1c. – V11. Broken leaves ...		...	...	1·50
193	12½c. – V10. Broken "Y" ...		...	...	4·00
	– V11. Broken leaves ...		...	...	1·75

POSTAGE DUE STAMPS

1947–58. [S. G. D4/6]

V4. Bolder "D". See Basutoland V3 (same position on sheet)
D6a   2d. – V4. Bolder "d"   ...   .   2·50

1961 (14 Feb). *Surcharges.* [S. G. D7/9E]

V8. Thick vertical spacing bar 12½mm. long between R. 1 Nos. 3 and 4, normally over left frame line of No. 4.

D8	2c. on 2d. (Type I)	– V4. Bolder "d"	... ...	1·75
	a.	Type II larger surcharge		
		– V4. Bolder "d"	... ...	2·00
		– V8. Spacing bar	... ...	35·00

1961 (15 Nov). [S. G. D10/12]

1c. Thick " c " in value (R. 2/6).

V9

D10	1c. – V9. Thick "c" ...	...	... ...	1·00

Belize

1973 (11 June). *Overprints.* [S. G. 347/59]

V1

½c. Scratch on plate by fish's tail-fin (Pl. 2A, R. 4/2)

347	½c. – V1. Plate scratch	... ...	1·25

1973 (14 Nov). *Royal Wedding.* [S. G. 360/1]

50c. Weak spot in background by Capt Phillips' head (Pl. 1C, R. 1/1).

V2

361	50c. – V2. Weak spot in background	... ...	2·00

1976 (30 Aug). *Surcharges.* [S. G. 445]

V3	V4	V5
" 2 " is clipped at top (Pl. 1A, R. 2/3).	Vertical line through " 2 " (Pl. 1A, R. 4/4).	Black spots by left wing resembling midges (Pl. 1A, R. 4/2).

Flaw between antenna and " 2 " resembles a bullet-hole (Pl. 1D, R. 4/3). Subsequently removed.

V6

445	20c. on 26c. – V3. Chipped "2"	...	...	1·75
	– V4. Line through "2"	...	...	1·75
	– V5. "Midges" by wing	...	...	1·75
	– V6. Bullet-hole by antenna	...		1·75

Bermuda

1953 (8 Dec). *Three Power Talks.* [S. G. 152E/3E]

Talks V4	A large dot joins "lk" of "Talks" (R.10/3).				
152E	3d. – V4. Joined "lk"	...	...	...	3·75
153E	1s.3d. – V4. Joined "lk"	...	...	...	3·75

1965 (22 June). *50th Anniv. United States – Bermuda Yacht race.* [S. G. 154/5]

OCEAN V1	8d. Dropped "o". This is probably caused by the piece of printers' type used for the "o" being inverted (R. 5/4). This does not occur on the 2nd setting.				
1956 V7	1s.3d. " 5 " of " 1956 " broken in two places (R. 2/3).				
1956 V8	1s.3d. " 5 " of " 1956 " broken in upright stroke (R. 7/4).				
154	8d. – V1. Dropped "o" ...	...	...	...	2·75
155	1s.3d. – V7. "5" broken twice	...	...	...	1·60
	– V8. "5" broken once	...	...	...	1·60

Two settings of the overprint have been reported.

1959 (29 July). *350th Anniv. of Settlement.* [S. G. 157/62]

Horiz red registration line close to S.W. part of right shield (R. 4/8).

V5

158E	3d. – V5. Registration line	...	...	...	2·50
160	8d. – V5. Registration line	...	...	...	3·00

1962 (26 Oct)–65. *Views.* [S. G. 163E/79]

V9

V22

2d. Inner frame line broken at upper left (Pl. 1A–1A–1A–1A, R.7/2).

Broken "a" in " Bermuda " (Pl. 1A, R. 11/5).

8d. The corner retouch formerly listed as **V6** which occurs in various degrees on different positions is now known to be not fully constant and so has been deleted.

1s. Damaged pinnacle at top of church tower (Pl. 1B–1B–1B–1B, R. 6/3).

V3

5s. Loop to top of " P " of " Postage " is broken (Pl. 1A–1A, R. 1/1). Corrected on No. 246.

V17

164E	2d.	*lilac, indigo, yellow and green*			
		– V9. Broken frame line	...	...	1·90
		– V22. Broken "a"	...	...	1·90
	Ed.	*Pale lilac, indigo, yellow and green*			
		– V9. Broken frame line	...	...	2·00
171	1s.	– V3. Damaged pinnacle	...	...	3·50
177E	5s.	– V17. Broken "P"	...	...	6·00

1965 (25 Oct). *International Co-operation Year.* [S. G. 187/88E]

V11. Broken leaves. See V6 of Antigua.

187	4d. – V11. Broken leaves	...	...	...	1·90
188E	2s.6d. – V11. Broken leaves	...	...	...	4·00

1966 (24 Jan). *Churchill Commemoration.* [S. G. 189/92]

V14. Dot by St. Paul's. See V2 of Antigua
V20. Flaw by Queen's ear. See V11 of Solomon Islands

189	3d. – V14. Dot by St. Paul's	...	...	...	1·75
190	6d. – V14. Dot by St. Paul's	...	...	...	2·25
	– V20. Flaw by Queen's ear	...	...	2·25
191	10d. – V20. Flaw by Queen's ear	...	...	2·50
192	1s.3d. – V14. Dot by St. Paul's	...	...	...	3·25

1966 (25 Oct)–69. *Views.* [S. G. 195/200]

195	2d. – V9. Broken frame line ...	...	...	...	2·00
198	1s. – V3. Damaged pinnacle	...	...	...	2·25

1966 (1 Dec). *20th Anniv. of U.N.E.S.C.O.* [S. G. 201/3]

1s.3d. Olive line over Queen's head (R. 4/1).

V10

202	1s.3d. – V10. Line over Queen's head	...	...	4·00

1967 (14 Sept). *Inauguration of Bermuda – Tortola Telephone Service.*   [S. G. 208/11]

1s. Cable broken above "R" of " BERMUDA " (R. 12/1).

V12

V13

V15

1s.6d. Dot on first rung of pylon (R. 10/5).

1s.6d. White spot at back of hair (R. 12/2).

208	1s. – V12. Broken cable	... ...	1·75
210	1s.6d. – V13. Dot on pylon	... ...	2·00
	– V15. Spot in hair	... ...	2·50

1968 (1 July). *New Constitution.*   [S. G. 216/19]

1s.6d. Line joining upper window a right with window below appearing as a rope (R. 2/4).

V16

218   1s.6d. – V16. "Rope" flaw   ...   .   1·50

1970 (6 Feb). *Decimal Currency.*   [S. G. 232E/48]
V9. See No. 164E

V18

2c

V19

1c. on 1d. Orange dot to right of " 1d " (Pl. 1A, R. 9/4).

2c. on 2d. in the surcharge the " 2 " is narrower giving the appearance of being tall (Pl. 1A, R. 2/2).

232E	1c. on 1d. – V18. Dot by value	... ...	1·25
233E	2c. on 2d. (wmk sideways)		
	– V9. Broken frame line	...	1·75
	– V19. Tall "2"	... ...	2·75
	c. Wmk upright (No. 164E)		
	– V9. Broken frame line	...	3·25
	– V19. Tall "2"	... ...	3·25
	– V22. Broken "a"	... ...	2·00
	d. Wmk upright (No. 164E*d*)		
	– V9. Broken frame line	...	2·75
	– V19. Tall "2"	... ...	2·75
240	12c. on 1s. – V3. Damaged pinnacle	...	2·25

1972 (20 Nov). *Royal Silver Wedding.*   [S. G. 291/2E]

V24. Dot on curtain. See V4 of Anguilla.
291   4c. – V24. Dot on curtain   ...   .   2·00

1975 (27 Jan). *World Bridge Championship, Bermuda.* [S. G. 324/7]

5c. "g" of "Bridge" with joined loop (Pl. 1A, R.1/4).

V21

324   5c. – V21. Joined "g"   ...   .   1·60

1976 (15 June). *Tall Ships Race, 1976.*   [S. G. 361/6]

$1 Dot over " P " (Pl. 1C, R. 4/1).

V23

366   $1. – V23. Dot over "P"   ...   .   4·00

Biafra

1968. *"SOVEREIGN BIAFRA"* overprint.　　　[S. G. 4/16]

　V15 Broken imprint see Nigeria.
16　£1 (185) – V15. Broken imprint　　...　　...　　...　　12·00

Botswana

1967 (3 Jan). *Birds.*   [S. G. 220/33]

V4

1c. White spot on bird's left claw (Pl. 1B, R. 3/6).

V7

20c. Frame line over " BO " of " BOTSWANA " is dented (Pl. 1A, R. 3/9).

V5

7c. Black dot over first "l" of "billed" (Pl. 1A. R. 5/2).

V14

7c. Flaw in tail-feathers causes them to appear broken (Pl. 1A, R. 3/6).

220	1c. – V4. White claw	...	...	...	...	1·75
225	7c. – V5. Dotted "l"	...	...	...	...	2·75
	– V14. Broken tail-feathers	...	...	...	2·75
228	20c. – V7. Dented top frame	...	...	...	2·75

1967 (2 Oct). *Chobe Game Reserve.*   [S. G. 238/40]

35c. White flaw above second fisherman resembling ghost (R. 8/6).

V2

240	35c. – V2. Ghost variety	...	...	...	...	3·00

1968 (8 Apr). *Human Rights Year.*   [S. G. 241/3]

15c. " s " in " RIGHTS " broken (R. 6/5).

V3

242	15c. – V3. Broken "s"	...	...	...	...	2·00

1968 (30 Sept). *Opening of National Museum and Art Gallery.*   [S. G. 244/8]

3c. Magenta dot appears in " o " of " OPENING " (Pl. 1B, R.1/5).

V6

244	3c. – V6. Dot in "o"	...	...	...	...	1·50

1969 (21 Aug). *22nd World Scout Conference, Helsinki.*   [S. G. 253/5]

V8   V9

3c. Green scratches on bottom bamboo frame appear as if the background is showing through splits in it (Pl. 1A, R. 5/5).

3c. Green spot over the " G " in " SCOUTING " (Pl. 1B, R. 1/2).

V10

15c. Black spot between " NC " of " CONFERENCE " and curved black line over right curve of the badge (Pl. 1C, R. 1/1).

253	3c. – V8. Split bamboo	...	...	...	...	2·00
	– V9. Spot over "G"	...	...	...	...	2·00
254	15c. – V10. Spot between "NC" and line over badge					3·00

1969 (6 Nov). *Christmas.*   [S. G. 256/60]

V11   V12

All Values. Brown line across the back of the woman's neck appears as a scar (Right pane, Pl. 1A–1A, R. 2/2).

All Values.
At the centre of the star there is a join between the long downward point and that to its right (Left pane, Pl. 1A–1A, R. 2/5).

1c. Blue dot below " t " of
" Cent " (Right pane Pl.
1A–1A, R. 4/3).

V13

256	1c. – V11. Scar on neck	...	...	...	...	1·25
	– V12. Flaw on star	...	...	...	...	1·25
	– V13. Spot below "t"	...	...	...	...	1·40
257	2c. – V11. Scar on neck	...	...	...	...	1·40
	– V12. Flaw on star	...	...	...	...	1·40
258	4c. – V11. Scar on neck	...	...	...	...	2·00
	– V12. Flaw on star	...	...	...	...	2·00
259	35c. – V11. Scar on neck	...	...	...	...	2·75
	– V12. Flaw on star	...	...	...	...	2·75

1977 (7 Feb). *Silver Jubilee.* [S. G. 391/3]

V15
25t. "Damage" to Cornation
Coach (Pl. 2A, R. 2/1).

V16
40t. Serif on "7" of "1977"
(Pl. 4C–3C–2C–1C,
R. 5/3).

392	25t. – V15. Damaged coach	...	...	...	...	4·25
393	40t. – V16. Serif on "7"	...	...	...	...	4·50

POSTAGE DUE STAMPS

1967 (1 Mar). *Overprints.* [S. G. D13/15]

V1. Thick "c". See V9 of Bechuanaland.

D13	1c. – V1. Thick "c"	...	...	...	...	1·00

British Antarctic Territory

1966 (24 Jan). *Churchill Commemoration.* [S. G. 16/19]

V1. Dot by St. Paul's. See V2 of Ascension.
V2. Flaw by Queen's ear. See V11 of Solomon Islands.

16	½d. – V1. Dot by St. Paul's	...	...	...	...	4·00
17	1d. – V1. Dot by St. Paul's	...	...	...	...	5·00
18	1s. – V1. Dot by St. Paul's	...	...	...	...	29·00
19	2s. – V2. Flaw by Queen's ear	...	...	...	...	45·00

1973 (23 Dec). *Royal Wedding.* [S. G. 59/60]

V3. Weak spot in background. See V2 of Belize.

59	5p. – V3. Weak spot in background	...	...	...	3·00

1977 (7 Feb). *Silver Jubilee.* [S. G. 83/85E]

RITOR   ITORY

V4
6p. Blob on "T" of
"TERRITORY" (Pl. 1D,
R.4/5).

V5
33p. Blob in "o" of
"TERRITORY" (Pl. 1D,
R.1/2).

83	6p. – V4. Blob on "T"	...	...	...	...	2·00
85E	33p. – V5. Blob in "o"	...	...	...	...	6·50

British Guiana

1954 (1 Dec).–63. *Views.* Wmk Script CA.   [S. G. 331/45]

3c. Green flaw on lily below second " I " of " BRITISH " resembling weed (R.3/10).

V4

3c. Black spot on claw of right-hand bird appearing as clubbed foot (R. 4/1).

V5

333E	3c. – V4. Weed flaw	...	...	...	...	...	2·50
	– V5. Clubbed foot	...	...	...	...		2·50

1963–65. *Views.* Wmk Block CA.   [S. G. 354/65]

48c. Blue dot under waterfall (R.2/1). Not known on Script wmk.

V2

362E	48c. – V2. Dot under waterfall	...	...	...	3·50

1965 (17 May). *I.T.U. Centenary.*   [S. G. 370/1]

V1. Broken "U" in "TELECOMMUNICATIONS". See V1 of Antigua

371	25c. – V1. Broken "U"	...	...	...	...	2·00

1965 (25 Oct). *International Co-operation Year.*   [S. G. 372/3]

V3. Broken "Y" in "YEAR". See V3 of Antigua.
V6. Broken leaves. See V6 of Antigua.

372	5c. – V3. Broken "Y"	...	...	...	...	5·00
	– V6. Broken leaves	...	...	...	...	1·75
373	25c. – V6. Broken leaves	...	...	...	...	2·75

British Honduras

1953 (2 Sept).–62. *Views.*   [S. G. 179E/190]

1c. Extension to outer frame line left of " BR " (R.8/4).

V1

179E	1c. (perf 13·3)	– V1. Frame line extension ...	2·00
	Ea. Perf 13·3 × 13·1	– V1. Frame line extension ...	2·00

1962 (15 Jan). *Hurricane Hattie Relief Fund.*   [S. G. 198/201]

198	1c. (179Ea) – V1. Frame line extension	...	...	2·10

1965 (25 Oct). *International Co-operation year.*   [S. G. 224/5]

V2. Broken leaves. See V6 of Antigua

224	1c. – V2. Broken leaves	...	...	...	...	1·75
225	22c. – V2. Broken leaves	...	...	...	...	1·75

1966 (24 Jan). *Churchill Commemoration.*   [S. G. 226/9]

1c. Broken " 6 " of " 1965 " (Pl. 1A, R 1/5).

V3

226	1c. – V3. Broken "6"	...	...	...	...	1·50

1971 (23 Sept). *Bridges of the World.*   [S. G. 320/3]

½c. Black spot on bridge under " O " of " OF " gives appearance of man's head (All Plates, R. 3/1).

V4

320	½c. – V4. "Man" on bridge	...	...	...	...	1·75

British Indian Ocean Territory

1968 (17 Jan). *Overprints.*   [S. G. 1E/15E]

45c. The optd full-stop after " B '' is damaged and almost missing (Pl. 1A, R.10/4).

V7

7E   45c. – V7. Damaged full-stop   ...   .   4·25

British Postal Agencies in Eastern Arabia

All V numbers are those of Great Britain where the varieties are illustrated. G.B. numbers in brackets.

1952–54. *Queen Elizabeth II.* Wmk Tudor Crown   [S. G. 42/51]

43   1a. on 1d. (516) – V32. Flaw on shamrock   ...   ...   2·50
48   4a. on 4d. (521) – V92. Dotted "R"   ...   .   3·00

1953 (10 June). *Coronation.*   [S. G. 52/55]

55   1r. on 1s. 6d. (535) – V63. Mis-shapen emblems   ...   4·75
                        – V93. Thistle flaw   ...   ...   4·75

1955 (23 Sept)–60. *Castles.* Waterlow ptgs.   [S. G. 56I/57I]

57I   5r. on 5s. (537)–V206. Major re-entry

1956–57. *Queen Elizabeth II.* Wmk St. Edward's Crown
                                                     [S. G. 58/64]

62   4a. on 4d. (546)   – V92. Dotted "R"   ...   ...   8·00
64   1r. on 1s.6d. (551) – V201. White flaw in Queen's hair
                                 below diadem   ...   ...   3·75
                        – V202. White flaw in Queen's hair
                                 opposite "N"   ...   ...   3·75

1957 (1 Apr)–59. *New Currency.*   [S. G. 65/75]

67   6np. on 1d. (541) – V32. Flaw on shamrock   ...   3·25
72   25np. on 4d. (546) – V92. Dotted "R"   ...   ...   4·50
74   50np. on 9d. (551) – V5. Frame break at upper right   4·00

1957 (1 Aug). *World Scout Jubilee Jamboree.*   [S. G. 76E/78]

76E 15np. on 2½d. (557) – V147. Retouch   ...   ...   4·00
77   25np. on 4d. (558) – V35. Solid pearl at right   ...   7·00

British Virgin Islands

1964 (23 Apr). *400th Anniv. of Birth of William Shakespeare.*
[S. G. 177]

This flaw consists of a horizontal white line projecting from Shakespeare's right eyebrow (R. 6/5).

V1

177   10c. – V1. Eyebrow flaw   ...   .   4·00

1965 (17 May). *I.T.U. Centenary.*
[S. G. 193/4]

V2. Broken "U" in "TELECOMMUNICATIONS". See V1 of Antigua.

193   4c. – V2. Broken "U"   ...   .   1·40
194   25c. – V2. Broken "U"   ...   .   3·00

1965 (25 Oct). *International Co-operation Year.*
[S. G. 195E/6]

V3. Broken "Y" in "YEAR". See V3 of Antigua.
V5. Broken leaves. See V6 of Antigua.

195E   1c. – V5. Broken leaves   ...   .   2·00
196   25c. – V3. Broken "Y"   ...   .   6·00
      – V5. Broken leaves   ...   .   2·40

1966 (1 Dec). *20th Anniv. of U.N.E.S.C.O.*
[S. G. 210/12]

60c. First lyre string broken near top (R. 7/1).

V4

212   60c. – V4. Broken lyre string   ...   .   4·50

1967 (18 Apr). *New Constitution.*
[S. G. 213/16]

10c. White spot on " s " of " CENTS " (R. 8/5).

V6

214E   10c. – V6. Spot on "s"   ...   .   2·75

1968 (2 Jan). *Game Fishing.*
[S. G. 220/3]

25c. Extra rock in seabed above and to left of " WAHOO " (R. 1/4).

V7

222   25c. – V7. Extra rock ...   .   2·50

1970 (16 Feb) – 74. *Ships.* Wmk Block CA sideways.
[S. G. 240/56]

V9
1c. Flaw at top of sail resembling a " blue rope '' (All Plates, R.3/5).

V10
5c. Right-hand bracket is broken at top (All plates, R.2/1).

$2. White spot over top wavy line to left of value tablet (Pl. 1A, R. 4/5).

V8

241a   1c. – V9. Blue rope flaw   ...   .   1·50
245   5c. – V10. Broken bracket   ...   .   1·25
254   $2. – V8. White spot beside value tablet   ...   ...   7·50

1973 (17 Oct). *Ships.* Wmk Block CA upright.
[S. G. 295/300]

298   5c. – V10. Broken bracket 2.00

1977 (7 Feb). *Silver Jubilee.*
[S. G. 364/6]

V11
30c. Blotch on "C" of "CENTS" (Pl. 1A, R. 3/5)

V12
30c. "A" of "ISLANDS" is split at the apex (Pl. 1B, 1C, R. 5/1).

365   30c. – V11. Blotch on "C"   ...   .   4·50
      – V12. Split "A" ...   .   4·50

Brunei

1973 (14 Nov). *Royal Wedding.*   [S. G. 200/1]

25c. Smudge at tip of Sultan's eyebrow (Pl. 1B, R. 1/2).

V1

200   25c. – V1. Eyebrow flaw   ...   .   2·25

1977 (7 June). *Silver Jubilee*   [S. G. 247/9]

75c. Red spot on Queen's cloak (Pl. 2A, R. 5/4).

V2

249   75c. – V2. Red spot on cloak   ...   .   4·00

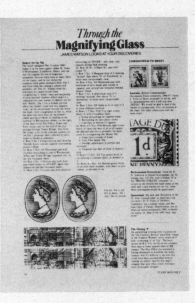

Canada

1964–66. *Provincial Emblems.* [S. G. 543/55]

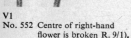

V1
No. 552 Centre of right-hand flower is broken R. 9/1).

V2
No. 551. Break in lily leaf (R.2/4).

| 551 | 5c. – V2. Broken leaf ... | ... | ... | ... | ... | 2·50 |
| 552 | 5c. – V1. Flaw in flower | ... | ... | ... | ... | 2·50 |

1971 (11 Aug). *Death Centenary of Paul Kane (painter).* [S. G. 686]

Mark near the top of the foremost wigwam (Each stamp in 1st vertical row).

V3

| 686 | 7c. – V3. Wigwam flaw | ... | ... | ... | ... | 2·00 |

1972–77. *Various designs.* [S. G. 693/711]

V6
8c. Spot beneath Queen's eye appears as "tear" (R. 2/3).

V5
$1 Broken "$" (R. 5/1, 2, 3, 4).

| 700 | 8c. – V6. Tear flaw ... | ... | ... | ... | ... | 1·50 |
| 707 | $1. – V5. Broken "$" | ... | ... | ... | ... | 15·00 |

1972 (29 Nov). *Death Centenary of Cornelius Krieghoff (painter).* [S. G. 749E]

Break in door frame at right (all stamps in 4th vertical row).

V4

749E	8c. – V4. Break in door frame	...	...	...	1·75
Eq.	Two fluorescent bands				
	– V4. Break in door frame	...	...	...	1·75

1975 (22 Oct). *Christmas.* [S. G. 822/7]

No. 823. Pink dots under " da " of " Canada " (R.2/10).

V7

| 823 | 6c. – V7. Pink dots | ... | ... | ... | ... | ... | 2·00 |

1976 (1 June). *Royal Military College Centenary.* [S. G. 840/1]

V8
No. 840. Line beneath jaw, before collar (R.5/4).

V9
Vertical line left of main tower appears as an extra flagstaff (R.4/5).

| 840 | 8c. – V8. Line beneath jaw | ... | ... | ... | ... | 2·00 |
| | – V9. "Extra flagstaff" | ... | ... | ... | ... | 2·00 |

1977 (4 Feb). *Silver Jubilee.* [S. G. 855]

Silver dot between "25" and last "A" of "CANADA" (R. 1/6).

V10

| 855 | 25c. – V10. Silver dot | ... | ... | ... | ... | 3·00 |

1977 (1 Mar).–79. [S. G. 856/85]

12 and 14c. Missing flagpole (Plates 1 and 2, R. 5/6 12c., and R. 3/4 14c.).

VII

872	12c. – V11. Missing flagpole	...	...	...	1·00
873E	14c. – V11. Missing flagpole	...	...	...	1·00

Cayman Islands

1965 (25 Oct). *International Co-operation Year.*   [S. G. 186/7]

V2. Broken leaves. See V6 of Antigua.
186	1d. – V2. Broken leaves	...	...	...	...	2·40
187	1s. – V2. Broken leaves	...	...	...	...	4·25

1966 (24 Jan). *Churchill Commemoration.*   [S. G. 188E/191]

V3. Dot by St. Paul's. See V2 of Ascension.
188E	½d. – V3. Dot by St. Paul's	...	...	...	1·25
189	1d. – V3. Dot by St. Paul's	...	...	...	1·50
190E	1s. – V3. Dot by St. Paul's	...	...	...	2·00
191	1s.9d. – V3. Dot by St. Paul's	...	...	...	3·00

1966 (1 July). *World Cup Football Championships.*   [S. G. 194/5]

V1

1s.9d. Coloured mark after "D" of "ISLANDS" resembles an apostrophe (R. 3/1).

195   1s.9d. – V1. "ISLAND'S"   ...   .   2·75

1966 (20 Sept). *Inauguration of W.H.O. Headquarters, Geneva.*
[S. G. 196/7]

V9. Dotted "r" in "Headquarters". See V5 of Dominica.
197   1s.3d. – V9. Dotted "r"   ...   .   6·00

1969 (8 Sept). *Decimal Currency.*   [S. G. 238/52]

7c. A green flaw appears as a line behind "AY" of "DAY" (Pl. 1A, R. 2/4).

V4

244   7c. on 8d. – V4. Green flaw ...   .   1·75

1972 (20 Nov). *Royal Silver Wedding.*   [S. G. 317/18E]

V5. Dot on curtain. See V4 of Anguilla.
318E   30c. – V5. Dot on curtain ...   .   3·00

1973 (14 Nov). *Royal Wedding.*   [S. G. 335/6]

V6. "Cotton" on dress. See V5 of Ascension
335   10c. – V6. "Cotton" on dress   ...   .   2·40

1977 (7 Feb). *Silver Jubilee.*   [S. G. 427E/29]

V7
8c. Black "mole" on Prince's cheek (Pl. 1D, R. 3/2).

V8
50c. "M" of "CAYMAN" is chipped at right (Pl. 1A, R. 3/2).

427E	8c. – V7. "Mole" on cheek	...	...	...	1·50
429	50c. – V8. Chipped "M"	...	...	...	3·50

Ceylon

1956 (26 Mar). *Prime Minister's 25 years of Public Service.*
[S. G. 437]

White stroke to left of " POSTAGE " (R. 2/6).

V3

437   10c. – V3. White stroke   ...   .   1·10

1957 (1 Apr). *Ceylon Stamp Centenary.*   [S. G. 442/5]

V2
10c. White flaw at top of " 1 " of " 10 " (R. 7/8).

V11
35c., 85c. Flaw at bottom of lion's rear leg (R.10/9).

443   10c. – V2.   Flaw on "1" of "10"   ...   .   1·10
444   35c. – V11. Lion's foot flaw   ...   .   1·50
445   85c. – V11. Lion's foot flaw   ...   .   2·50

1958 (15 Jan). *Overprint.*   [S. G. 446E/7]

V8. The obliteration square is 3 mm wide instead of 4 mm (R. 2/3 and R. 10/1).

447   10c. – V8. Narrower Square   ...   .   1·00

1961 (8 Jan). *Prime Minister Bandaranaike Commemoration.*
[S. G. 471]

Stop after "CEYLON" (R. 8/9).

471a   10c. (redrawn portrait) – V1. Stop after "CEYLON"   1·75

1963 (1 June). *Surcharge.*   [S. G. 477]

Normal   Variety
V4

The tail of the centre character on the bottom line of surcharge is broken (R.6/4). A similar variety occurs on R.4/10. Also on R.2/7 and 3/3. Plates 1–6.

477   2c. on 4c. – V4. Broken character   ...   .   1·10

1964–70. *Pictorials.*   [S. G. 485/500a]

10c. Flaw over right eye-brow (R. 7/2).

V12

486   10c. – V12. Flaw over eye   ...   .   1·60

1966 (8 Oct). *Inauguration of W.H.O. Headquarters, Geneva.*
[S. G. 513/4]

1r. Broken character (R. 4/10).

V13

514   1r. – V13. Broken character ...   .   2·00

1966 (25 Oct). *International Rice Year.*   [S. G. 515/6]

V6. 6c. Comma after " INTERNATIONAL " (R. 1/7).

30c. Blue flaw on map shows as " lake " on R. Nile (R. 9/9).

V7

515   6c. – V6. Comma after "INTERNATIONAL" ...   ...   1·25
516   30c. – V7. "Lake" on R. Nile   ...   .   2·40

1969 (20 Mar). *Silver Jubilee of National Savings Movement.*
[S. G. 548]

Yellow blob below the right arm of pylon appears as Sun (R. 7/8). Later retouched.

V5
548   3c. – V5. Sun spot   ...   .   1·75

1970 (21 Dec). *International Education year.* [S. G. 573]

A brown flaw above the value impinges upon the " 5 " and also appears less noticeably to the right of the value and extending upwards past the scroll (R. 3/2).

V9

Large white flaw at top to right of U.N. emblem appears as a centipede (R. 6/5).

V10

573	15c. – V9.	Value flaw	...	...	...	...	1·50
	– V10.	"Centipede" flaw		...	...	...	1·50

Christmas Island

Cocos (Keeling) Islands

1958 (15 Oct). *Queen Elizabeth II.* [S. G. 1/10]

V1 Normal at top, variety below

All values. Retouch below " AUSTRALIA " resulting in thinner white frame line (Right pane, R. 4/10).

1	2c. – V1. Retouch	...	...	...	...	...	2·10
2	4c. – V1. Retouch	...	...	...	...	...	2·25
3	5c. – V1. Retouch	...	...	...	...	...	2·50
4	6c. – V1. Retouch	...	...	...	...	...	3·00
5	8c. – V1. Retouch	...	...	...	...	...	3·00
6	10c. – V1. Retouch	...	...	...	...	...	3·00
7	12c. – V1. Retouch	...	...	...	...	...	3·25
8	20c. – V1. Retouch	...	...	...	...	...	6·50
9	50c. – V1. Retouch	...	...	...	...	...	9·00
10	$1. – V1. Retouch	...	...	...	...	...	35·00

1969 (10 Nov). *Christmas.* [S. G. 32]

Short first string of harp missing, (lower pane, R. 5/10).

Normal V2

2	5c. – V2. Missing harp string	...	...	...	...	2·75

1969 (9 July). *Decimal Currency.* [S. G. 8/19]

V1 V2

1c. Vertical lines of disturbance across the background in lower left corner (Lower pane, R. 5/5).

30c. White flaw below " 0 " of " 30 " appears as large comma (Left-hand pane, R. 7/5).

8	1c. – V1. Background disturbance	...	...	...	2·50
17	30c. – V2. Comma flaw	...	...	...	...	5·00

1976 (29 Mar). *Ships.* [S. G. 20/31]

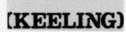

20c. Broken "N" in Keeling (Right pane R. 3/1).

V3

25c. Blue circle in water (Upper pane R. 5/8).

V4

25	20c. – V3. Broken "N" ...	...	...	...	...	3·00
26	25c. – V4. Circle in water	...	...	...	...	3·00

Cook Islands

1966 (24 Jan). *Churchill Commemoration.*   [S. G. 179/84]

V1. Missing dot on "i" in "Memoriam" (R. 1/8 and 6/10, all values and also R. 7/8 and 12/10 on 2s., 3s. and 5s.).
V2. Long hyphen between "1874–1965" (R. 2/6 all values and also R. 8/6 on 2s., 3s. and 5s.).
V3. "I" for "1" in "1874" (R. 6/5 all values and also R. 12/5 on 2s., 3s., and 5s.).
Numerous other more minor varieties also exist.

179	4d. – V1. Missing dot	...	...	...	...	1·75
	– V2. Long hyphen	...	...	...	...	2·00
	– V3. "I" for "1"	...	...	...	...	2·50
180	10d. – V1. Missing dot	...	...	...	...	2·00
	– V2. Long hyphen	...	...	...	...	2·50
	– V3. "I" for "1"	...	...	...	...	3·00
181	1s. – V1. Missing dot	...	...	...	...	2·50
	– V2. Long hyphen	...	...	...	...	3·00
	– V3. "I" for "1"	...	...	...	...	3·50
182	2s. – V1. Missing dot	...	...	...	...	4·00
	– V2. Long hyphen	...	...	...	...	4·50
	– V3. "I" for "1"	...	...	...	...	4·75
183	3s. – V1. Missing dot	...	...	...	...	4·50
	– V2. Long hyphen	...	...	...	...	5·00
	– V3. "I" for "1"	...	...	...	...	5·50
184	5s. – V1. Missing dot	...	...	...	...	6·00
	– V2. Long hyphen	...	...	...	...	7·50
	– V3. "I" for "1"	...	...	...	...	12·00

The overprinting was done in a setting of 10 × 6 and Nos. 182/4 being originally in sheets of 120 were first split in half resulting in the varieties appearing in two positions. Nos. 179/81 were already in sheets of 60.

1967 (3 April–6 June) *Decimal Currency.*   [S. G. 205/18]

c
V4   1c. Condensed letter " c " (R. 2/4, 3/8, 6/2, 8/4).

1c
V5   1c. Thin letter " c " (R. 3/5, 8/1).

1c
V6   1c. Thin figure " 1 " (R. 3/6, 8/2).

1c
V7   1c. Thin figure " 1 " and letter " c " (R. 3/7, 8/3).

2c
V8   2c. Thin figure " 2 " and letter " c " (R. 2/1, 8/8).

c
V9   2c. Condensed letter " c " (R. 4/8, 5/4).

2½c
V10   2½c. Thin figures " 2½ " and letter " c " (R. 6/5).

.2½c
V11   2½c. Thin " 2 ", thin " c " and stop to left of surcharge (R. 3/4).

2½c.
V12   2½c. Thin " 2 ", thin " c " and stop to right of surcharge (R. 9/2).

3c
V13   3c. Thin figure " 3 " and letter " c " (R. 3/6, 4/10, 5/7, 6/3).

4c
V14   4c. Thin figure " 4 " and letter " c " (R. 5/4, 7/5).

.4c
V15   4c. Thin figure " 4 ", thin " c " and stop to left of surcharge (R. 2/8).

5c
V16   5c. Thin figure " 5 " and letter " c " (No. 211, R. 2/8, 8/7; No. 212, R. 5/10, 6/6).

.5c
V17   5c. Thin figure " 5 " thin " c " and stop to left of surcharge (No. 211, R. 6/4; No. 212, R. 4/5).

c
V18   5c. Condensed letter " c " (R. 2/4, 3/9).

7c
V19   7c. Thin figure " 7 " and letter " c " (R. 7/1, 8/5).

.7c
V20   7c. Thin figure " 7 ", thin " c " and stop to left of surcharge (R. 3/8, 6/4).

10c
V21   10c. Thin figures " 10 " and letter " c " (R. 3/4, 5/5, 9/8).

1;0c
V22   10c. Flaw between figures " 1 " and " 0 " (R. 9/3).

30c
V23   30c. Thin figures " 30 " and letter " c " (R 3/10).

50c
V24   50c. Thin figures " 50 " and letter " c " (R. 2/1, 3/7, 5/4, 4/10).

10/-
V25 $1 No top serif to figure " 1 " of " 10/– " (R. 3/2).

10/-
V26 $1 No bottom serif to figure " 1 " of " 10/– " (R. 5/7).

$1.00
V27 $1 Figure " 1 " of " $1 " damaged (R. 5/8).

Other minor varieties exist.

205	1c. on 1d. (No. 163)	– V4. Condensed "c"	...		1·0
		– V5. Thin "c"	...	...	1·2
		– V6. Thin "1"	...	...	1·2
		– V7. Thin "1c"	...	...	1·2
206	2c. on 2d. (No. 164)	– V8. Thin "2c"	...	...	1·2
		– V9. Condensed "c"	...	...	1·2
207	2½c. on 3d.				
	(No. 165) (I)	– V10. Thin "2½c"	...	...	1·2
208	2½c. on 3d.				
	(No. 165) (II)	– V11. Thin "2½c" and stop to left	...	...	1·2
		– V12. Thin "2½c" and stop to right	...	...	1·2

209	3c. on 4d. (No. 175)	– V13. Thin "3c"	...	...	90
210	4c. on 5d. (No. 166)	– V14. Thin "4c"	...	...	1·50
		– V15. Thin "4c" and stop	...		1·75
211	5c. on 6d. (No. 167)	– V16. Thin "5c"	...	...	90
		– V17. Thin "5c" and stop	...		1·10
212	5c. on 6d. (No. 174)	– V16. Thin "5c"	...	...	2·50
		– V17. Thin "5c" and stop	...		3·00
		– V18. Condensed "c"			2·50
213	7c. on 8d. (No. 168)	– V19. Thin "7c"	...	...	1·10
		– V20. Thin "7c" and stop	...		1·10
214	10c. on 1s. (No. 169)				
		– V21. Thin "10c"	...	...	1·25
		– V22. Flaw between "1" and "0"	...	...	1·50
216	30c. on 3s. (No. 172)				
	(R). – V23. Thin "30c"	...	...		12·00
217	50c. on 5s. (No. 173)				
	(R.) – V24. Thin "50c"	...			7·50
218	$1. on 10s. on 10d.				
	(No. 176) (R.) – V25. No top serif to "1" of "10/–"		...	...	20.00
		– V26. No bottom serif to "1" of "10/–"	...	...	20·00
		– V27. Damaged "1" of "$1"			20·00

1971 (8 Sept). *Fourth South Pacific Games, Tahiti.*   [S. G. 351/9]

eetc

Nos. 351/2, 354/5, 357/8. " c " for E in " PAPEETE " (R. 2/5).

V29

351	10c.	– V29. "c" for "E"	...	...	...	2·75
352	10c. + 1c.	– V29. "c" for "E"	...	...	...	2·75
354	25c.	– V29. "c" for "E"	...	...	...	3·25
355	25c. + 1c.	– V29. "c" for "E"	...	...	...	3·25
357	30c.	– V29. "c" for "E"	...	...	...	4·00
358	30c. + 1c.	– V29. "c" for "E"	...	...	...	4·00

1972 (24 May) *Hurricane Relief.*   [S. G. 392/400]

V28. The " Plus 2c " is 16 mm. long instead of the normal 18 mm. (R. 1/1 and R. 1/3). Our listing is of a *se-tenant* pair, one with V28 and the other normal.

393	5c. + 2c.	– V28. Shortened "Plus 2c"	...	...	1·00
395	10c. + 2c.	– V28. Shortened "Plus 2c"	...	...	1·50
397	25c. + 2c.	– V28. Shortened "Plus 2c"	...	...	2·50
399	30c. + 2c.	– V28. Shortened "Plus 2c"	...	...	3·00

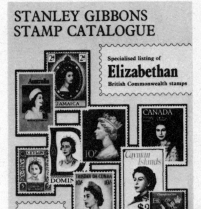

Cyprus

1962 (14 May). *Malaria Eradication.*   [S. G. 209/210]

V1

10m. Blob in Globe at right and line of arctic latitude extended to right of Globe (R. 10, Nos. 1/5).

209   10m. – V1. Blob on Globe   ...   .   2·00

1962 (17 Sept). *Views.*   [S. G. 211/23]

V2

30m. Break in dark wall near centre of stamp (R. 9 Nos. 1/10).

216   30m. – V2. Break in wall   ...   .   2·00

1964 (5 May). *U.N. Security Council's Cyprus Resolutions, March 1964.*   [S. G. 237/41]

1964

V3
Damaged and slanting " 1 " in " 1964 " (R. 7/3).

V4
Outside line at top right of Globe is broken (R. 6/5).

238   30m. – V2. Break in wall   ...   .   2·25
        – V3. Slanting "1"   ...   .   2·75
        – V4. Broken Globe   ...   .   3·25
239   40m. – V3. Slanting "1"   ...   .   3·00
        – V4. Broken Globe   ...   .   3·50
240   50m. – V4. Broken Globe   ...   .   3·25

THE ELIZABETHAN

All other aspects of the stamps of the present reign are fully covered by the *Elizabethan Specialised Stamp Catalogue,* published annually.

1964 (6 July). *Olympic Games, Tokyo.*   [S. G. 246/8]

V7

10m. Brown flaw covering face of right-hand runner gives the appearance of a mask (R. 9/2).
      As these stamps were printed in sheets of 400, divided into four post office sheets of 100, the variety was only constant on one sheet in four. Moreover, it was quickly discovered and many were removed from the sheets by post office clerks.

246   10m. – V7. "Blind runner"   ...   .   85·00

1966 (31 Jan). *U.N. General Assembly's Cyprus Resolutions, 18 December 1965.*   [S. G. 270/3]

272   30m. – V2. Break in wall   ...   .   2·25

1966 (25 Apr). *1900th Death Anniv. of St. Barnabas.*   [S. G. 274/77]

Normal   V5

15m. Left-hand tassel and part of middle tassel omitted (R. 2/3).

V6

25m. Grey patch left of door appearing as extra brick in wall (R. 1 Nos. 1–5).

274   15m. – V5. Missing tassel   ...   .   1·75
275   25m. – V6. Extra brick   ...   .   2·00

1966 (21 Nov). *Views.*   [S. G. 283/96]

V8

15m. Right hand vertical of letter " N " in " CENT " is extended at top and bottom (R. 2/8).

286   15m. – V8. Extended "N"   ...   .   1·50

1968 (2 Sept). *20th Anniv. of W.H.O.* [S. G. 323]

V9

V10

50m. Black spot on shoulder appearing as a mole (R. 3/6).

50m. Spot between " s " & " κ " in inscription (R. 7/2).

323	50m. – V9. Mole flaw	...	...	...	...	2·00
	– V10. Dot between "s" and "κ"		...	...	2·00

1969 (28 Apr). *Europa.* [S. G. 331/3]

150m. A white flaw appears as a spot left of the foot of " P " in " EUR-OPA " (R. 7/6).

V11

333	150m. – V11. Spot by "p"	...	...	...	...	3·50

1969 (7 July). *Birds of Cyprus.* [S. G. 334/9]

15m. Pale blue diagonal line in sea above value (R. 10/5).

V12

335	15m. – V12. Diagonal flaw	...	...	...	...	1·50

1969 (24 Nov). *Christmas.* [S. G. 340/2E]

20m. Dark brown patch, above the Madonna's head, overlaps the blue and appears as a Moon (R. 1/5).

V13

340	20m. – V13. Moon flaw	...	...	...	...	2·25

1970 (3 Aug). *European Conservation Year.* [S. G. 348/50]

10 and 50m. Black line joins emblem to star (R. 2/7).

V14

349E	50m. – V14. Line in emblem	...	...	...	2·50

1971 (22 Feb). *Pictorials.* [S. G. 358/71]

V17 V15

25m. An ornament by the right-hand border of the mosaic is broken (every 4th sheet, R.1/9).

50m. Flaw on the crown of the head appears as tuft of hair (every 4th sheet, R. 9/10).

363	25m. – V17. Broken mosaic	...	...	...	...	2·40
366	50m. – V15. Hair tuft	...	...	...	...	2·75

1974 (14 Oct). *U.N. Security Council Resolution 353.* [S. G. 431/4]

V16

10m. and 40 m. Broken " I " in " SECURITY " (R. 8/6).

431	10m. – V16. Broken "I"	...	...	...	...	2·00
432	40m. – V16. Broken "I"	...	...	...	...	2·00

1975 (13 Oct). *Telecommunications Achievements.* [S. G. 449/50]

100m. Flaw on globe appears as a "lake" in Asia (every 8th sheet, R. 4/4).

V18

450	100m. – V18. Lake in Asia	...	...	...	...	3·00

Turkish Cypriot Posts

1974 (27 July*). *50th Anniv. of Republic of Turkey.*   [S. G. 1/7]

20m. Blue mark above "2" appears as a
tadpole (R. 4/10).

V2

5   20m. – V2. Blue "tadpole" flaw   ...   .   2·50
   * This is the date on which Nos. 1/7 became valid for international mail.
The stamps were first issued for local use on 29th October, 1973.

1975 (3 Mar). *Proclamation of the Turkish Federated State of
Cyprus.*   [S. G. 8/9]

30m. Optd date is broken (R.9/2).

V1

8   30m. on 20m. – V1. Broken date   ...   .   60·00
                    – V2. Blue "tadpole" flaw   ...   ...   3·00

1977 (2 Dec). *Turkish Buildings in Cyprus.*   [S. G. 54/57]

V3

40m. Broken "B" in "BAF KALESI"
   (R. 10/3).

55   40m. – V3. Broken "B"   ...   .   1·50

Dominica

1954 (1 Oct)–62. *Views.* [S. G. 140/58]

V1

¼c. "V" flaw. A "V" shaped coloured flaw is to be found above the tiara (R. 10/2, Pl. 1).

V2

4c. Cracked plate affecting the lower right corner of the stamp and the sheet margin (R. 6/5, Pl. 1a–1a).

140	¼c. – V1. "V" flaw	...	...	...	...	1·25
145	4c. – V2. Cracked plate	...	...	...		2·75

1963 (16 May)–65. *Views.* [S. G. 162/78]

V4

24c. White patch on Queen's forehead retouched (Pl. 1A R. 3/4 and 4/4).

V11

$2.40 Broken "F" in "TRAFALGAR" (Pl. 1A, R.5/3).

173	24c. – V4. Retouch	...	...	...	...	5·00
177	$2·40 – V11. Broken "F"	...	...	...		7·50

1965 (17 May). *I.T.U. Centenary.* [S. G. 183/4]

V3. Broken "U" in "TELECOMMUNICATIONS". See V1 of Antigua.

183	2c. – V3. Broken "U"	...	...	...	...	2·00

1965 (25 Oct). *International Co-operation Year.* [S. G. 185/6]

V6. Broken leaves. See V6 of Antigua.

185	1c. – V6. Broken leaves	...	...	...		2·25
185	15c. – V6. Broken leaves	...	...	...		3·00

1966 (20 Sept). *Inauguration of W.H.O. Headquarters, Geneva.* [S. G. 195/6]

V5

5c. Dot over "r" of "Headquarters" (Pl. 1B, R, 2/1).

195	5c. – V5. Dotted "r"	...	...	...	...	2·25

1968 (8 July). *Associated Statehood.* [S. G. 214/31]

V4. See No. 173 V4.
V9. The word "STATEHOOD" is 11½ mm. long instead of the normal 12 mm. (R. 4/4).
V11. See No. 177 V11.

226	24c. – V4. Retouch	...	...	...	...	1·50
227a	48c. – V9. Short "STATEHOOD"		...	...	...	14·00
230	$2·40 – V11. Broken "F"	...	...	...		6·00

1968 (3 Nov). *National Day.* [S. G. 232/6]

V8

1c., 3c., $1.20. Broken " 3 " (R.10/4).

232	1c. – V8. Broken "3"	...	...	...	...	2·00
234	3c. – V8. Broken "3"	...	...	...		1·25
236	$1·20 – V8. Broken "3"	...	...	...		3·50

1969 (3 Nov). *National Day.* [S. G. 268/71]

V7

6c. White flaw below 'R" of " E II R '' appears as a dot (R.2/3).

268	6c. – V7. Dot under "R"	...	...	...	...	1·50

1974 (25 Nov). *Birth Centenary of Sir Winston Churchill.* [S. G. 434/40]

IC'A

V10

2c. Flaw between " c " and " A " of " DOMINICA " appears as an apostrophe (Pl. 1B, R. 2/3).

436	2c. – V10. Apostrophe flaw	...	...	...		1·75

East Africa

1964 (21 Oct), *Olympic Games, Tokyo.*   [S. G. 1/4]

V1

50c. Colon between " KENYA " and " TANGANYIKA " (R. 10/1).

2   50c. – V1. Colon variety   ...   .   1·75

1966 (2 Aug). *Eighth British Empire and Commonwealth Games, Jamaica.*   [S. G. 21/24]

V2

2s.50 Short "z" in TANZANIA (R. 9/8).

24   2s.50. – V2. Short "z" ...   .   2·50

1968 (4 Mar). *Mountains of East Africa.*   [S. G. 38/41]

V8   V3.

30c.

V8. Extra ledge to mountain at right (R. 7/2 and 7/3).

V3. Normal ledge removed, appearing as an avalanche (R. 8/10).

38   30c. – V8. Extra ledge ...   .   1·75
     – V3. "Avalanche" flaw ...   .   1·75

1969 (20 Jan). *Water Transport.*   [S. G. 50/53]

V4

50c. Flaw in ship's hull below anchor appears as a hole (Pl. 1A, R. 2/1).

V5   V6

2s.50 Large white flaw over car appears as a water-spout (Pl. 1A, R. 10/5).

2s.50 Small white flaw to left of superstructure appears as a shirt fluttering (Pl. 1A. R. 10/9).

51   50c. – V4. Hole in hull   ...   .   1·50
53   2s.50 – V5. Waterspout flaw   ...   .   3·00
     – V6. Shirt flaw ...   .   3·00

1971 (5 Apr). *Railway Transport.*   [S. G. 86/90]

V7

1s.50. Missing gold background under " NZ " leaving thicker white frameline (Pl. 1B, R. 3/4).

88   1s.50 – V7. Thick frame under "NZ" ...   .   3·00

1971 (28 Oct). *Centenary of Livingstone and Stanley meeting at Ujiji.*   [S. G. 95]

V9

5s. Two brown dots left of " AT " (All plates, R. 1/4, both ptgs).

95   5s. – V9. "AT" flaw   ...   .   4·50

1973 (16 July). *24th World Scout Conference, Nairobi.* [S. G. 123/6]

V16

2s.50. Flaw on the hat brim (Pl. 1A, R.5/1).

126   2s.50 – V16. Hat flaw   ...   .   4·50

PHILATELIC TERMS ILLUSTRATED

The essential philatelic dictionary. Terms covering printing methods, papers, errors, varieties, watermarks, perforations and much more are explained and illustrated, many in full colour. See the preliminary pages of this Catalogue for details of the current edition.

1973 (24 Sept). I.M.F./World Bank Conference.   [S. G. 127/31]

V14

40c. Line over "I" of "IMF" (All plates, all stamps on Row 1).

V15

2s.50. Dot on globe (All plates, all stamps on Row 4).

127	40c. – V14. Line over "I"	...	...	...	...	90
130	2s.50 – V15. Dot on globe	...	...	...	...	2·50

1974 (9 Oct). Centenary of Universal Postal Union.   [S. G. 153/6]

V11

1s.50. Flaw appears to "break" the top row of windows (Pl. 1B, R. 1/3).

V12

2s.50. Flaw shaped like "C" beneath aircraft's tail (Pl. 1C, R. 2/4).

155	1s.50 – V11. Broken windows	...	...	...	2·25
156	2s.50 – V12. "c" beneath tail	...	...	...	3·00

1975 (24 Feb). East Africa Game Lodges.   [S. G. 161/4]

2s.50 Base of left tusk has a protuberance appearing like a " black nail " (Pl. 1C, R. 5/5).

V10

Red, diagonal "accent" over "K" of "Kenya" (Pl. 1A, R. 3/3).

V13

164	2s.50 – V10. Black nail flaw ...	...	...	...	3·00
	– V13. Accent over "K"	...	...	...	3·00

Falkland Islands

1960 (10 Feb)–63. *Birds.* Wmk Block CA (upright).

[S. G. 193E/207]

¼d., 1d., 2d., 2s. Weak entry under "FA" of "FALKLAND" (D.L.R. Pl. 2, R. 12/5).

V3

THRUSH ¼d. Extended cross-bar to first "H" in "THRUSH" (D.L.R. Pl. 1 (black), R. 2/2).

V4

193Ea	¼d. – V3. Weak entry	...	...	...	...	2·10
	– V4. "H" flaw ...	...	...	...	...	2·10
194Ea	1d. – V3. Weak entry	...	...	...	...	2·25
195Ea	2d. – V3. Weak entry	...	...	...	...	3·50
204Ea	2s. – V3. Weak entry	...	...	...	...	9·00

1965 (25 Oct). *International Co-operation Year.* [S. G. 221/2]

V1. Broken leaves. See V6 of Antigua.

221	1d. – V1. Broken leaves	...	...	...	...	3·25
222	1s. – V1. Broken leaves	...	...	...	...	4·50

1966 (24 Jan). *Churchill Commemoration.* [S. G. 223/6]

V2. Dot by St. Paul's. See V2 of Ascension
V8. Flaw by Queen's ear. See V11 of Solomon Islands

223	¼d. – V2. Dot by St. Paul's	...	...	...	1·50
224E	1d. – V2. Dot by St. Paul's	...	...	...	2·00
225E	1s. – V2. Dot by St. Paul's	...	...	...	3·00
	– V8. Flaw by Queen's ear	...	...	...	3·00
226	2s. – V2. Dot by St. Paul's	...	...	...	5·50
	– V8. Flaw by Queen's ear	...	...	...	5·50

1966 (25 Oct). As 193Ea but wmk. Block CA sideways. [S. G. 227]

227	¼d. – V3. Weak entry ...	...	...	...	...	2·00
	– V4. "H" flaw	...	...	...	...	2·00

1968 (9 Oct)–71. *Flowers.* [S. G. 232/45E]

¼d. Missing grey colour in diadem appears as a damaged crown (Pl. 1A, R. 2/2).

V7

V5. 3s. The lavender is omitted from small bud at left (Pl. 1A, R. 3/11).

V9   V6

5s. Extra pink bud by centre leaf of flower at right (Pl 1A, R. 2/3).

£1. Green spot on lowest orange stalk (Pl. 1A, R. 2/9).

£1. Accent over "1" (Pl. 1A, R. 4/5).

V16

232	¼d. – V7. Crown damaged	...	...	...	1·50
243	3s. – V5. Lavender omitted from bud	...	...	8·00
244	5s. – V9. Extra pink bud	...	...	...	9·00
245Ea	£1 – V6. Spot on stalk	...	...	...	17·00
	– V16. Accent over "1"	...	...	...	17·00

1970 (30 Apr). *Golden Jubilee of Defence Force.* [S. G. 254E/57]

6d. Broken inscription in "JUBILEE" (Pl 1a, R. 1/3).

V29

6d. Frame break by sandbags at lower left also a break above "N" of "FALKLAND" in the top frame line. (Pl. 1a, R. 2/3).

V30

255	6d. – V29. Broken inscription	...	...	...	2·00
	– V30. Frame break	...	...	...	2·00

PHILATELIC TERMS ILLUSTRATED

The essential philatelic dictionary. Terms covering printing methods, papers, errors, varieties, watermarks, perforations and much more are explained and illustrated, many in full colour. See the preliminary pages of this Catalogue for details of the current edition.

1971 (15 Feb). *Decimal Currency.* [S. G. 263/75]

10p. on 2s. Broken crown (Pl. 1A, R. 5/2).

V17

263	½p. on ½d. – V7. Crown damaged	...	...	...	1·50
273	10p. on 2s. – V17. Broken Crown	...	...	...	7·00
275	25p. on 5s. – V9. Extra pink bud	...	...	...	8·00

1972 (1 June). *Decimal Currency.* [S. G. 276/88]

V10

½p. Dark flaw on Queen's hair above ear (Pl. 1A, R. 1/7).

V11

½p. Smudge over second "i" in "decipiens" (Pl. 1A, R. 3/12).

1p. Black spot on leaf. (Pl. 1A, R. 12/2).

V31

5p. Dot on stem of "d" of "Falkland" (Pl. 1A, R. 4/5).

V12

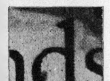

6p. Dot in "d" of Islands" (Pl. 1A, R. 9/4).

V13

6p. Extended serif to bottom of "p" of value (Pl. 1A, R. 8/3).

V14

276	½p. – V10. Flaw on hair	...	...	...	...	2·50
	– V11. Smudge over "i"	...	...	...	...	2·50
277E	1p. – V31. Black spot on leaf	...	...	...	1·50
283	5p. – V12. Dot on "d"	...	...	...	3·50
284	6p. – V13. Dot in "d"	...	...	...	6·50
	– V14. Serif to "p"	...	...	...	6·50
288	25p. – V9. Extra pink bud	...	...	...	5·50

1973 (14 Nov). *Royal Wedding.* [S. G. 291/2]

V15. "Cotton" on dress. See V8 of Ascension.

291	5p. – V15. "Cotton" on dress	...	...	...	2·75
292	15p. – V15. "Cotton" on dress	...	...	...	4·00

1974 (31 July). *Centenary of Universal Postal Union.* [S. G. 300/3]

2p. Figure on the left of the U.P.U. emblem has a broken foot (Pl. 1B, R.1/5).

Normal V24

V18

8p. Yellow bar left of U.P.U. emblem (Pl. 1D, R. 1/5).

V19

16p. Omission of colouring dots results in a "white patch" (Pl. 1C, R. 4/1).

300	2p. – V24. Broken foot	...	...	...	...	2·10
302	8p. – V18. Yellow bar	...	...	...	...	1·75
303	16p. – V19. White patch	...	...	...	...	2·50

1974 (13 Dec). *35th Anniv. of the Battle of the River Plate.* [S. G. 307E/10E]

6p. Diagonal scratch on ship's bridge (Pl. 1A, R. 2/1).

V20

308E	6p. – V20. Scratch on bridge	...	...	2·10

1975 (28 Oct). *50th Anniv. of Heraldic Arms.* [S. G. 311/4]

2p. Black tip to Queen's crown, and flaw behind bull's croup appearing as a " yellow road '' (All plates, R. 5/4).

V21

7½p. Flaw appearing as an upright spar on mizzen mast (Pl. 1B and 1D, R. 1/5).

V22

311   2p. – V21. Black tip and yellow road   ...   ...   2·00
312   7½p. – V22. Extra spar   ...   .   2·50

1975 (31 Dec). *New Coinage.* [S. G. 316E/20]

10p. Red flaw on stone appears as a blade of grass (Pl. 1A, R. 3/1).

V23

319   10p. – V23. Extra blade of grass   ...   .   3·00

1976 (28 Apr). *Sheep Farming Industry.* [S. G. 321/4]

2p. Flaw resembling an accent over "I" of "Islands" (Pl. 1D, R. 2/1).

V25

321   2p. – V25. Accent over "ɪ"   ...   .   2·40

1977 (7 Feb–1 Nov). *Silver Jubilee.* [S. G. 325/7b]

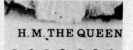

V26   V27

6p. Black dot on "6" (Pl. 1C, R. 1/1).

33p. Flaw on "I'' of "JUBILEE'' gives the appearance of a large serif (Pl. 1C, R.1/5).

H.M. THE QUEEN

V37

33p. Extra dot after "м" (Booklet pane R. 1/1).

325   6p. – V26. Dot on "6"   ...   .   2·25
327   33p. – V27. Large serif   ...   .   3·00
     a.   Booklet pane of 4 with blank margins
       – V37. Extra dot ...   .   8·00

1977 (24 Oct). *Telecommunications.* [S. G. 328/30]

40p. White scratch left of globe (Pl. 1A, R. 1/5).

V28

ıal Telex and Service 1967-

40p. Black flaw joins "r" and "v" of "Service" (Pl. 1A, R. 4/3).

V32

330   40p. – V28. White scratch   ...   .   2·25
       – V32. Joined "rv"   ...   .   2·25

1978 (28th Apr). *26th Anniv. of First Direct Flight, Southampton– Port Stanley.* [S. G. 346/7]

33p. "White island" on Australia (Pl. 1B, R. 3/5).

V33

347   33p. – V33. "White island" flaw   ...   .   3·00

1978 (8 Aug). *Centenary of First Falkland Is. Postage Stamp.*
[S. G. 351/4]

All values. White spot above perforations. (Pl. 1B, R. 3/3).

V34

351	3p. – V34. White spot	...	...	...	1·50
352	11p. – V34. White spot	...	...	...	2·25
353	15p. – V34. White spot	...	...	...	2·50
354	22p. – V34. White spot	...	...	...	3·00

1979 (1 May). *Opening of Stanley Airport.*
[S. G. 360/63]

11p. White flaw under "o". (Pl. 1, 2, 3, 4. R. 8/5).

V35

361E	11p. – V35. Flaw under "o"	...	...	...	2·50

1980 (25 Feb). *Dolphins and porpoises.*
[S. G. 371/76]

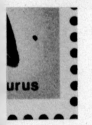

15p. Black spot flaw (Pl. 1B × 3. R. 5/5).

V36

375	15p. – V36. Spot flaw ...	...	...	...	...	2·00

Falkland Islands Dependencies

1954 (1 Feb)–62. *Ships.*
[S. G. G26E/40]

1d. There are a number of retouches of the cross-hatching in the clouds where lines have been deepened. The one illustrated is on R. 12/1 and other prominent retouches occur on R. 8/1 and R. 10/1 but there are other less marked ones. These were corrected in the D.L.R. printing.

V1

V2

Re-entry. Whole of bottom frame line doubled (R. 11/3). Also corrected in the D.L.R. printing.

3d. V3. Top frame line weak or broken over "NDS" on R. 2/3.
V4. In the second state the frame line has been heavily re-cut.

G27E	1d. – V1. Retouches to cross-hatching *From*	...	...		...	2·00
	– V2. Re-entry ...	...	...	...	...	2·50
G31	3d. – V3. Broken frame line	...	...	...	4·50
	– V4. Frame line re-cut	...	...	...	3·75

1956 (30 Jan). *Trans-Atlantic Expedition.*
[S. G. G41/44]

G41	1d. – V1. Retouches to cross-hatching *From*	...	...		...	2·75
	– V2. Re-entry	...	...	...	...	3·75
G43	3d. – V3. Broken frame line	...	...	...	7·50
	– V4. Frame line re-cut ...	...	...	...	6·50

Fiji

1954–59. *Views.* [S. G. 280/95]

½d. Owing to weak entry, lines of shading are missing (R. 6/10).

V1

280　½d. – V1. Weak entry ... ... 1·50

1959–63. *Views.* Wmk Script CA. [S. G. 298/310]

4s. Dent in left frame line (R. 4/2).

V2

308　4s. – V2. Dented frame line ... ... 9·00

1962–66. *Views.* Wmk Block CA (upright). [S. G. 311/25]

3d. Red spot on the medal ribbons appears as an extra adornment (Pl. 1A R. 1/10).

V16

313E　3d. – V16. Medal flaw ... ... 2·00
321　4s.　*red, yellow–green, blue* and *green*
　　　　　– V2. Dented frame line ... ... 6·50
322　4s.　*red, green blue* and *slate-green*
　　　　　– V2. Dented frame line ... ... 8·00

1964 (4 Aug). *50th Anniv. of Fijian Scout Movement.* [S. G. 336/7]

1s. Coloured line appearing as a pocket in the " sulu " (R. 1/1).

V6

337　1s. – V6. Pocket in skirt ... ... 2·25

1964 (24 Oct). *25th Anniv. of First Fiji–Tonga Airmail Service.* [S. G. 338/40]

V3　　　　　　　　　　V4

3d. Flaw in hair above ear-ring (R. 2/5).　　　3d. Frame of neck shaved at left (R. 7/1).

1s. White patch on cheek (R. 3/3).

V5

338　3d. – V3. Flaw in hair ... ... 2·75
　　　　　– V4. Frame of neck shaved ... ... 3·00
340　1s. – V5. White face ... ... 3·25

1965 (25 Oct). *International Co-operation Year.* [S.G. 343/4]

V8. Broken leaves. See V6 of Antigua.
344　2s.6d. – V8. Broken leaves ... ... 2·50

1966 (24 Jan). *Churchill Commemoration.* [S. G. 345/8]

V9. Dot by St. Paul's. See V2 of Ascension.
V19. Flaw by Queen's ear. See V11 of Solomon Islands.
345　3d. – V9. Dot by St. Paul's ... ... 1·75
346　9d. – V9. Dot by St. Paul's ... ... 3·00
347　1s. – V9. Dot by St. Paul's ... ... 3·00
348　2s.6d. – V19. Flaw by Queen's ear ... ... 6·00

1966 (1 July). *World Cup Football Championships.* [S. G. 349/50]

V23

2s. One line of latitude broken (R. 6/2).

V24

Two lines broken (R. 7/2).

| 350 | 2s. – V23. One line broken | ... | ... | ... | ... | 2·10 |
| | – V24. Two lines broken | ... | ... | ... | ... | 3·25 |

1966 (20 Sept). *Inauguration of W.H.O. Headquarters, Geneva.*
[S. G. 354/5]

V7. Dotted "r" in "Headquarters". See V5 of Dominica.

| 354 | 6d.–V7. Dotted "r" | ... | ... | ... | ... | ... | 3·25 |

1967 (16 Feb). As No. 321 but wmk Block CA sideways.
[S. G. 359]

| 359 | 4s. – V2. Dented frame line | ... | ... | ... | ... | 6·00 |

1968 (5 June). *40th Anniv. of Kingsford Smith's Pacific Flight via Fiji.*
[S. G. 367/70]

V10

2d. Black spot on Queen's neck below ear-ring (R. 2/5).

V11

2d. Green spot above trees above the tail of the 'plane (R. 10/3).

V12

6d. Retouch on Queen's nose (R. 9/5).

V13

6d. White dot on radio mast (R. 12/3).

2s. Brown spot appears as extra tree top above airplane cockpit (R. 2/3).

V14

V21 2s. Hyphen between "MONOPLANE" and "LADY" (R. 12/4).

367	2d. – V10. Spot on neck	...	...	...	...	2·50
	– V11. Spot over trees	...	...	...	...	2·50
368	6d. – V12. Retouch	...	...	...	...	3·00
	– V13. Radio mast flaw	...	...	...	...	3·00
370	2s. – V14. Extra tree top	...	...	...	...	3·00
	– V21. Hyphen flaw	...	...	...	...	2·15

1968 (9 Dec). *20th Anniv. of World Health Organisation.*
[S. G. 388/90]

3s. Blue mark in the wake of the speed boat appears as a shark's fin (Pl. 1B, R. 11/5).

V15

| 390 | 3s. – V15. Shark's fin | ... | ... | ... | ... | ... | 5·50 |

1969 (13 Jan) – 70. *Decimal Currency.* [S. G. 391/407]

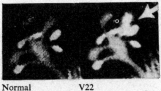

1c. Extra yellow pollen on left-hand flower (Pl. 1A R. 4/5).

Normal   V22

| 391 | 1c. – V22. Extra yellow pollen | ... | ... | ... | 1·00 |

1969 (18 Aug). *Third South Pacific Games, Port Moresby.*
[S. G. 411E/13]

Normal   V17

4c. Grey shading on the right of the vest and the black (biceps) of the right arm partly omitted (Pl. 1A, R. 10/3).

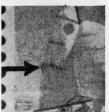

8c. Grey flaw on outer edge of sail on small yacht by second stay up (R. 3/3).

V18

| 411E | 4c. – V17. White shirt and missing biceps | ... | 2·75 |
| 412 | 8c. – V18. Sail flaw | ... | ... | ... | 2·75 |

1970 (18 Aug). *Explorers and Discoverers.* [S. G. 424E/7]

25c. Severed frame spike and mis-shapen corner ornament (R. 6/4).

V20

427   25c. – V20. Severed frame spike mis-shapen corner ornament   ...   .   4·00

1971–72. *Birds and Flowers.* Wmk Block CA (upright). [S. G. 435/50]

4c. Extra "red leaf" at base of plant (Pl 2B, R.2/7).

V25

438   4c. – V25. Red leaf   ...   .   2·10

1973 (26 Oct). *Festivals of Joy.* [S. G. 485/8]

3c. Crease on veil (Pl. 1B, R. 1/1).

V26

485   3c. – V26. Crease in veil   ...   .   1·75

1974 (21 Feb). *Cricket Centenary.* [S. G. 492E/4]

3c. Yellow flaw on ground between bowler's legs resembles a dandelion (Pl. 1A, R. 1/2).

V27

492E   3c. – V27. Dandelion flaw ...   .   2·00

1975–77. *Birds and Flowers.* Wmk CA Diagonal. [S. G. 505/20]

V28   V29

1c. Damaged "C" in face-value (Pl. 1A, R. 9/3).   2c. Black "feather" on bird at left (Pl. 3A–2A–3A–3A, R. 1/2).

3c. Blue "flower" occurs on the orchid blossom second from left (Pl. 2A–2A–3A–2A, R. 6/6).

V30

4c.   V25.   See No. 438 V25.

5c. Black scratch over "5c" (Pl. 2A, R. 6/3).

V31

505   1c.   (wmk sideways)
        – V28. Damaged "c"   ...   .   1·10
506   2c. – V29. Black feather   ...   .   1·50
507   3c. – V30. Blue flower   ...   .   1·25
508   4c. – V25. Red leaf   ...   .   1·25
509   5c. – V31. Scratch over "5c"   ...   .   1·50

1977 (7 Feb). *Silver Jubilee.* [S. G. 536/8E]

30c. Blue dot under "R" of "SILVER" (Pl. 1C. R. 4/2).

V32

538E   30c. – V32. Blue dot   ...   .   3·00

Gambia

1963 (4 Nov). *Birds.* [S. G. 193/205]

½d. Diagonal blue line causing shadow under right leg (R. 6/6).

V1

193   ½d. – V1. Shadow under leg ...   .   2·00

1965 (18 Feb). *Independence overprint.* [S. G. 215/27]

215   ½d. – V1. Shadow under leg ...   .   1·50

1967 (20 Dec). *International Tourist Year.* [S. G. 250/2]

All values. Dark cloud in background colour over Adonis Hotel (R. 1/4).

V2

250   2d. – V2. Thunder cloud ...   .   2·10
251   1s. – V2. Thunder cloud ...   .   2·25
252   1s.6d. – V2. Thunder cloud ...   .   3·00

1972 (1 July). *Tenth Anniv. of Radio Gambia.* [S. G. 287/9]

4b. Diagonal white line through right wall passing through " AD " of " RADIO " (Pl. 1A, R. 1/4).

V3

287   4b. – V3. Line through wall ...   .   2·00

Ghana

1957 (6 Mar). *Independence Commemoration.*   [S. G. 166/9]

2d. Retouch to background between S.W. Africa and " GH " of " GHANA " (R. 3/1, Pl. 1B).

V8

2½d. Retouch to background above eagle's right wing (R. 3/4, Pl. 1B).

V1

4d. Retouch over Nkrumah's left eye (R. 1/6, Pl. 1B).

V9

1s.3d. There are a number of retouches to the background on this value. The one illustrated shows part of R. 2/1 and other prominent retouches occur on R. 1/1, R. 3/1 and R. 4/2.

V2

166	2d. – V8. Retouched background	...	...	1·25
167	2½d. – V1. Retouched background	...	...	1·25
168	4d. – V9. Black eye retouch	...	...	1·40
169	1s.3d. – V2. Retouches to background. *From*	...	1·50

1957 (6 May)–58. *Independence overprints.*   [S. G. 170E/81]

MARCH. Dot between " AR " of " MARCH " (R. 7/3).
V10

171	1d. – V10. Dot between "AR"	...	...	...	1·10
176	4d. – V10. Dot between "AR"	...	...	...	1·50
179	2s. – V10. Dot between "AR"	...	...	...	1·75
180	5s. – V10. Dot between "AR"	...	...	...	2·25

1958 (18 July). *Prime Minister's Visit to the U.S.A. and Canada.* Nos. 166/9 overprinted.   [S. G. 197/200]

U.S.A. Malformed " U " in " U.S.A." (R. 2/1).
V11

197	2d. – V8. Retouched background	...	...	1·10
	– V11. Malformed "U"	...	...	1·10
198	2½d. – V1. Retouched background	...	...	1·10
	– V11. Malformed "U"	...	...	1·25
199	4d. – V9. Black eye retouch	...	...	1·10
	– V11. Malformed "U"	...	...	1·40
200	1s.3d. – V2. Retouch to background *From*	...	1·75

1959 (5 Oct)–61. *Pictorials.*   [S. G. 213/27]

5s. White stop after " 5 ", later retouched (Pl. 1A, R. 2/6).

V5

224	5s. – V5. Stop after "5"	...	...	...	5·00

1959 (15 Oct). *West African Football Competition 1959.*   [S. G. 228/32]

Normal   V6
3d. Part of brown covering goalkeeper's right boot missing (Pl. 1A, R. 3/1).
230   3d. – V6. Boot variety   ...   .   1·25

THE ELIZABETHAN

Uniform with this volume, the *Elizabethan Specialised Stamp Catalogue* covers all other aspects of the stamps of the present reign, from both Great Britain and the British Commonwealth, in considerable detail. See the preliminary pages of this Catalogue for details of this annual publication.

1965 (15 Nov). *African Soccer Cup Competition.*   [S. G. 400/2]

24p. Green line behind footballer at left appearing as a tail (R. 3/4).

V13

402   24p. – V13. Tail flaw ...   .   2·50

1966 (7 Feb). *"Black Stars" Victory in African Soccer Cup Competition.*   [S. G. 412/4]

V18. No dot after "Nov" in opt (R. 5/1).

412   6p. – V18. No dot after "Nov"   ...   .   2·10
414   24p. – V13. Tail flaw   ...   .   2·00
       – V18. No dot after "Nov"   ...   .   2·50

1967 (23 Feb). *New Currency.*   [S. G. 445/54]

V14. 2nc. No stop after "2" (R. 6/5).

452   2nc. – V14. no stop after "2"   ...   .   19·00

1969 (1 Oct). *New Constitution.*   [S. G. 541/55]

Damaged first " I " in " CONSTITUTION " (R. 3/4 on 1½np. and 2nc. 50; R. 2/3 on horizontal designs; R. 4/2 on the remainder).

V16

" CO " of " CONSTITUTION " joined (R. 2/5 on 1½np. and 2nc. 50; R. 1/2 on horizontal designs; R. 4/2 on the remainder).

V17

542   1½np. – V16. Damaged "I" ...   .   1·10
            – V17. "co" joined ...   .   1·10
543   2np. – V16. Damaged "I" ...   .   1·10
            – V17. "co" joined ...   .   1·10
544   2½np. – V16. Damaged "I" ...   .   1·25
            – V17. "co" joined ...   .   1·25
545   3np. – V16. Damaged "I" ...   .   1·25
            – V17. "co" joined ...   .   1·25
547   6np. – V16. Damaged "I" ...   .   1·00
            – V17. "co" joined ...   .   1·00
549   9np. – V16. Damaged "I" ...   .   1·25
            – V17. "co" joined ...   .   1·25
550   5np. – V16. Damaged "I" ...   .   1·50
            – V17. "co" joined ...   .   1·50
551   20np. – V16. Damaged "I" ...   .   1·75
            – V17. "co" joined ...   .   1·75
552   50np. – V16. Damaged "I" ...   .   2·50
            – V17. "co" joined ...   .   2·50
553   1nc – V16. Damaged "I" ...   .   3·00
            – V17. "co" joined ...   .   3·00
554   2nc – V16. Damaged "I" ...   .   6·00
            – V17. "co" joined ...   .   6·00
555   2nc.50 – V16. Damaged "I" ...   .   8·00
            – V17. "co" joined ...   .   8·00

POSTAGE DUE STAMPS

1958 (25 June). *Overprints.*   [S. G. D9/13]

V4.   Upright stroke. See V1 of Gold Coast
V7.   Missing serif. See V2 of Gold Coast
V15. Bolder "d". See V3 of Basutoland

D10   2d. – V15. Bolder "d"   ...   .   2·00
D11   3d. – V7. Missing serif   ...   .   2·00
D13   1s. – V4. Upright stroke   ...   .   2·50

1958 (1 Dec).   [S. G. D14/18]

Notch in frame of top left ornament and circle dented (R. 1/2).

V12

D14   1d. – V12. Damaged ornament   ...   .   1·75
D15   2d. – V12. Damaged ornament   ...   .   2·00
            – V15. Bolder "d"   ...   .   2·25
D16   3d. – V7. Missing serif   ...   .   2·50
            – V12. Damaged ornament   ...   .   2·50
D17   6d. – V12. Damaged ornament   ...   .   3·50
D18   1s. – V4. Upright stroke   ...   .   2·00
            – V12. Damaged ornament   ...   .   2·00

1965. *New Currency.*   [S. G. D19/23]

D19   1p. on 1d. – V12. Damaged ornament   ...   ...   1·75
D20   2p. on 2d. – V12. Damaged ornament   ...   ...   1·75
            – V15. Bolder "d"   ...   .   1·50
D21   3p. on 3d. – V7. Missing serif   ...   .   1·50
            – V12. Damaged ornament   ...   .   2·50
D22   6p. on 6d. – V12. Damaged ornament   ...   ...   3·25
D23   12p. on 1s. – V4. Upright stroke ...   .   2·00
            – V12. Damaged ornament   ...   .   3·50

1968 (Feb)–70. *Surcharges.*   [S. G. D24/26]

D24   1½np. on 2p. on 2d. – V12. Damaged ornament ...   7·00
            – V15. Bolder "d"   ...   ...   7·00
D25   2½np. on 3p. on 3d. – V7. Missing serif ...   ...   2·50
            – V12. Damaged ornament   ...   ...   2·50
D26   5np. on 6p. on 6d. – V12. Damaged ornament ...   2·50

Gibraltar

1953 (2 June). *Coronation.* [S. G. 144]

Stop before "2" in "½" in right-hand value tablet (Pl. 1A–5A, R. 4/4).

V5

144 ½d. – V5. Stop before "2" in "½" ... ... 3·25

1953 (19 Oct)–59. *Views.* [S. G. 145/58]

5d. Major re-entry causing doubling of "ALTA" of "GIBRALTAR" (R. 4/6).

V1

1s. Re-entry causing doubling of lines of sea wall and buildings (R.6 Nos. 3 to 5) (MG 9.56).

V2

152E	5d. *maroon*	– VI. Re-entry	...	...	6·00
	Ea. Deep maroon	– VI. Re-entry	...	...	5·00
154E	1s. *pale blue and red-brown*	– V2. Re-entry *each*	...	...	3·75
	Ea. Pale blue and deep red-brown	– V2. Re-entry *each*	...	...	3·50

1960 (29 Oct)–62. *Views.* [S. G. 160/73]

V26

1d. Brown flaw over upper right turret appears as a guard (Pl. 1B, R. 1/3).

V27

1d. Jagged brown flaw in wall to right of gate appears as a crack (Pl. 1B, R. 2/5).

1d. Retouch right of flag appears as an extra flag (Pl. 1B, R. 5/5).

V32

V18

2d. Retouch on "OR" of "GEORGE'S" (Pl. 1B, R. 6/4).

V8

6d. Large white spot on map S.W. of "CEUTA" (Pl. 1B, R. 4/5).

V19

6d. Brown flaw on map over "C" of "AFRICA" appearing as an extra oasis (Pl. 1A, R. 1/9).

V20

6d. Brown dot on map by source of river appearing as an extra hill (Pl. 1A, R. 1/10).

V21

7d. Large grey blob on stay of mast (Pl. 2A, R. 3/1).

V22

1s. Green vertical branch joining two main branches at right, is broken (Pl. 1B, R. 2/2).

161	1d.	– V26. Guard on battlements	...	...	...	1·75
		– V27. Crack in wall	...	...	...	1·75
		– V32. "Phantom flag"	...	...	...	2·25
162	2d.	– V18. Retouch on "OR"	...	...	...	1·50
166	6d.	– V8. White spot on map	...	...	...	2·00
		– V19. "Oasis" flaw	...	...	...	2·00
		– V20. Extra hill ...	...	...	...	2·00
167	7d.	– V21. Blob on stay	...	...	...	2·00
169	1s.	– V22. Broken branch	...	...	...	2·50

1964 (23 Apr). *400th Anniv. of Birth of William Shakespeare.*
[S. G. 177]

Retouch over " 1 " of "1964"
(R. 10/1).

V6

| 177 | 7d. – V6. Retouch | ... | ... | ... | ... | ... | 4·00 |

1964 (16 Oct). *New Constitution*   [S. G. 178/9]

1964.
V3

6d. The serif on " 1 " of " 1964 " is broken, giving the appearance of a wrong fount (R. 1/2).

| 179 | 6d. – V3. Broken serif on "1" in "1964" | ... | ... | 4·00 |
| | – V8. White spot on map | ... | ... | ... | 3·50 |

1965 (25 Oct). *International Co-operation Year.*   [S. G. 182/3]

V11. Broken leaves. See V6 of Antigua.

| 182 | ½d. – V11. Broken leaves | ... | ... | ... | ... | 2·00 |

1966 (24 Jan). *Churchill Commemoration.*   [S. G. 184E/7]

1d. Broken second " N " in " WINSTON " (Pl 1A, R. 3/3).

V9

V12. Dot by St. Paul's. See V2 of Ascension.

184E	½d. – V12. Dot by St. Paul's ...	...	...	...	2·00
185	1d. – V9. Broken "N"	...	...	...	2·00
	– V12. Dot by St. Paul's ...	...	...	...	2·50
186	4d. – V12. Dot by St. Paul's ...	...	...	...	3·75
187	9d. – V12. Dot by St. Paul's ...	...	...	...	5·00

1966 (27 Aug). *European Sea Angling Championships, Gibraltar.*
[S. G. 190/2]

4d. Break at top right corner of " d " of value (R. 9/3).

V28

| 190 | 4d. – V28. Broken "d" | ... | ... | ... | ... | 2·10 |

1966 (20 Sept). *Inauguration of W.H.O. Headquarters, Geneva.*
[S. G. 193/4]

V10. Dotted "r" in "Headquarters". See V5 of Dominica.

6d. South America missing from emblem (R. 8/1).

V33

| 193 | 6d. – V10. Dotted "r" | ... | ... | ... | ... | 4·00 |
| | – V33. South America missing | ... | ... | ... | 6·00 |

1967 (3 Apr)–69. *Ships.*   [S. G. 200E/13]

V13

½d. Gash in shape of boomerang in topsail (Pl. 1A, R. 8/4).

V14

½d. Grey mark in topsail resembling a stain (Pl. 1A, R. 8/6).

V29

½d. Break in " o " of " VICTORY " (Pl. 1A, R. 3/1).

V30

1d. White spot on cross-bar of First " A " in " GIBRALTAR " (Pl. 1A, R. 3/3).

V15

2d. Rope near front funnel is broken (Pl. 1A, R. 7/4).

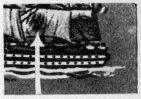

V7

7d. Bold shading on sail appearing as patch (Pl. 1A, R. 10/5).

£1 White spot in hair just below front of tiara resembling jewel (Pl. 1A, R. 3/6).

V16

200E	½d. – V13. Gash in sail	...	...	...	...	1·10
	– V14. Stained sail	...	...	...	...	1·10
	– V29. Broken "o"	...	...	...	...	1·10
201E	1d. – V30. Spot in "A"	...	...	...	...	1·50
202	2d. – V15. Broken rope	...	...	...	...	1·50
207E	7d. – V7. Patched sail	...	...	...	...	2·00
213	£1 – V16. Jewel in hair	...	...	...	...	45·00

1967 (1 Nov). *Christmas.*   [S. G. 217E/18E]

V17

2d. Black line across babe's
arm resembling a brace-
let (Pl. 1A, R. 10/4).

6d. White retouch above Queen's lip
(R. 5/8).

V23

217E	2d. – V17. Bracelet flaw	...	...	...	...	1·75
218E	6d. – V23. Retouch on lip	...	...	...	...	2·25

1968 (27 Mar). *60th Anniv. of Gibraltar Scout Association.*
                                       [S. G. 223/6]

1s. Top of "1" of "GIBRALTAR"
is short (R. 12/2).

V24

226	1s. – V24. Short "1"	...	...	...	...	2·10

STAMP VARIETIES EXPLAINED

In this *Stanley Gibbons Guide* James Watson presents
the knowledge essential to every philatelist—the various
processes that are used to print stamps. By demonstrating just how varieties occur, he enables collectors to
assess their relative importance and shows what contribution, if any, they can make to philatelic study. See the
preliminary pages of this Catalogue for details of the
current edition.

POSTAGE DUE STAMPS

1956 (1 Dec).   [S. G. D1/3]

V25

4d. Ball of " d " broken and serif at top damaged
(R. 9/5). This variety also occurs in Tristan da
Cunha. Other stamps in 9th vertical row show
slight breaks to ball of " d ".

V4.   Bolder "d". See V3 of Basutoland

D2	2d. – V4. Bolder "d"	...	...	...	...	12·00
D3	4d. – V25. Broken "d"	...	...	...	...	20·00

Gilbert and Ellice Islands

Gilbert Islands

1956 (1 Aug)–62. *Pictorials.*   [S. G. 64/75]

½d. Short line along top of "Y" in "PENNY" (Pl. 1, R. 10/1).

V2

64   ½d. – V2. "Y" flaw   ...   .   2·50

1964 (20 July). *First Air Service.* Wmk Block CA sideways.
    [S. G. 82E/84]

3d. Line extending from inner engine of left wing almost to tailplane (R. 6/5).

V1

82E   3d. (wmk Crown to left)   – V1. Line variety   ...   2·50
    Ea. (wmk Crown to right)   – V1. Line variety   ...   2·25

1965 (25 Oct). *International Co-operation Year.*   [S. G. 104/5]

V3. Broken leaves. See V6 of Antigua.
104   ½d. – V3. Broken leaves   ...   .   2·10

1966 (24 Jan). *Churchill Commemoration.*   [S. G. 106/9]

V4. Dot by St. Paul's. See V2 of Ascension.
V5. Flaw by Queen's ear. See V11 of Solomon Islands.
106   ½d. – V4. Dot by St. Paul's   ...   .   2·50
107   3d. – V4. Dot by St. Paul's   ...   .   2·50
108   3s. – V4. Dot by St. Paul's   ...   .   5·00
    – V5. Flaw by Queen's ear   ...   .   5·00
109   3s.7d. – V4. Dot by St. Paul's   ...   .   5·50
    – V5. Flaw by Queen's ear   ...   .   5·50

1976 (2 Jan). *Overprint.*   [S. G. 3/22]

PANDANUS   20c. Broken second "A" in "PANDANUS" (Pl. 2A, R. 4/5).
V1

18   20c. – V1. Broken "A" ...   .   3·50

Gold Coast

POSTAGE DUE STAMPS

1951–52 [S. G. D5/8]

V3. Bolder "d". See V3 of Basutoland.

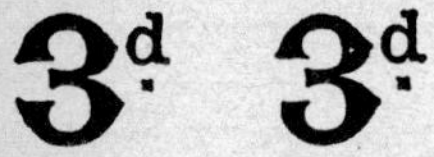

Normal V2

3d. Lower serif at left of "3" missing (R.9/1).

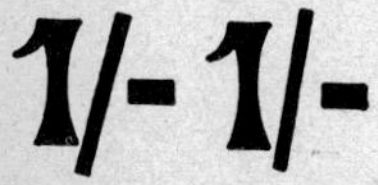

Row 4 Row 5

V1

1s. The stroke in the value is more upright than the normal. (All rows, No. 5.)

The degree of inclination of the stroke varies in the different rows as follows: Rows 1, 2 and 6, 104°, row 3, 108°, row 4, 107° and row 5 100°. Our price is for stamps from row 5.

D5 2d. – V3. Bolder "d" ... ... 3·00
D6 3d. – V2. Missing serif ... ... 3·00
D8 1s. – V1. Upright stroke ... ... 3·50

Grenada

1961 (1 June). *Centenary of First Grenada Postage Stamp.*
[S. G. 208/10]

V1

3c. Grey flaw on corner of building (Pl. 1A–1A, R. 6/4).

208 3c. – V1. Flaw on building ... ... 1·75

1965 (25 Oct). *International Co-operation Year.* [S. G. 223/4]

V3. Broken leaves. See V6 of Antigua.

223	1c. – V3. Broken leaves	...	...	...	2·25
224	25c. – V3. Broken leaves	...	...	...	2·50

1966 (1 Apr). *Views.* [S. G. 231/45]

V8

V13

1c. Blue line joining top of first " o " of " HILLSBOROUGH " to "U" of "CARRIACOU" (Pl. 1A, R. 8/3).

50c. Green blob in margin (R. 4/5)

231	1c. – V8. Line flaw ...	...	...	...	1·00
242	50c. – V13. Green blob	...	...	...	2·75

1966 (20 Sept). *Inauguration of W.H.O. Headquarters, Geneva.*
[S. G. 248/9]

V7. Dotted "r" in "Headquarters". See V5 of Dominica.

248 8c. – V7. Dotted "r" ... ... 1·90

THE ELIZABETHAN

All other aspects of the stamps of the present reign are fully covered by the *Elizabethan Specialised Stamp Catalogue*, published annually.

1968 (17 Feb). *World Scout Jamboree, Idaho.* [S. G. 283/8]

V4

V5

All values. Dot in colour of panel projecting below panel under emblem (R. 2/6).

1c. and 35c. Prominent white spot on hat (R. 4/8).

V6

V9

1c. and 35c. White mark on neck resembling a collar (R. 4/7).

1c. and 35c. Light colouring to hat appearing as stripes over it (R. 4/6).

283	1c. – V4. Dot below panel	...	...	...	...	1·25
	– V5. Dot in hat ...	...	...	...	...	1·25
	– V6. White collar	...	...	...	...	1·25
	– V9. Banded hat	...	...	...	...	1·25
284	2c. – V4. Dot below panel	...	...	...	...	1·25
285	3c. – V4. Dot below panel	...	...	...	...	1·40
286	35c. – V4. Dot below panel	...	...	...	...	1·75
	– V5. Dot in hat ...	...	...	...	...	2·00
	– V6. White collar	...	...	...	...	2·00
	– V9. Banded hat	...	...	...	...	2·00
287	50c. – V4. Dot below panel	...	...	...	...	2·50
288	$1 – V4. Dot below panel	...	...	...	...	3·75

1968 (Oct)–71. *Pictorials.* [S. G. 306/21]

V14

$5. White spot over "s" of "NUDIGENIS" (R. 2/4).

321 $5 – V14. Spot over "s" ... ... 20·00

1970 (18 Mar). *Surcharge.* [S. G. 371]

V16

Top of the "5" is damaged (R. 9/1).

371 5c. – V16. Damaged "5" ... ... 1·10

1972 (20 Nov). *Royal Silver Wedding.*   [S. G. 530/1]

V10. Dot on curtain. See V4 of Anguilla.

530	8c. – V10. Dot on curtain	...	...	...	...	1·25
531	$1 – V10. Dot on curtain	...	...	...	...	3·50

1973 (3 Aug). *Carriacou Regatta.*   [S. G. 565/72]

GR 1c. White streak in "GRENADA" extends from the "G" to the top of the "R" (Pl. 1B, R. 2/5).

V15

566   1c. – V15. White streak   ...   .   1·60

1973 (10 Dec). *Christmas.*   [S. G. 585/93]

Child ½c. Flaw at the bottom of the stamp resembles a candle (Pl. A, R. 1/3).

V11

585   ½c. – V11. "Candle" flaw   ...   .   1·60

1974 (19 Aug). *Independence.*   [S. G. 613/18]

3c. White scratch above "D" of "GRENADA" (Pl. 1A, R. 5/4).

V12

613   3c. – V12. White scratch   ...   .   2·10

Grenadines of Grenada

1975 (27 Oct). *Pan-American Games, Mexico City.*   [S. G. 103/10]

½c. Accent on second "A" of "AMERICAN" (Pl. 1C, R. 6/2).

V1

103   ½c. – V1. Accent flaw ...   .   1·60

1977 (8 Feb). *Silver Jubilee.*   [S. G. 215/17]

$4 Missing dot after "I" (R. 2/4).

V2

217   $4 – V2. Missing dot after "I"   ...   .   3·00

Grenadines of St. Vincent

1974 (24 Apr). *Overprints.*   [S. G. 3/17]

RENA
OF
V1

Various values. Misplaced " OF " in overprint (Pl. 1A, R. 10/1).

V2. "B" for "R" flaw. See V8 of St. Vincent.
V3. Broken claw. See V9 of St. Vincent.

3	1c. – V1. Misplaced "OF"	...	...	...	...	2·00
	– V3. Broken claw	...	...	...	...	2·00
4E	2c. – V1. Misplaced "OF"	...	...	...	...	2·00
5	3c. – V1. Misplaced "OF"	...	...	...	...	2·00
7	5c. – V2. "B" for "R" flaw	...	...	...	...	2·00
8	6c. – V1. Misplaced "OF"	...	...	...	...	2·00
9	8c. – V1. Misplaced "OF"	...	...	...	...	2·50
12	20c. – V1. Misplaced "OF"	...	...	...	...	3·00

Guyana

1966 (26 May)–67. *Independence overprints.*   [S. G. 379/407A]

V4 and V5. See V4/5 of British Guiana (No. 333E).
V3. Dot under waterfall. See V2 of British Guiana.

380	3c. – V4. Weed flaw	...	...	...	...	6·50
	– V5. Clubbed foot	...	...	...	...	6·50
403A	48c. – V3. Dot under waterfall	...	...	...	7·50

1967 (23 Feb). *World's Rarest Stamp Commemoration.* [S. G. 414/5]

V1

5c. Square left leg to first " A " in " GUIANA "
(Pl. 1A and 1B, R. 10/4).

V2

25c. Extra stop after " GUIANA " (Pl. 1A,
R. 10/5).

414	5c. – V1. Square leg to "A" ...	...	...	...	1·50
415	25c. – V2. Extra stop of "GUIANA" ...	...	...	1·75

1967–68. *Independence overprints.*   [S. G. 420E/40]

V3. Dot under waterfall. See V2 of British Guiana.

437	48c. – V3. Dot under waterfall	...	...	...	3·50

1968 (4 Mar). *Pictorials.* No wmk.   [S. G. 448/62]

V6

$1 Nick in the shadow below head
(Pl. 1A, R. 2/7).

460	$1 – V6. Hole in ground	...	...	...	...	3·00

1969–71. *Pictorials.* Wmk Lotus Blossoms   [S. G. 485/99]

497	$1 – V6. Hole in ground	...	...	...	...	3·00

1969 (17 Nov). *Christmas.*   [S. G. 511/14]

60c. Broken " h " in " Christmas "
(R. 5/2, both plates).

V7

V8. All values. Inverted first " s '
in " Christmas " (R. 2/2, 2/10
and 5/4 on T 47; R. 4/2 on
T 48).

511	5c. – V8. Inverted "s"	...	...	...	...	1·50
512	6c. – V8. Inverted "s"	...	...	...	...	4·50
513	25c. – V8. Inverted "s"	...	...	...	...	3·00
514	60c. – V7. Broken "h"	...	...	...	...	2·50
	– V8. Inverted "s"	...	...	...	...	4·50

1978 (4 Sept). *National Science Research Council.*   [S. G. 694/7]

V10

10c. Faint "HY" in "PHYSICIAN" (Pl.
1B, R. 1/2).

694	10c. – V10. Faint "HY"	...	...	...	...	1·50

POSTAL FISCAL STAMPS

1975 (1 Nov). *"Revenue only". Overprints.*   [S. G. F1/10]

V9

No. F4a. Break in rule and
first " E " of " REVENUE "
(Pl. 1D, R. 1/1).

F4a	25c. (No. 550) – V9. Damaged overprint	...	...	13·00

Hong Kong

1954 (5 Jan)–62. *Queen Elizabeth II.* [S. G. 178/191E]

V7

5c. Pearl at left of Crown almost missing (Pl. 1, R. 1/6).

V1

30c. The left ornament above the central cross on the crown, on the right, is missing (Pl. 1, R. 4/7).

V2

30c. The jewels at the foot are joined to the main part of the crown, on the right, by a grey-coloured flaw (Pl. 1, R. 5/7).

壹 壹 ←

Normal   V3

$1 The two horizontal strokes in the centre of the upper left character joined at the left-hand end (Pl. 1–1, R. 1/6).

↓
香 香

Normal   V4

$2 The top stroke in the right-hand upper character is shortened (Pl. 1–1, R. 6/4).

Normal   V8

$10 Two dots in bottom left character (Pl. 1–1, R. 5/3).

178	5c. – V7. Damaged pearl	...	...	...	...	3·00
183E	30c. *grey*					
	– V1. Ornament missing	...	...	...	7·00
	– V2. Joined pearls	...	...	...	7·00
Ea.	*Pale grey*					
	– V1. Ornament missing	...	...	...	7·00
	– V2. Joined pearls	...	...	...	7·00
187	$1 – V3. Joined character	...	...	...	7·50
189E	$2 *reddish violet and scarlet*					
	– V4. Short character	...	...	...	15·00
Ea.	*Light reddish violet and scarlet*					
	– V4. Short character	...	...	...	15·00
191E	$10 *reddish violet and bright blue*					
	– V8. Two dots in character	...	...	...	40·00
Ea.	*Light reddish violet and bright blue*					
	– V8. Two dots in character	...	...	...	40·00

1962 (4 May). *Stamp Centenary.* [S. G. 193/5]

Normal   V9

10c. White spot over character in lower right corner (Pl. 1A–1A, R. 1/3).

Normal   V5

50c. The short tail at the foot of the right-hand central character is broken (R. 8/3).

193	10c. – V9. Spot on character	...	...	...	...	4·50
195	50c. – V5. Broken character	...	...	...	...	7·50

1962 (4 Oct)–73. *Queen Elizabeth II (After Annigoni).* Wmk Block CA (upright). [S. G. 196/210E]

Normal   V6   V11

5c. The horizontal bar of the " 5 " is missing (Pl. 1A, R.3/1 and Pl. 1B, R. 2/2) (MG 3.63, 4.63).

10c. Large flaw on collar in first printing, retouched in second printing (Pl. 1C, R. 2/1).

196	5c. – V6. Broken "5"	...	...	...	...	6·00
197E	10c. – V11. Flaw on collar	...	...	...	...	2·00

1963 (4 June). *Freedom from Hunger.* [S. G. 211]

V10. The two characters at left are retouched (R.1/5). In the normals the characters are dotted but in the retouch they are clear-cut and the lower left part of the bottom character is more pointed.

211	$1·30 –.V10. Retouched characters	...	...	...	55·00

1965 (25 Oct). *International Co-operation Year.* [S. G. 216E/17E]

V14. Broken leaves. See V6 of Antigua.

216E	10c. – V14. Broken leaves	...	...	...	...	4·50
217E	$1·30 *dp. bluish green and lavender*					
	– V14. Broken leaves	...	...	...	10·00
Ea.	*Blue-green and lavender*					
	– V14. Broken leaves	...	...	...	12·00

1966 (24 Jan). *Churchill Commemoration.*   [S. G. 218E/21]

$1.30 Deformed " U " in " CHURCHILL " (R. 7/5).

V15

220   $1·30 – V15. Deformed "U" ...   .   6·00

1966–72. *Queen Elizabeth II.* Wmk Block CA (sideways).
                                              [S. G. 222/36]

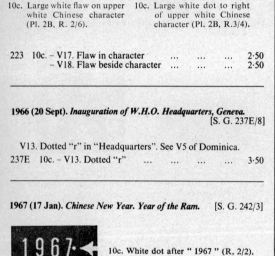

V17

10c. Large white flaw on upper
      white Chinese character
      (Pl. 2B, R. 2/6).

V18

10c. Large white dot to right
      of upper white Chinese
      character (Pl. 2B, R.3/4).

223   10c. – V17. Flaw in character   ...   .   2·50
      – V18. Flaw beside character   ...   .   2·50

1966 (20 Sept). *Inauguration of W.H.O. Headquarters, Geneva.*
                                              [S. G. 237E/8]

V13. Dotted "r" in "Headquarters". See V5 of Dominica.
237E   10c. – V13. Dotted "r"   ...   .   3·50

1967 (17 Jan). *Chinese New Year. Year of the Ram.*   [S. G. 242/3]

10c. White dot after " 1967 " (R. 2/2).

V12

242   10c. – V12. Dot after "1967"   ...   .   2·50

1968 (23 Jan). *Chinese New Year. Year of the Monkey.* [S. G. 245/6]

Normal   V19

10c. Missing
right gold
segment to
diadem in
centre of
crown
(R. 5/4).

245   10c. – V19. Diadem flaw   ...   .   3·00

1968 (24 Apr). *Sea Craft.*   [S. G. 247/52]

10c. Malformed Crown at bottom
      right (Pl. 1C, R. 10/2).

V16

247   10c. – V16. Chipped Crown ...   .   1·25

1972 (8 Feb). *Chinese New Year. Year of the Rat.*   [S. G. 276/7E]

10c. Lower right character of
      central inscription has
      two strokes at upper left
      instead of one (R. 7/4).

V20

276   10c. – V20. Character flaw   ...   .   2·50

1972 (20 Nov). *Royal Silver Wedding.*   [S. G. 279/80E]

V22. Dot on curtain. See V4 of Anguilla.
279   10c. – V22. Dot on curtain   ...   .   3·00

PHILATELIC TERMS ILLUSTRATED

The essential philatelic dictionary. Terms covering
printing methods, papers, errors, varieties, watermarks
perforations and much more are explained and illustrated, many in full colour. See the preliminary pages o
this Catalogue for details of the current edition.

1973 (12 June)–74. *Queen Elizabeth II.*   [S. G. 283/96]

V21

No. 283a. White vertical line (throughout one entire roll)

No. 288 As V21, a white vertical line occurred on sheet stamps and is caused by streaks in the paper coating.

283a	10c.	(Wmk side-ways (from coils))			
		– V21. White line	... ...	4·25
288	40c. – V21. White line	... ...	6·00

1976 (23 Apr). *Girl Guides Diamond Jubilee.*   [S. G. 354/55E]

 20c. Short "N" in Hong (Plate 1B. R. 4/4).

V27

354E   20c. – V27. Short "N"   ... ...   1·50

1977 (7 Feb). *Silver Jubilee.*   [S. G. 361E/3]

V23
20c. White spot in "O" of face-value (Pl. 1A, R. 1/3).

V24
$2 Break in border above orb (Pl. 1B, R. 1/4).

361E	20c. – V23. White spot in "0"	... ...	5·50
363	$2 – V24. Break in border	... ...	6·00

1978 (2 June). *25th Anniv. of Coronation.*   [S. G. 373/74]

 $1·30 Red accent on "I" (Right pane R. 3/1).

V25

374   $1·30 – V25. Red accent   ... ...   1·10

1979 (20 June). *Butterflies.*   [S. G. 380/83]

 $2. Short right leg to "R" (Plate 1B. R. 4/5).

V26

383   $2 – V26. Short right leg   ... ...   2·00

India

1961 (7 May). *Birth Centenary of Rabindranath Tagore.* [S. G. 439]

15np. Extra spur to dot above "i" (R. 5/4).

V1

439   15np. – V1. Damaged dot   ...   .   1·25

1965 (27 May). *First Anniv. of Nehru's Death.* [S. G. 501]

15p. Absence of screening dots results in pink patches on pillar (R. 5/3).

V2

501   15p. – V2. Pink patches   ...   .   1·00

1966 (26 Jan). *Indian Armed Forces.* [S. G. 527]

15p. Spot after "A" of "India" (R. 7/5).

V3

527   15p. – V3. Spot after "A"   ...   .   2·00

1969 (24 Nov). *International Union for the Conservation of Nature and Natural Resources Conference, New Delhi.* [S. G. 603]

20p. White spot after "E" of "NATURE" (R. 4/3).

V4

603   20p. – V4. White spot   ...   .   1·75

1971 (7 Aug). *Abanindranath Tagore Commemoration.* [S. G. 640]

20p. Plant at left has extended leaf at right (Pane with cross in upper left margin, R. 4/6).

V5

640   20p. – V5. Extended leaf   ...   .   1·75

1974 (20 Aug). [S. G. 721/38]

V6

2p. White dot on "2" (R. 5/7).

V7

2p. White spur on the left-hand arch of character (R. 1/1).

724   2p. – V6. White dot   ...   .   1·25
       – V7. White spur ...   .   1·25

1974 (2 Dec). *19th International Dairy Congress.* [S. G. 751]

V8

25p. Tail flaw (R. 1/1).

751   25p. – V8. Tail flaw   ...   .   1·60

1977 (22 Mar). *Death of President Ahmed.* [S. G. 842]

25p. "P" for "R" in "PRESIDENT" (R. 2/1).

V9

842   25p. – V9. "P" for "R"   ...   .   2·00

1978 (15 Jan). *Conquest of Kanchenjunga.* [S. G. 874/5]

1R. "o" for "Q" in "CONQUEST" (R. 2/5).

V10

875 1R. – V10. "o" for "Q" ... ... 2·00

1978 (10 Dec). *Birth Centenary of Mohammad Ali Jauhar.* [S. G. 903E]

25p. Extra spur to last character in the top panel (R. 3/5).

V11   Normal

903E 25p. – V11. Damaged character ... ... 2·00

1978 (24 Dec). *Centenary of Ravenshaw College.* [S. G. 906]

/12

25p. Diagonal scratch crosses central pillars (Pane with cross in upper right margin, R. 1/5).

906 25p. – V12. Diagonal scratch ... ... 3·00

1979 (2 July). *Centenary of Indian Postcards.* [S. G. 915]

50p. Retouch to bottom right of magnifying glass (Pane with marginal inscription in the left-hand margin, R. 5/3).

13

15 50p. – V13. Retouch ... ... 1·25

1979 (21 Oct). *Centenary of Electric Light bulb.* [S. G. 922]

1r. Broken "T" in "ELECTRIC" (R. 1/6).

V14

922 1r. – V14. Broken "T" ... ... 1·50

1979 (21 Dec). *500th Birth Anniv. of Guru Amar Das.* [S. G. 929]

30p. Break in "G" of "GURU" (R. 5/4).

V15

929 30p. – V15. Break in "G" ... ... 1·00

Ireland (Republic)

1940–68. *Various designs.*   [S. G. 111E/25E]

5s. White line above left value tablet joining bottom horizontal line to ornament (R. 3/7).

V2

124E   5s. – V2. Line flaw ...   .   20·00

1948 (7 Apr)–65. *Air.*   [S. G. 140/3*b*]

V1 3d. Re-entry consists ot partial doubling of the " 3 ", the " H " of " HIBERNIÆ " and the bottom frame line (R. 6/3).

1s. 5d. Strong retouch above trees at left (Pl. 2B, R. 10/5).

V3

141   3d. – V1. Re-entry ...   .   42·00
143*b* 1s.5d. – V3. Retouch ...   .   17·00

1954 (24 May). *Marian Year.*   [S. G. 158/9]

3d. Shading and four blue spots on Child's right hand (Pl. 1B, R. 3/5).

V8

158   3d. – V8. Hand flaw ...   .   60·00

1964 (20 July). *New York World's Fair.*   [S. G. 201/2]

Both values. White " ledge " on the right of the central tower (R. 4/2, bottom pane).

V32

201   5d. – V32. Ledge on tower   ...   .   20·00
202   1s.5d. – V32. Ledge on tower   ...   .   55·00

1965 (16 Aug). *International Co-operation Year.*   [S. G. 209/10]

3d. Blue line projecting into top margin above date (Lower pane, R. 5/9).

V4

209   3d. – V4. Blue projection   ...   .   7·00

1966 (3 Aug). *50th Death Anniv. of Roger Casement (patriot).*   [S. G. 221/2]

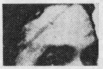

5d. Scar on forehead (R.1/6)

V40

221   5d. – V40. Scar on forehead ...   .   15·0

1967 (30 Nov). *300th Birth Anniv. of Jonathan Swift.*   [S. G. 237/8]

V5   V21

3d. Circular flaw at top of hat resembling a bullet hole (left pane, R. 3/5).   Flaw in throat, resembling bullet-hole (R.2/6).

237   3d. – V5. Bullet hole in hat ...   .   4·0
            – V21. Bullet hole in throat   ...   .   4·0

1968 (29 Apr). *Europa.* [S. G. 239/40]

7d. Long diag-
onal line
beneath key
(lower pane.
R. 7/1).

V41

239   7d. – V41. Diagonal line   ...   .   7·00

1968 (23 Sept). *Birth Centenary of Countess Markievicz (patriot).*
[S. G. 243/4]

V6

3d. Scratch down the nose and extending across the face right
into the right-hand margin (Lower pane, R. 4/6).

243   3d. – V6. Scratch through face   ...   .   6·00

1968 (23 Sept). *Birth Centenary of James Connolly (patriot).*
[S. G. 245/6]

6d. and 1s. Small white flaw above
2nd button resembling top button
(left pane, R. 5/1).

V7

245   6d. – V7. Extra button   ...   .   6·00
246   1s. – V7. Extra button   ...   .   6·00

STAMP VARIETIES EXPLAINED

In this *Stanley Gibbons Guide* James Watson presents
the knowledge essential to every philatelist—the various
processes that are used to print stamps. By demonstrating just how varieties occur, he enables collectors to
assess their relative importance and shows what contribution, if any, they can make to philatelic study. See the
preliminary pages of this Catalogue for details of the
current edition.

1969 (28 Apr). *Europa.* [S. G. 267/8]

9d. Blue line below " E " of
" CEPT " (Lower pane, R. 5/6).

V9

267   9d. – V9. Line below "E" of "CEPT" ...   .   6·00

1969 (1 Sept). *Contemporary Irish Art* (1st issue).   [S. G. 271]

1s. Short " 1 " in " 1894 " (R.
2/1).

V10

271   1s. – V10. Short "1" in "1894"   ...   .   3·00

1970 (26 Oct). *Death Anniversaries of Irish Patriots.*   [S. G. 281/4]

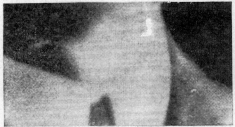

V12
No. 282.   White flaw on throat (R. 6/14).

No. 284. White line left of
value (R. 2/3).

V13

282   9d. – V12. "Cut throat"   ...   .   5·00
284   2s.9d. – V13. White line   ...   .   7·00

1970 (2 Nov). *50th Death Anniv. of Kevin Barry (patriot).*
[S. G. 285/6]

V14

6d. Prominent flaw on lip (Cyl. 1, upper pane, R. 3/1).

V33

1s.2d. White ring flaw beneath right ear (R. 1/1).

285   6d. – V14. "Cut lip" ... ... 12·00
286   1s.2d. – V33. Flaw beneath ear ... ... 6·00

1971 (3 May). *Europa.*
[S. G. 302/3]

Retouch above " PT " of " CEPT " (R. 2/7).

V11

302   4p. – V11. Retouch ... ... 3·00
303   6p. – V11. Retouch ... ... 5·50

1972 (6 Dec). *50th Anniv. of the First Irish Postage Stamp.*
[S. G. 323/4]

No. 323. Inlet on the west coast is filled in, forming a headland (R. 5/9).

Normal   V15

323   6p. – V15. Missing inlet ... ... 4·50

1973 (1 Jan). *Entry into European Communities.*
[S. G. 325/6]

6p. Celtic head motifs are joined together (R. 9/1).

V16

325   6p. – V16. Joined motifs ... ... 4·00

1973 (1 Nov). *Christmas.*
[S. G. 334/5]

Both values. Smudge above Joseph's head (R. 3/1).

V17

334   3½p. – V17. Smudge above head ... ... 2·00
335   12p. – V17. Smudge above head ... ... 4·00

1974 (28 Mar). *150th Anniv. of Royal National Lifeboat Institution.*
[S. G. 336]

Flaw to right of lightship's beacon appears as " red star " (R. 5/9).

V18

336   5p. – V18. "Red Star" flaw ... ... 3·00

1974 (29 Apr). *Europa.*
[S. G. 337/8]

V22

5p. " r " damaged at top (R. 7/9).

V23

7p. Dot between serifs of " E " (R. 6/1).

337   5p. – V22. Damaged "r" ... ... 9·00
338   7p. – V23. Dot between serifs ... ... 7·50

1974 (9 Sept). *Centenary of Irish Rugby Football Union.*
[S. G. 363E/4]

V19

Re-entry consists of a double impression of the bottom frame-line. Doubling also occurs on other portions of the stamp (R. 4/1 or R. 9/1, occurring on one sheet in two).

363E   3½p. – V19. Re-entry ... ... 50·00

1974 (14 Nov). *Christmas.*
[S. G. 367/8]

Both values. Break in frame above Madonna's head (R. 8/8).

V20

367   5p. – V20. Frame-break ... ... 2·50
368   15p. – V20. Frame-break ... ... 2·75

1975 (24 Mar). *International Women's Year.*   [S. G. 369/70]

V24   V25

Both values. Flaw on central leaf   15p. Lower leaf
resembles a caterpillar (R. 3/5).   shows broken
                                       outline (R. 2/2).

369   8p. – V24. Caterpillar flaw ...   .   2·50
370   15p. – V24. Caterpillar flaw ...   .   3·00
        – V25. Broken outline of leaf   ...   .   3·00

1975 (28 Apr). *Europa.*   [S. G. 371/2]

V26   V27

7p. Flaw above huntsmen's   Crescent-shaped flaw in upper
heads resembles a   right-hand corner (R. 4/4).
football (R. 8/6).

                9p. Flaw in front of huntsman
                appears as a whip (R. 10/2).

V28

371   7p. – V26. Football flaw   ...   .   3·00
        – V27. Crescent flaw   ...   .   3·00
372   9p. – V28. Whip flaw   ...   .   4·50

1975 (26 June). *Ninth European Amateur Golf Team Championship,*
Killarney.   [S. G. 373/4]

                9p. Flaw before "E" of "European"
                resembles an apostrophe (R. 8/4).

V29

374   9p. – V29. Apostrophe flaw ...   .   4·00

1975 (28 June). *Contemporary Irish Art* (7th issue).   [S. G. 375]

                Vertical flaw on bird's foot
                appears as an "Extra claw"
                (R. 9/4).

V30

375   15p. – V30. Extra claw   ...   .   6·00

1976 (21 Jan). *Birth of James Larkin (Trade Union Leader).*
                                                          [S. G. 387/8]

                Both values. White flaw
                on eye resembles a sty
                (All stamps, seventh
                vertical row).

V34

387   7p. – V34. Sty in eye   ...   .   2·50
388   11p. – V34. Sty in eye   ...   .   3·00

1976 (10 Mar). *Telephone Centenary.*   [S. G. 389/90]

                15p. Flaw on "5" of face-
                value resembles a serif
                (R. 5/1).

V35

390   15p. – V35. Seriffed "5"   ...   .   9·00

1976 (1 July). *Europa.*   [S. G. 396/7]

                9p. Gap in shadow within the flourish
                of the "D" (R. 10/1).

V36

396   9p. – V36. Gap in shadow   ...   .   2·00

1976 (30 Aug). *Contemporary Irish Art* (8th issue).   [S. G. 398]

                Two green blobs to the right of the
                man's head (R. 6/4).

V37

398   15p. – V37. Green blobs   ...   .   3·00

1976 (11 Nov). *Christmas.*   [S. G. 401/3]

V38   V39

All values. Magenta flaw   All values. Yellow
shaped like a puddle   dot just above the
beneath the infant Jesus   frame-line (R. 2/7).
(R. 2/2).

401   7p. – V38. Magenta puddle   ...   .   2·00
        – V39. Yellow dot   ...   .   2·00

402	9p. – V38. Magenta puddle	...	...	...	2·50
	– V39. Yellow dot	...	...	...	2·50
403	15p. – V38. Magenta puddle	...	...	...	3·00
	– V39. Yellow dot	...	...	...	3·00

1978 (20 Mar). No wmk.   [S. G. D24/26]

D25	4p. – V44. Frame broken at right	...	...	...	90
	– V45. Frame broken at left	...	...	...	90

POSTAGE DUE STAMPS

1940–70.   [S. G. D5E/14]

1d. Inverted " Q " for " o " in " POSTAGE " (R. 10/1).

V31

D6E	1d. – V31. Inverted "Q"	...	...	...	...	10·00

1971 (15 Feb). *Decimal Currency.*   [S. G. D15E/21]

V42   V43   V44

3p. Damaged frame at bottom right (R. 2/2).

3p. Stone-coloured dot in corner (R. 7/1).

4p. Broken frame at top right (R. 4/5). Partly repaired on No. D25.

4p. Broken frame at top left (R.10/5).

V45

8p. White blob in upper left corner (R. 2/2).

V47

7p. Damaged right-hand frame (R. 9/2).

V46

D15E	1p. – V31. Inverted "Q"	...	...	...	...	1·50
D17E	3p. – V42. Damaged frame	...	...	...	...	1·75
	– V43. Dot in corner	...	...	...	...	1·75
D18	4p. – V44. Frame broken at right	...	...	...	2·00
	– V45. Frame broken at left	...	...	...	2·00
D20E	7p. – V46. Damaged frame	...	...	...	...	1·25
D21	8p. – V47. White blob	...	...	...	...	1·25

Jamaica

1953 (25 Nov). *Royal Visit.* [S. G. 154]

2d. Green spot on shoulder resembling a mole (R. 2/5).

V6

154 2d. – V6. Mole on shoulder ... ... 2·50

1962 (8 Aug)–63. *Independence.* Wmk Script CA. [S. G. 181/92]

Wide "9" in date at right (R.8/5). This has been seen on the 1d. Pl. 2A–5A and on the 2½d. Pl. 1A–5A.

V1

182 1d. – V1. Wide "9" at right ... ... 2·50
183 2½d. – V1. Wide "9" at right ... ... 2·75

1962 (11 Aug). *Ninth Central American and Caribbean Games, Kingston.* [S. G. 197/200]

2s. White flaw between "96" of "1962" (Pl. 1B, R. 9/2). Later retouched showing as deep blue lines.

V2   V3 Retouched

200 2s. – V2. "96" flaw ... ... 3·00
       – V3. Do. retouched ... ... 3·00

1963–64. *Independence.* Wmk Block CA. [S. G. 205/13]

206 1d. – V1. Wide "9" at right ... ... 5·00
207 2½d. – V1. Wide "9" at right ... ... 5·00

1964 (4 May). *Pictorials.* [S. G. 217/32]

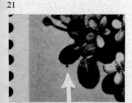

1d. " LISNUM " for " LIGNUM " (Pl. 1C, R. 9/6).

21

1d. Green extension to leaf. (Plate 1B. R. 9/1).

V38

2d. First " NA " of " NATIONAL " joined by white flaw (Pl. 1D, R. 6/9).
In this stamp there are also smaller white dots under " R " of " TREE " (Pl. 1B, R. 5/3) and over second " E " of " TREE " (Pl. 1D, R. 1/9). These were retouched on No. 281.

V7

2d. Cape on Jamaica's southern coast has forked to form an extra cape (Pl. 1D, R. 6/2).

V22

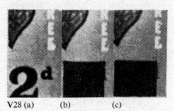

2d. Damaged last " E " in " TREE " (Pl. 1D, R. 1/9). For subsequent states see Nos. 281 and 306.

V28 (a)   (b)   (c)

217 1d. – V21. "LISNUM" flaw ... ... 2·25
      – V38. Leaf flaw ... ... 2·25
219E 2d. – V7. "NA" joined ... ... 2·25
      – V22. Extra cape ... ... 2·25
      – V28a. Damaged "E" ... ... 2·25

1966 (5 Dec). *150th Anniv. of "Jamaica Letter".* [S. G. 259E]

8d. White spot under stars in flag (R. 1/8).

V4

259E 8d. – V4. Flag flaw ... ... 3·00

1967 (28 Aug). *Sangster Memorial Issue.* [S. G. 262/3]

3d. Vertical black scratch over left eye and two purple dots on nose (R. 1/3). As these are printed in sheets of 240, divided into four post office sheets of 60, the variety only occurs on one sheet in four.

V5

262 3d. – V5. Scratch over eye ... ... 3·25

1967 (28 Nov). *Centenary of the Constabulary Force.*   [S. G. 264/6]

1s.6d. Dot over " A " of JAMAICA (R. 10/5).

V23

266   1s.6d. – V23. Dot over "A"   ...   .   3·25

1969 (8 Sept). *Decimal Currency.*   [S. G. 280/92]

The following broken type varieties do not necessarily appear on all plates and probably occurred during the course of printing so that they are not fully constant. Other similar varieties exist and a " quad " variety, similar to V8, has been seen on the 4 c. on R. 4/1 and R. 10/1 and on the 10c. on R. 9/6

1c. on 1d.   Two black bars between " 8th " and " September " (R. 10/1).

V8

V24   V25
2c. on 2d. Long tail   2c. on 2d. Broken
to " Y " of " C-DAY "   " 9 " of " 1969"
(Pl. ?, R. 4/5).   (Pl. ?, 4/9).

   3c. on 3d. The " 8 " of " 8th " is sliced, and the
                       " S " of " September " broken (R. 10/1).
V10

[checkerboard varieties image]   3c. on 3d. Half chequers at right
                                 missing at bottom and almost
                                 missing at top (R. 7/5).

Normal   V14

4c   4c. on 4d. Segment of " c " in " 4c " missing (R 3/3).
V11

4c   4c. on 4d. " c " in " 4c " damaged (R. 5/4).
V12

V26. 4c. on 4d. "8t" of "8th" omitted (Pl. ?, R. 10/1).

10c   10c. on 1s. Right-hand side of " 0 " in " 10 "
V13   broken (R. 6/1).

[15c image]   15c. on 1s. 6d. Broken serif on " 1 "
              (Pl. 1B, R. 10/6).

V29

280	1c. on 1d.	– V8.	Lines between "8th" and "s"	1·75
		– V21.	"LISNUM" flaw	2·50
		– V38.	Leaf flaw	2·25
281E	2c. on 2d.	– V7.	"NA" joined	2·50
		– V22.	Extra cape	2·50
		– V24.	Long tail to "Y" ...	2·50
		– V25.	Broken "9"	2·50
		– V28b.	Damaged "E"	2·50
		– V28c.	Damaged "E"	2·50
282	3c. on 3d.	– V10.	Sliced "8" and broken "s"	2·50
		– V14.	Missing half chequers ...	2·00
283	4c. on 4d.	– V8.	Lines between "8th" and "s"	2·75
		– V11.	Segment of "c" missing in "4c"	2·75

		– V12.	Damaged "c" in value ...	2·75
		– V26.	"8t" omitted ...	25·00
286	10c. on 1s.	– V13.	Damaged "0" in "10" ...	3·50
287	15c. on 1s.6d.	– V29.	Broken Serif	4·00

1969 (25 Oct). *Christmas.*   [S. G. 293/5]

5c. Blue dot in frame
    (Pl. 1B, R. 2/1).

V30

294   5c. – V30. Blue dot in frame ...   .   2·00

1970 (16 July). No. 219 surcharged.   [S. G. 306]

The retouched state of variety V7 has two large dots which distinguishes it from the normal.

306	2c. on 2d.	– V7.	"NA" joined	2·25
		– V7a.	Retouched	2·25
		– V22.	Extra Cape	2·25
		– V28c.	Damaged "E"	2·25

1970. *Decimal Currency.*   [S. G. 307/19]

2c. Last " E " of " TREE " has a flaw
    resembling an extra serif (Pl. 1A, R. 3/7).

V31

[GYPSUM images]

Normal

Normal

V15   V16

5c. " U " shaped flaw on   8c. White spur to cloud
butterfly's upper left   (Pl. 1A, R. 10/4).
wing (Pl. 1B, R. 5/2).

V17   V18

20c. Parallel vertical lines   50c. White spot over " CI " of
after " MINING " (Pl.   " CITY " (Pl. 1A, R. 2/10).
1A, R. 9/3).

308	2c.—V31. Damaged "E"	2·00
311	5c. – V15. "U" variety	2·00
312	8c. – V16. Spur to cloud	2·00
	a. Wmk sideways	
	– V16. Spur to cloud	2·00
315	20c. – V17. Vertical lines	2·50
317	50c. – V18. Spot over "CI"	3·75

1972. *Views.* [S. G. 344/58*a*]

V19

V20

2c. Black " v " flaw under " c " of value and smaller " v " in " 2 " (Pl. 1D, bottom pane, R. 2/3).

3c. Curved black line left of inscription (Pl. 1A and 1D, R. 3/9).

V32

V33

3c. Black spot under " X " (Pl. 1E–1E–2E–1E and 1E (×4), R. 2/1).

5c. Black flaw on " I " of "JAMAICA" appears as a serif (Pl. 1A, R. 2/3).

V34

5c. Diagonal flaw extends through " 5c " (Pl. 1E, R. 3/1).

V35

V36

$1 Black dot in "A" of "JAMAICA" (Pl. 1A, R. 4/3).

Black dot under "HOUSE" (Pl. 1A, R. 5/4).

345	2c. – V19. "v" flaws ...	...	...	...	...	1·75
346	3c. – V20. Curved line	...	...	...	...	1·75
	– V32. Black spot under "X"	...	...	...	1·75
348E	5c. – V33. Serif on "I"	...	...	...	...	1·75
	– V34. Broken "s"	...	...	...	...	1·75
357E	$1. – V35. Black dot in "A" ...	...	...	...	2·50
	– V36. Black dot under "HOUSE"	...	...	2·50

1972 (8 Aug). *Tenth Anniv. of Independence.* [S. G. 359E/61]

359E 3c. – V20. Curved line ... ... 1·75

1973 (9 July). *Flora.* [S. G. 369/74]

15c. Dot on " c " of " 15c " (Pl. 1A, R. 5/5).

V27

372 15c. – V27. Dot on "c" ... ... 3·00

1974 (8 Apr). *Mail Packet Boats.* [S. G. 380/84]

5c. Blue dot under " Mary " (Pl. 1C, R. 4/1).

V37

380	5c. (perf 13½)	– V37. Dot under "Mary"	...	2·00
	a. Perf 14	– V37. Dot under "Mary"	...	18·00

Johore

1960 (10 Feb). *Coronation of Sultan.*   [S. G. 154]

10c. Line forming acute accent over " E "
of " CENTS " (R. 3/2).

V1

154   10c. – V1. Accent flaw   ...   .   1·50

1965 (15 Nov). *Flowers.* Wmk PTM (upright).   [S. G. 166E/72]

V2   Normal   **V3**

1c. Turquoise flaw on   All values except 6 and 15c. Top
pink petal, below   of Cap Badge shaved almost
" L " of " MALAYSIA "   level with cap rim (Pl. 1A,
appears as a cater-   R. 2/10).
pillar (Pl. 1A, R. 5/3).

V4   **V5**

1c. Magenta line across petal   1c. Dot under first " A " of
at right near arms (Pl.   " VANDA " (Pl. 1B, R.
1B, R. 10/9).   4/4).

5c. Stroke through " c " of
" 5c " is short, not reach-
ing bottom of name
tablet (Pl. 1A, R. 10/10).

Normal   **V6**

THE ELIZABETHAN

Uniform with this volume, the *Elizabethan Specialised
Stamp Catalogue* covers all other aspects of the stamps
of the present reign, from both Great Britain and the
British Commonwealth, in considerable detail. See the
preliminary pages of this Catalogue for details of this
annual publication.

Normal   V7

10c. Shortened stroke through " c " of " 10c " (Pl. 1B
R. 10/10).

20c. Brown blotches on
orchids at left (Pl. 1B
R. 1/8).

V8

V9   **V10**   **V11**

1c. Black spot   1c. Black dot at   1c. Black dot on
on petal,   the top of the   top petal of
above "VANDA"   flower at   blossom at left
(Pl. 1A, R.   right (Pl.   (Pl. 1B, R. 10/5).
2/8).   1A, R. 10/1).

V12   **V13**   **V14**

5c. "A" and   5c. Dot under   5c. Dot under "5c"
"P" of   "H" of   (Pl. 1B, R. 4/6).
latin name   latin name
joined (Pl.   (Pl. 1A,
1A, R.   R. 10/3).
8/3).

V15

Line at the left of the country-name, dot at the right (Pl. 1B, R. 10/6).

166E   1c. – V2. Caterpillar flaw   ...   .   1·0
            – V3. Shaved cap badge   ...   .   1·5
            – V4. Line through petal   ...   .   1·0
            – V5. Dot under "A" ...   .   1·6
            – V9. Spot above "VANDA"   ...   .   1·6
            – V10. Dot on flower ...   .   1·6
            – V11. Dot on top petal   ...   .   1·6

167	2c.	– V3.	Shaved cap badge	...	...	...	1·50
168E	5c.	– V3.	Shaved cap badge	...	...	...	1·50
		– V6.	Short stroke	...	...	...	1·50
		– V12.	"A" and "P" joined	...	...	...	1·60
		– V13.	Dot under "H"	...	...	...	1·60
		– V14.	Dot under "5"	...	...	...	1·60
		– V15.	Flaws on country name	...	...	1·90
170	10c.	– V3.	Shaved cap badge	...	...	...	1·60
		– V7.	Short stroke	...	...	...	1·60
172	20c.	– V3.	Shaved cap badge	...	...	...	1·60
		– V8.	Brown blotches	...	...	...	1·60

1970. As Nos. 166 and 170 but wmk PTM (sideways).

[S. G. 173/4]

173	1c.	– V2.	Caterpillar flaw	...	...	...	1·00
		– V3.	Shaved cap badge	...	...	...	1·50
		– V4.	Line through petal	...	...	...	1·00
		– V5.	Dot under "A"	...	...	...	1·90
		– V11.	Dot on top petal	...	...	...	1·60
174	10c.	– V3.	Shaved cap badge	...	...	...	1·90
		– V7.	Short stroke	...	...	...	1·90

Kedah

1965 (15 Nov). *Flowers.*Wmk PTM (upright).   [S. G. 115/21E]

V2/15. See corresponding varieties on Johore Nos. 166/72.

All values except 6 and 15c. The two dots in the inscription above Sultan's head are partly shaved (Pl. 1A, R. 5/4).

V16

115	1c. – V2.	Caterpillar flaw	...	...	...	1·00
	– V4.	Line through petal	...	...	...	1·00
	– V5.	Dot under "A"	...	...	...	1·60
	– V9.	Spot above "VANDA"	...	...	...	1·60
	– V10.	Dot on flower	...	...	...	1·60
	– V11.	Dot on top petal	...	...	...	1·60
	– V16.	Shaved dots	...		...	1·25
116	2c. – V16.	Shaved dots	...	...	...	1·60
117	5c. – V6.	Short stroke	...		...	1·50
	– V12.	"A" and "P" joined	...	...	...	1·60
	– V13.	Dot under "H"	...	...	...	1·60
	– V14.	Dot under "5c"	...	...	...	1·60
	– V15.	Flaws on country name	...	...	...	1·90
	– V16.	Shaved dots	...	...	...	1·50
119	10c. – V7.	Short stroke	...	...	...	1·50
	– V16.	Shaved dots	...	...	...	1·50
121E	20c. – V16.	Shaved dots	...	...	...	1·60

1970 (27 May). As Nos. 115 and 119 but wmk PTM (sideways)
[S. G. 122/23]

122	1c. – V2.	Caterpillar flaw	...		...	1·00
	– V4.	Line through petal	...	...	...	1·00
	– V5.	Dot under "A"	...	...	...	1·50
	– V9.	Spot under "VANDA"	...	...	...	1·60
	– V10.	Dot on flower	...		...	1·60
	– V11.	Dot on top petal	...	...	...	1·60
	– V16.	Shaved dots	...	...	...	1·50
123	10c. – V6.	Short stroke	...	...	...	1·90
	– V16.	Shaved dots	...	...	...	1·90

Kelantan

1951 (11 July)–55.   [S. G. 61/81]

Normal   V1

2c. Stop under " c " almost omitted (R. 1/2).

62E	2c. – V1.	Stop omitted	...	...	...	...	3·00

1965 (15 Nov). *Flowers.* Wmk PTM (upright).   [S. G. 103/9]

V2, V4/7 and V9/15. See corresponding varieties on Johore Nos. 166/72.

6c. and 15c. Malay character broken above second " A " of " KELANTAN " (Pl. 1B. R. 4/8).

V16

V17

6c. and 15c. Dot over letter completely missing. (Plate 1B, R. 8/2).

103	1c. – V2.	Caterpillar flaw	...	...	...	1·00
	– V4.	Line through petal	...	...	...	1·00
	– V5.	Dot under "A"	...	...	...	1·50
	– V9.	Spot above "VANDA"	...	...	...	1·60
	– V10.	Dot on flower	...	...	...	1·60
	– V11.	Dot on top petal	...	...	...	1·60
105	5c. – V6.	Short stroke	...	...	...	1·50
	– V12.	"A" and "P" joined	...	...	...	1·60
	– V13.	Dot under "H"	...	...	...	1·60
	– V14.	Dot under "5c"	...	...	...	1·60
	– V15.	Flaws on country name	...	...	...	1·90
106	6c. – V16.	Broken character	...	...	...	1·50
	– V17.	Missing dot	...	...	...	1·50
107E	10c. – V7.	Short stroke	...	...	...	1·50
108	15c. – V16.	Broken character	...	...	...	1·50
	– V17.	Missing dot	...	...	...	1·50

1970 (20 Nov). As Nos. 103 and 107 but wmk PTM (sideways).   [S. G. 110/11]

110	1c. – V2.	Caterpillar flaw	...	...	...	1·1
	– V4.	Line through petal	...	...	...	1·1
	– V5.	Dot under "A"	...	...	...	1·6
	– V9.	Spot above "VANDA"	...	...	...	1·7
	– V10.	Dot on flower	...	...	...	1·7
	– V11.	Dot on top petal	...	...	...	1·7
111	10c. – V6.	Short stroke	...	...	...	1·7

Kenya

1966 (12 Dec)–71. *Animals.* Chalk-surfaced paper. [S. G. 226/39]

5c. Flaw in front of gazelle's nose, appearing like a carrot (Pl. 1A, R. 7/2).

V3

V1   V2

15c. Grey flaw under snout of bear resembling a small antheap (Pl. 1A, R. 10/5).

15c. Two orange dots under snout which could be taken for ants (Pl. 1B, R. 9/7).

V4   V5

15c. Definite break in line of ant bear's back (Pl. 1B, R. 4/5).

15c. Depression in back in a different position (Pl. 1B, R. 5/8).

V6   V8

50c. White spot to left of buffalo's right horn (Pl. 1A. R. 8/9).

70c. Black line by ostrich's leg appears as a grass stem (Pl. 1B, R. 6/6).

2s.50. Flaw on left of " o " of value, appearing as reversed "Q" (Pl. 1A, R. 2/9).

V7

226	5c. – V3. "Carrot" flaw	...	...	...	...	1·75
228	15c. – V1. "Antheap"	...	...	...	...	2·25
	– V2. "Ants" ...	...	...	...	...	2·25
	– V4. Break in back	...	...	...	...	3·25
	– V5. Depression in back	...	...	...	3·25
232	50c. – V6. Spot by horn	...	...	...	...	1·25
233a	70c. – V8. Black grass stem	...	...	...	2·00
	b. Glazed, ordinary paper					
	– V8. Black grass stem	...	...	...	2·00
236	2s.50 – V7. Reversed "Q" for "0" ...	...	...	3·00

1976 (15 Apr). *Telecommunications Development.* [S. G. 260/64]

1s. Break in " к " of " KENYA " (Pl. 1D, R. 2/5).

V9

261	1s – V9. Break in "к"	...	...	...	...	2·00

1976 (4 Oct). *Railway Transport.* [S. G. 270/4]

V10   V11   V12

3s. Black dot after " N " of " KENYA " (Pl. 1A, R. 7/2).

Red flaw between boiler and cab resembles a rivet (Pl. 1A, R. 7/3).

Black, curving line on " RAIL " (Pl. 1A, R. 8/4).

273	3s – V10. Dot after "N"	...	...	...	...	2·75
	– V11. Red rivet ...	...	...	...	...	2·75
	– V12. Line on "RAIL"	...	...	...	...	2·75

Kenya, Uganda and Tanganyika

1960 (1 Oct)–61. *Queen Elizabeth II.*　　　[S. G. 183/98]

V5

5c. White flaw on upper right sisal leaf (Pl. 2A, R. 6/3).

V1

15c. Serif at left of base of " Y " in " TAN-GANYIKA " (Pl. 1, R. 2/7). This was later retouched but traces still remained.

V2

1s. Re-entry. Whole of " TANGANYIKA " is doubled (Pl. 1–1 and 1–2, R. 9/4).

183	5c. – V5.	Leaf flaw ...	...	...	...	1·60
185	15c. – V1.	Serif variety	...	...	...	2·25
	– V1a.	Serif retouched	...	...	...	2·25
192	1s. – V2.	Re-entry ...	...	...	...	4·50

OFFICIAL STAMPS

1959 (1 July). *Overprints.*　　　[S. G. O1/12]

OFFICIAL　Damaged second " F " in " OFFICIAL " (R. 8/3, first printing only).

V3

OFFICIAL　£1 Broken "O" in "OFFICIAL" (R. 1/6).

V4

O1	5c. – V3.	Damaged 2nd "F"	...	...	...	1·25
O2	10c. – V3.	Damaged 2nd "F"	...	...	...	1·40
O4	20c. – V3.	Damaged 2nd "F"	...	...	...	1·50
O5	30c. – V3.	Damaged 2nd "F"	...	...	...	1·60
O6	50c. – V3.	Damaged 2nd "F"	...	...	...	1·75
O12	£1 – V4.	Broken "O"	...	...	...	20·00

1960 (18 Oct). *Overprints.*　　　[S. G. O13/20]

O13	5c. – V5.	Leaf flaw ...	...	...	...	2·75
O15	15c. – V1.	Serif variety	...	...	...	3·25
	– V1a.	Serif retouched	...	...	...	3·25
O19	1s. – V2.	Re-entry ...	...	...	...	6·50

Kuwait

All V numbers are those of Great Britain where the varieties are illustrated. G.B. numbers in brackets.

1952–54. *Queen Elizabeth II.* Wmk Tudor Crown.　[S. G. 93/102]

94	1a. on 1d. (516) – V32. Flaw on shamrock	... ...	6·50
99	4a. on 4d. (521) – V92. Dotted "R"		4·00

1953 (3 June). *Coronation.*　　　[S. G. 103/6]

106	1r. on 1s.6d. (535) – V63. Mis-shapen emblems	...	7·50
	– V93. Thistle flaw	... ...	7·50

1955 (23 Sept)–57. *Castles.* Waterlow ptgs.　　[S. G. 107I/91]

109I	10r. on 10s. (538) – V8. Weak entry	... ...	50·00
109I/II	10r. on 10s. (538) – V8. Weak entry	... ...	£150

1956. *Queen Elizabeth II.* Wmk St. Edward's Crown.
　　　[S. G. 110/19]

111	1a. on 1d. (541) – V32. Flaw on shamrock	:..	6·00
112	1½a. on 1½d. (542) – V9. Spot between rose and		
		shamrock	6·00
116	4a. on 4d. (546) – V92. Dotted "R"	... ...	6·00

1957 (1 June)–58. *New Currency.*　　　[S. G. 120/30]

122	6np. on 1d.	(541) – V32. Flaw on shamrock		6·00
123	9np. on 1½d.	(542) – V9. Spot between rose and		
		shamrock	... ...	6·00
124	12np. on 2d.	(543Eb) – V46. Dot on shamrock	...	7·00
127	25np. on 4d.	(546) – V92. Dotted "R" ...	...	7·00
129	50np. on 9d.	(551) – V5. Frame break at upper		
		right	... ...	8·50

Leeward Islands

1954 (22 Feb). *Queen Elizabeth II.* [S. G. 126/40]

V1
½c. Extra line to "L" of "LEEWARD" (R. 6/3).

V3
½c. to $1·20. Loop flaw on top left scroll (R. 2/2).

V4
½c. Upper line of value tablet dented (R.3/9).

$2.40 and $4.80. Upper right scroll broken (R. 4/3).

V2

126	½c. – V1. "L" flaw	...	...	...	...	1·50
	– V3. Loop flaw	...	...	...		1·25
	– V4. Value tablet dented	...	...		2·00
127	1c. – V3. Loop flaw	...	...	...		1·50
128	2c. – V3. Loop flaw	...	...	...		1·75
129	3c. – V3. Loop flaw	...	...	...		2·00
130	4c. – V3. Loop flaw	...	...	...		2·00
131	5c. – V3. Loop flaw	...	...	...		2·25
132	6c. – V3. Loop flaw	...	...	...		3·00
133	8c. – V3. Loop flaw	...	...	...		3·25
134	12c. – V3. Loop flaw	...	...	...		3·50
135	24c. – V3. Loop flaw	...	...	...		4·50
136	48c. – V3. Loop flaw	...	...	...		5·00
137	60c. – V3. Loop flaw	...	...	...		6·00
138	$1.20 – V3. Loop flaw	...	...	...		7·00
139	$2.40 – V2. Broken scroll	...	...		12·00
140	$4.80 – V2. Broken scroll	...	...		17·00

Lesotho

1966 (1 Nov). *Overprints.* A. Wmk Script CA. [S. G. 110A/20B]

LESOTHO
V1 Broken first "o" in "LESOTHO" (R. 6/5). Developed during printing.
V2. Weak entry. See V2 of Basutoland

111A	1c. – V1. Broken "o"	...	...	...	...	1·75
112A	2c. – V1. Broken "o"	...	...	...	...	2·75
114A	3½c. – V1. Broken "o"	...	...	...	...	3·75
115A	5c. – V1. Broken "o"	...	...	...	...	4·50
	– V2. Weak entry	...	...	...	...	4·00
116A	10c. – V2. Weak entry	...	...	...	...	3·50
118A	25c. – V1. Broken "o"	...	...	...	...	11·00
	– V2. Weak entry	...	...	...	...	3·50
119A	50c. – V1. Broken "o"	...	...	...	...	11·00

B. Wmk Block CA.

113B	2½c. – V1. Broken "o"	...	...	...	3·50
115B	5c. – V1. Broken "o"	...	...	...	3·50
117B	12½c. – V1. Broken "o"	...	...	...	9·00
119B	50c. – V1. Broken "o"	...	...	...	11·00

1966 (1 Dec). *20th Anniv. of U.N.E.S.C.O.* [S. G. 121/4]

2½c. Green line across arm of microscope (R. 5/6).

V3

121	2½c. – V3. Broken arm of microscope	...	...	2·00

1969 (11 Mar). *Centenary of Maseru.* [S. G. 167/70]

V4
2½c. White spot under "HO" of "LESOTHO" (R. 6/4).

V5
12½c. Black flaw on 8th window from left appears as a broken window (Pl. 1B, R 7/2).

167	2½c. – V4. Spot under "HO"	...	...	...	1·10
169	12½c. – V5. Broken window	...	...	...	1·75

Malacca

1965 (15 Nov). *Flowers.* Wmk PTM (upright).   [S. G. 61/67E]
V2, V4/8 and V9/15. See corresponding varieties on Johore Nos. 166/72.

On all values except 20c. Black diagonal line through centre of coat of arms (Pl. 1B, R. 6/8).

V16

6c. and 15c. Broken leg of left hand Pelandok (Mouse deer) in coat of arms (Pl. 1B, R. 5/2).

V17

61	1c. – V2. Caterpillar flaw	...	...	...	1·60
	– V4. Line through petal	...	...	...	1·60
	– V5. Dot under "A" ...	...	...	...	1·60
	– V9. Spot above "VANDA"	...	...	...	1·60
	– V10. Dot on flower ...	...	...	...	1·60
	– V11. Dot on top petal	...	...	...	1·60
	– V16. Line through shield	...	...	...	1·60
62	2c. – V16. Line through shield	...	...	...	1·60
63E	5c. – V6. Short stroke	...	...	...	1·60
	– V12. "A" and "P" joined	...	...	...	1·60
	– V13. Dot under "H" ...	...	...	...	1·60
	– V14. Dot under "5c"	...	...	...	1·60
	– V15. Flaws on country name	...	...	...	2·00
	– V16. Line through shield	...	...	...	1·60
64	6c. – V16. Line through shield	...	...	...	1·60
	– V17. Broken leg	...	...	...	1·60
65	10c. – V7. Short stroke	...	...	...	1·60
	– V16. Line through shield	...	...	...	1·60
66	15c. – V16. Line through shield	...	...	...	1·60
	– V17. Broken leg	...	...	...	1·60
67E	20c. – V8. Brown blotches	...	...	...	1·60
	Ea. Red-brn background				
	– V8. Brown blotches	...	...	...	1·60

In No. 67E the background is purple-brown.

1970. As Nos. 61 and 65 but Wmk PTM (sideways).   [S. G. 68/9]

68	1c. – V2. Caterpillar flaw ...	...	...	...	2·25
	– V4. Line through petal	...	...	...	2·25
	– V5. Dot under "A" ...	...	...	...	2·25
	– V9. Spot above "VANDA"	...	...	...	1·60
	– V10. Dot on flower ...	...	...	...	1·60
	– V11. Dot on top petal ...	...	...	...	1·60
	– V16. Line through shield	...	...	...	1·60
69	10c. – V7. Short stroke	...	...	...	2·50

Malawi

1964 (6 July)–65. *Pictorials.* No wmk.   [S. G. 215/27]

V1. 5s. " Lake Nyasa ". See V5 of Nyasaland.

5s. " Lake Malawi ". Large white flaw over mountains in top right corner appears as a moon (Pl. 1A, R. 3/1).

V2

225	5s – V1. Cloud reflections elongated	...	...		4·50
225a	5s – V2. Moon flaws	...	...	...	...	4·50

No. 225a is inscribed "LAKE MALAWI" instead of "LAKE NYASA"

1966–67. *Pictorials.* Wmk Cockerels.   [S. G. 252/62]

260	5s. – V2. Moon flaw	...	...	...	...	...	4·50

No. 260 is inscribed "LAKE MALAWI"

1976 (24 Mar). *Centenary of the Telephone.*   [S. G. 520/4]

3t. Broken " R " in " FIRST " (Pl. 1B, R. 3/4).

V3

520	3t. – V3. Broken "R" ...	...	...	...	...	1·75

1976 (6 Dec). *Christmas.*   [S. G. 537/41]

FORTH.
SON..

10t. Inscription at top ends with two stops instead of three (Pl. 1B, R. 3/1)

V4

538	10t. – V4. Missing stop	...	...	...	...	2·00

Malayan Federation

1957 (5 May)–63. Wmk Block CA.   [S. G. 1E/4E]

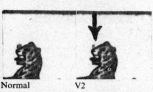

12c. Lion at right has only two whiskers instead of three (Pl. 1B. R. 2/7).

Normal   V2

V3. 12c. Occurs on Pl. ?, R. 3/1.

2	12c. – V2. Missing whisker	...	...	...	...	1·50	
	– V3. "STRF. NGTH" for "STRENGTH"		...	...	1·25	

1961 (4 Jan). *Installation of Yang di-Pertuan Agong.*   [S. G. 19]

10c. Flaw in head-dress resembling extra notch (R. 3/2).

V1

19   10c. – V1. Extra notch ...   .   1·50

Malayan Postal Union

POSTAGE DUE STAMPS

1964 (14 Apr)–65.   [S. G. D22/8]

POSTAGE   4c. Closed " G " in " POSTAGE " (R. 3/4).
V1   This was corrected on No. D24a.

D24   4c. – V1. Closed "G"   ...   .   1·75

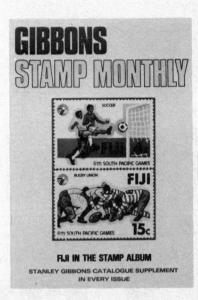

Malaysia

1965 (27 Aug). *Opening of National Mosque. Kuala Lumpur.*
[S. G. 15/17]

15c. Coloured spot at bottom left of minaret (R. 8/3).

V2

16   15c. – V2. Minaret spot   ...   .   1·75

1965 (9 Sept). *Birds.*   [S. G. 20E/27]

V3

75c. White flaw in " Y " of " MALAYSIA " (Pl. 1A, R. 5/9).

V4

White flaw in Malay inscription above " s " of " MALAYSIA ", giving appearance of malformed character (Pl. 1A, R. 9/4).

V9

75c. Black dot below first " G " of " ENGGANG " (Pl. 1A, R. 7/3).

V5

$1 Light patch below " M " of " MALAYSIA " (Pl. 1A, R. 3/3).

V6

$1 White flaw in Malay inscription above " s " of " MALAYSIA " (different from V4) (Pl. 1A, R. 9/3).

V10

$1 White diagonal line in top right corner (Pl. 1A, R.4/5).

V7

$2 White flaw above " K " of " KUANG " resembling egg (Pl. 1A, R. 5/6).

V12

$2 Serif on Malay character above " s " of " MALAYSIA " (Pl. 1B, R. 9/9).

V18

$5 Extra dot under Malay inscription (Pl. 1B, R. 4/8).

V13

$10 Additional diagonal stroke on Malay character above " I " of " MALAYSIA " (Pl. 1A, R. 6/1).

23E	75c. – V3.	Dot in "Y"	...	...	...	...	1·75
	– V4.	Flaw above "s"	...	...	...	...	1·75
	– V9.	Dot below "G"	...	...	...	...	2·00
24E	$1 – V5.	Patch below "M"	...	...	...	...	2·25
	– V6.	Flaw above "s"	...	...	...	...	2·25
	– V10.	Line in corner	...	...	...	...	2·50
25E	$2 – V7.	"Egg" flaw	...	...	...	...	3·25
	– V12.	Serif above "s"	...	...	...	...	3·50
26E	$5 – V18.	Extra dot ...	...	...	...	...	7·00
27	$10 – V13.	Diagonal stroke above "I"	...	...	...	14·00

1966 (8 Feb). *National Monument, Kuala Lumpur.*   [S. G. 31E/32]

20c. Gap in rocks at left (Pl. 1B, R. 9/10).

V1

32   20c. – V1. Gap in rocks   ...   .   1·75

PHILATELIC TERMS ILLUSTRATED

The essential philatelic dictionary. Terms covering printing methods, papers, errors, varieties, watermarks, perforations and much more are explained and illustrated, many in full colour. See the preliminary pages of this Catalogue for details of the current edition.

1967 (30 March). *Completion of Malaysia – Hong Kong Link of SEACOM Telephone Cable.* [S. G. 42/43]

75c. Gap in white coastline by Guyana (R. 5/1).

V8

43   75c. – V8. Missing coastline   ...   .   3·00

1968 (12 Oct). *Olympic Games, Mexico.* [S. G. 54/55]

30c. White dot over left leg of " M " in " MEXICO " (Pl. 1a, R.5/1–10).

VII

54   30c. – V11. Dot over "M" of "MEXICO"   ...   ...   1·75

1969 (8 Dec). *National Rice Year.* [S. G. 59/60]

V14. 75c. Missing dot over "i" of "Malaysia" (R. 3/7).

59   15c. – V14. Missing dot over "i"   ...   .   1·10

1970 (6 Apr). *Satellite Earth Station.* [S. G. 61/63]

V15

15c. Blue spot over " a " of " satelit " (R. 1/1).

V16

15c. Hair flaw above " he " of " seteshen " (R. 7/9).

15c. Blue flaw on top of cloud under first " a " of " malaysia " (R. 8/9).

V17

61   15c. – V15. Blue spot over "a"   ...   .   1·25
     – V16. Hair flaw   ...   .   1·25
     – V17. Flaw on top of cloud   ...   .   1·25

1970 (31 Aug). *Butterflies.* [S. G. 64/71]

$5 Missing line in upper ball in " y " (Pane with colour dabs at left, R. 2/10).

V19

70   $5 – V19. "Y" variety   ...   .   6·50

Malta

1954 (8 Sept). *Centenary of Dogma of the Immaculate Conception.* [S. G. 263/5]

V32

V7

1½d. Dark green blotch behind " M " of " MALTA " appears as a shadow (R. 5/2).

3d. White flaw on " o " of " OF " at top of stamp (R. 2/7).

V1

1s. " Halo " variety consists of retouch. over heads of Cherubim (R. 2/4) (MG 12.54.)

263	1½d. – V32. Shadow behind "M"	...	...	...	1·75
264	3d. – V7. Flaw on "o" of "OF"	...	...	...	1·75
264	1s. – V1. "Halo" variety	...	...	...	5·00

1957 (15 Apr). *15th Anniv. of George Cross Award.* [S. G. 283/5]

V2

1s. White flaw over first " a " of " Malta " (R. 5/10).

Normal   V8

1s. Extensive retouch across the buildings (R. 6/2).

| 285 | 1s. – V2. Flaw over "a" | ... | ... | ... | ... | 2·50 |
| | – V8. Retouch | ... | ... | ... | ... | 3·25 |

1958 (15 Feb). *Technical Education in Malta.* [S. G. 286/8]

V20

V9

3d. Retouch to right of value (Pl. 1A, R. 6/1).

1s. Retouch consisting of large black flaw on end of left-hand building (Pl. 1A, R. 8/5).

| 287 | 3d. – V20. Retouch | ... | ... | ... | ... | 2·25 |
| 288 | 1s. – V9. Retouch | ... | ... | ... | ... | 4·00 |

1958 (15 Apr). *16th Anniv. of George Cross Award.* [S. G. 289/91E]

V10

3d. White flaw on third gun from right appearing as larger gunflash (Pl. 1A R. 5/7).

V3

1s. Queen's face heavily retouched showing a series of spots (Pl. 1B, R. 10/1). (MG 5.58.)

Normal   V11

Man's hand appears white as shading mostly omitted (Pl. 1A, R. 9/2).

290	3d. – V10. Gunflash flaw	...	...	...	...	3·00
291E	1s. – V3. Retouch on face	...	...	...	...	4·00
	– V11. White hand	...	...	...	...	4·00

1959 (15 Apr). *17th Anniv. of Geroge Cross Award.*   [S. G. 292/4]

V12   V13

1½d. Retouch on stretcher above   1s. Flaw on head-shawl
rescuer's forearm (Pl. 1A,   above child's hand
R. 6/8).   (Pl. 1B, R. 4/1).

| 292 | 1½d. – V12. Retouch | ... | ... | ... | ... | 3·00 |
| 294 | 1s. – V13. Flaw over child's hand | ... | ... | ... | 4·00 |

1960 (9 Feb). *19th Centenary of the Shipwreck of St. Paul.*
[S. G. 295/300]

3d. Retouch on halo over left shoulder
(Pl. 1A, R. 2/1).

V14

8d. White stroke after
" K " of " SHIP-
WRECK " (Pl. 1A–1A
R. 2/10).

V4

8d. Two white flaws in " PAUL "
one giving the " P " the appearance of " R " and other a blob
over the " L " (Pl. 1A–1A
R. 5/2).

V5

296E	3d. – V14. Halo retouch	...	...	...	...	2·75
298	8d. – V4. Flaw over "K"	...	...	...	...	3·75
	– V5. "RAUL" flaw	...	...	...	...	3·75

1960 (1 Dec). *Stamp Centenary.*   [S. G. 301E/3]

V6. 3d. with right-hand bottom corner of the 1860 stamp blank
on R. 4/7 comes from early trial plates and the sheets containing
this error should have been destroyed; however some were mis-
sorted into the good material and were issued at a post office.

| 302 | 3d. – V6. Blank corner | ... | ... | ... | ... | 80·00 |

1964 (5 Sept). *First European Catholic Doctors' Congress,
Valletta.*   [S. G. 318/20]

2d. Retouched background to " O " of
" CONGRESS " showing as dark
diagonal line (R. 4/6).

V15

| 318 | 2d. – V15. Retouch | ... | ... | ... | ... | 2·25 |

1964 (3 Nov). *Christmas.*   [S. G. 327/9]

V16   V17

4d. White flaw on Virgin's   4d. White flaw on face of
head-shawl appearing as   left-hand figure giving
earring (Pl. 1B–2B. R.   appearance of mouth being
6/1).   open (Pl. 1A–2A, R. 6/6).

V18   V19

4d. White flaw in sky behind   8d. White patch on St. Joseph's
crook appearing as extra   cloak (Pl. 1A–2A, R. 4/5).
star (Pl. 1A–2A, R. 7/6).

328	4d. – V16. Earring flaw	...	...	...	...	2·75
	– V17. Open mouth	...	...	...	...	3·50
	– V18. Extra star	...	...	...	...	3·50
329	8d. – V19. Patch on cloak	...	...	...	...	6·50

1965 (7 Jan)–71. *History of Malta.*   [S. G. 330E/48E]

Normal   V33   V21

½d. The coil behind the first " A "   1½d. Red spot on toga at
of " MALTA " has brown   top right (Pl. 1B,
missing and shows as gold   R. 2/1).
(Pl 1A, R. 2/2)

2s. Green flaw on doorstep gives appearance of battering (Pl. 1A, R. 10/1).

V34

330E	¼d. – V33. Bright coil	...	...	...	...	1·25
332	1½d. – V21. Red spot on toga	...	...	...	1·25
343	2s. – V34. Battered doorstep	...	...	...	1·75

1965 (1 Sept). *400th Anniv. of Great Siege.* [S. G. 352/8]

V23

2d. White spot on " 2 " (R. 5/1).

V22

2s.6d. White dot between " 2/6 " (R. 4/5).

352	2d. – V23. Spot on "2"	...	...	...	...	2·25
358	2s.6d. – V22. Dot between "2/6"	...	...	...	12·00

1965 (7 Oct). *Christmas.* [S. G. 359/61]

All values. Patch in robe of right-hand figure (R. 3/5).

V25

359	1d. – V25. Patch in robe	...	...	...	...	1·75
360	4d. – V25. Patch in robe	...	...	...	2·50
361	1s.3d. – V25. Patch in robe	...	...	...	4·50

1966 (24 Jan). *Churchill Commemoration.* [S. G. 362/5]

V24

2d. Black scar on nose (R. 1/5).

V26

2d. Light patch on forehead (R. 4/10).

1s.6d. White flaw in bottom arm of cross (R. 6/7).

V35

362	2d. – V24. Scar on nose	...	...	...	...	1·75
	– V26. Light patch on head	...	...	...	1·75
365	1s.6d. – V35. Flaw in cross	...	...	...	3·50

1968 (2 May). *Human Rights Year.* [S. G. 399/401]

V36

2d. Brown spot on buildings above " F " of " FOR " appears as a broken chimney (Pl. 1B, R. 6/5).

V27

6d. Break in blue fold of white garment above flame (Pl. 1A, R. 7/5).

399	2d. – V36. Broken chimney	...	...	...	...	1·50
400	6d. – V27. Gap in garment	...	...	...	2·75

1968 (1 June). *Malta International Trade Fair.* [S. G. 402/4]

V28

All values. White line to right of Maltese Cross is broken (Pl. 1A R. 5/1).

V37

All values. Dark smudge between vertical lines below Maltese cross (Pl. 1A, R. 10/4).

402	4d. – V28. Broken line	...	...	...	...	1·50
	– V37. Smudge flaw	...	...	...	1·50
403	8d. – V28. Broken line	...	...	...	2·25
	– V37. Smudge flaw	...	...	...	2·25
404	3s. – V28. Broken line	...	...	...	4·00
	– V37. Smudge flaw	...	...	...	4·00

1968 (3 Oct). *Christmas.* [S. G. 409/11]

V29

V38

1d. Brown line below neck of reclining shepherd is broken (Pl. 1A, R. 1/6).

8d. Retouch to background above " It " of " Malta " shows as white patch (R.8/3).

409 1d. – V29. Broken line ... ... 1·50
410 8d. – V38. Retouch ... ... 2·25

1968 (21 Oct). *Sixth Food and Agricultural Organisation Regional Conference for Europe.* [S. G. 412/14]

V30

V31

2s.6d. black spot on left breast of figure (Right pane, R. 1/6).

2s.6d. Large white flaw on chest (Left pane. R. 1/10).

414 2s.6d. – V30. Spot on breast ... ... 4·00
– V31. White chest ... ... 4·00

1969 (20th Sept). *Fifth Anniv. of Independence.* [S. G. 422/6]

V39

2d. Black line from second tree across " cloud " above monument extending through " MALTA " (R. 2/1).

422 2d. – V39. Black scratch 90

1970 (21 Mar). *13th Council of Europe Art Exhibition.* [S. G. 430/7]

5d. Gold stop before " L-EUROPA " (R. 1/1).

V41

432 5d. – V41. Gold stop variety ... ... 1·75

1975 (30 May). *International Women's Year.* [S. G. 539/42]

5c. Green flaw beneath I.W.Y. emblem resembling a hyphen (Pl. 1C, R. 4/6).

V42

541 5c. – V42. Green hyphen ... ... 5·50

1977 (20 Jan). *Suits of Armour.* [S. G. 572/4]

2c. Yellow glow around " Jean de " (Pl. 1C, R. 10/4).

V43

572 2c. – V43. Yellow glow ... ... 1·75

Mauritius

1953 (3 Nov)–58. *Views.*   [S. G. 293/306]

V11
3c. Break in oval below
and to right of crown
(R. 3/2).

V1
4c. White spot between
" U " and " S " of
" MAURITIUS " (Pl. 2,
R. 6/2).

V2
4c. Curved line linking first
two windows of white
house (Pl. 2, R. 10/8).

V3
10c. White blob on " C "
of " CENTS " (Pl. 1
R. 5/2).

V16
15c. White blob causes
a break in the
crown (Pl. 2, R. 1/8).

V4
20c. Retouched back-
ground under " ITI "
of " MAURITIUS "
(Pl. 2, R. 1/10).

294	3c. – V11. Break in oval	...	...	...	...	1·50
295E	4c. – V1. Spot between "U" and "S"		...	...	1·75
	– V2. Linked windows	...	...	...	1·75
297E	10c. – V3. Blob on "C"	...	...	...	1·40
298	15c. – V16. Broken Crown	...	...	...	2·50
299E	20c. – V4. Retouch	...	...	...	1·75

1965 (16 Mar). *Birds.*   [S. G. 317E/31]

2c. Smudged " U " in " MAURITIUS "
(Pl. 1A, R. 2/4).

V17

V5
4c. Right-hand claw broken
(R. 9/5).

V7   Normal
4c. Bough is cut short at left
instead of having a ragged
end (R. 1/1).

4c. Nick in branch under bird (R. 2/5).

V8

317E	2c. – V17. Smudged "U"	...	...	...	...	2·25
319E	4c. – V5. Broken claw	...	...	...	...	1·40
	– V7. Sawn-off bough	...	...	...	...	1·00
	– V8. Nick in branch	...	...	...	...	1·25

1965 (25 Oct). *International Co-operation Year.*   [S. G. 334/5]

V6. Broken "Y" in "YEAR". See V3 of Antigua
V9. Broken leaves. See V6 of Antigua

334	10c. – V9. Broken leaves	...	...	...	...	2·75
335	60c. – V6. Broken "Y"	...	...	...	...	5·50
	– V9. Broken leaves	...	...	...	...	3·50

1967 (1 Sept). *Self Government.*   [S. G. 345E/8]

60c. White scratch across Queen's
throat (R. 2/1).

V12

ME·NT

1r. Small black dot between " E " and
" N " of " GOVERNMENT " (R. 5/4).

V10

347	60c. – V12. Scratched throat	...	...	...	3·00
348	1r. – V10. Stop between "E" and "N"	...	...	3·50

1967 (1 Dec). *Self Government Overprint.*   [S. G. 349E/63]

351E	4c. (319E) – V5. Broken claw	...	...	...	1·75
	– V7. Sawn-off bough	...	...	...	1·75
	– V8. Nick in branch	...	...	...	1·75

1968 (12 July). *Birds.* [S. G. 370/5]

370E 2c. – V17. Smudged "u" ... ... 2·25

1968 (2 Dec). *Bicentenary of Bernardin de St. Pierre's Visit.*
[S. G. 376/81]

2c. Blue blob by Dominique's hand (Pl. 1A, R. 2/3).

V18

376 2c. – V18. Blue blob flaw ... ... 1·60

1969 (12 Mar)–73. *Pictorials.* Chalk-surfaced paper.
[S. G. 382E/99]

Wmk Block CA (sideways on 2, 3, 4, 5, 10, 15, 60 and 75c.).

V19

10c. Flourish at top of "м" is broken (Pl. 1A, R. 1/2). Later retouched on printing (*j*) of No. 441.

V20

Serif at foot of "a" is cleft, leaving a dot (Pl. 1A, R.7/4).

Normal

V14

5c. Bottom serif of "u" and serif of "r" shortened in "Mauritius" (Pl. 1B, R. 5/5). Retouched on Diagonal watermark printing as V24, and for printing (*j*) of No. 442 was further retouched so that the serifs appear normal.

21

0c. Frame at bottom right is damaged and thus askew (Pl. 1B, R. 1/2).

V13

2r.50 At the centre of the bottom frame there is an indentation (Pl. 1A, R. 10/4). Retouched on No. 397a.

Normal   V15

5r. Black line around pink fin mostly missing (Pl. 1A, R. 10/5). Retouched on No. 453.

386E	10c. – V19. Broken flourish	...	...	...	1·60
	– V20. Broken serif	...	...	...	1·60
387E	15c. – V14. Shortened serifs of "u" and "r"		...	1·60
394	60c. – V21. Damaged frame	...	...	...	2·50
397	2r.50 – V13. Damaged frame	...	...	...	3·50
398E	5r. – V15. Fin variety	...	...	...	4·00
	a. Glazed, ordinary paper				
	– V15. Fin variety	...	...	...	4·00

1969 (1 July). *Birth Centenary of Mahatma Gandhi.* [S. G. 400/6]

AS A LAW

2c. Flaw extends the foot of the "A" (Pl. 1B, R. 5/5).

V22

400 2c. – V22. Extended "A" ... ... 1·75

1970 (7 Apr). *World Fair, Osaka.* No. 394 overprinted.[S. G. 413/4]

413 60c. – V21. Damaged frame ... ... 2·25

1972–74. As No. 386E etc., but wmk Block CA upright.
[S. G. 437/54]

A. Glazed, ordinary paper.
B. Chalk-surfaced paper.

		A.	B.
441	10c. – V19. Broken flourish	1·75	1·75
	– V20. Broken serif	1·75	1·75
442	15c. – V14. Shortened serifs of "u" and "r"	1·75	1·75
449E	60c.– V21. Damaged frame	2·25	2·25

1974 (4 Dec). *Centenary of Universal Postal Union.* [S. G. 473/4]

THE UNION

1r. Dot over "u" of "union" (Pl. 1A, R. 2/5).

V23

474 1r. – V23. Dot over "u" ... ... 2·75

1975–77. As No. 386E etc., but wmk CA Diagonal. [S. G. 475/91]

15c. Variety V14 is now retouched resulting in the ragged appearance of
the right-hand side of the " r " of
" Mauritius ".   The serifs of the
" u " and the " r " are now back to
their correct length (Pl. 1B, R. 5/5).

V24

480   15c. (wmk sideways) – V24. Retouched "r"   ...   1·75

1975 (5 Dec). *International Women's Year.*   [S. G. 498]

Blue flaw on " U " of " MAURITIUS "
shaped like a chevron (Pl. 1D,
R. 1/2).

V25

498   2r.50 – V25. Blue chevron   ...   .   3·00

Montserrat

1964 (23 Apr). *400th Anniv. of Birth of Shakespeare.*   [S. G. 156]

Light patch in wall of theatre (R. 6/2).

V4

156   12c. – V4. Patch in wall   ...   .   2·50

1965 (17 May). *I.T.U. Centenary.*   [S. G. 158/9]

V1. Broken "U" in "TELECOMMUNICATIONS". See V1 of Antigua
158   4c. – V1. Broken "U" ...   .   3·25

1965 (16 Aug). *Fruits etc.* Wmk Block CA (upright).
    [S. G. 160E/76]

48c. White flaw over second "R" in "MONTSERRAT" appears as a grave accent (R. 4/10).

V6

172   48c. – V6. Accent over "R"   ...   .   4·00

1965 (25 Oct). *International Co-operation Year.*   [S. G. 177/8]

V3. Broken leaves. See V6 of Antigua
177   2c. – V3. Broken leaves   ...   .   2·75
178   12c. – V3. Broken leaves   ...   .   3·25

1966 (20 Sept). *Inauguration of W.H.O. Headquarters, Geneva.*
    [S. G. 185/6]

V2. Dotted "r" in "Headquarters". See V5 of Dominica
185   12c. – V2. Dotted "r"   ...   .   2·75

1968 (6 May). *Surcharges.*   [S. G. 194/9]

V5. Obliterating bars are 1½mm. apart instead of 2mm. (outside measurements) (R. 5/10).
194   15c. on 12c. – V5. Narrow bars   ...   .   1·75
195   25c. on 24c. – V5. Narrow bars   ...   .   2·00

196   50c. on 48c. – V6. Accent over "R" ...   .   2·25

1969 (17 Mar)–70. Wmk Block CA (sideways).   [S. G. 213/22]

222   50c. on 48c. – V6. Accent over "R" ...   .   5·00

1972 (20 Nov). *Royal Silver Wedding.*   [S. G. 307/8E]

V7. Dot on curtain. See V4 of Anguilla.
307   35c. – V7 Dot on curtain   ...   .   2·50

1974 (2 Oct). *Surcharges.*   [S. G. 335E/9]

V8
Upper obliterating bar is short (Pl. 1A, R. 1/1).

V9
Staggered bars (Pl. 1A, R. 2/2).

V10

The figure " 2 " is wrong fount, now being seriffed instead of sans-serif (Pl. 1B, R. 3/1).

V11. Bottom bar is missing from surcharge (Pl. 1B, all stamps of the fifth row).

338   20c. on $1 (No. 252B) – V8.   Short bar ...   ...   12·00
                              – V9.   Staggered bars   ...   12·00
                              – V10.   Wrong fount "2" ...   12·00
                              – V11.   Missing bar   ...   18·00

1977 (28 Oct). *Royal Visit.*   [S. G. 409/11]

V14. "Short bars". All obliterating bars on the first vertical row are 9½–10 mm. long, instead of 12 mm. on the remainder.

V15
"Comma" in surcharge, between "SILVER" and "ROYAL" (R. 1/2).

V16
Double bars in the upper position (R. 3/4).

409    $1 on 55c. – V14. Short bars   ...   .   1·50
                  – V15. Comma flaw   ...   .   3·50
                  – V16. Double bars   ...   .   3·50
410    $1 on 70c. – V14. Short bars   90
                  – V15. Comma flaw   ...   .   1·75
                  – V16. Double bars   ...   .   1·75
411    $1 on $2.50 – V14. Short bars   90
                   – V15. Comma flaw   ...   .   1·75
                   – V16. Double bars   ...   .   1·75

OFFICIAL STAMPS

1976 (12 Apr). *O.H.M.S. Overprint.*   [S. G. O1/6]

5c., 10c. and 45c. Line
through " O " of opt
(Pl. 1A, R. 5/5).

V13

O1	5c. – V13. Line through "o"	...	...	...	5·00
O2	10c. – V13. Line through "o"	...	...	...	5·00
O4	45c. on 3c. – V13. Line through "o"	...	...	...	9·00

The prices quoted are for used copies.

1976 (1 Oct). *Larger overprint*   [S. G. O7/15E]

V12. all values. Stop after "S" of "O.H.M.S." is missing (R. 1/3 and 3/5).

Nos. O7/15 were not available in an unused condition, and were sold to the public cancelled-to-order.

O7	5c. – V12. Missing stop	...	...	...	...	1·50
O8	10c. – V12. Missing stop	...	...	...	...	1·50
O9E	15c. – V12. Missing stop	...	...	...	...	1·50
O10	20c. – V12. Missing stop	...	...	...	...	1·50
O11	25c. – V12. Missing stop	...	...	...	...	1·50
O12	55c. – V12. Missing stop	...	...	...	...	2·00
O13	70c. – V12. Missing stop	...	...	...	...	2·25
O14	$1 – V12. Missing stop	...	...	...	...	3·50
O15E	$5 – V12. Missing stop	...	...	...	...	6·00

Morocco Agencies

All V numbers with the exception of V3, are those of Great Britain where the varieties are illustrated. G.B. number in brackets.

A. British Currency

1952–55. *Queen Elizabeth II.* Wmk Tudor Crown.   [S. G. 101/10]

102	1d. (516) – V32.	Flaw on shamrock	...	...		4·75
106	4d. (521) – V92.	Dotted "R"	...	...	...	6·00
107	5d. (522) – V193.	Spot by "E"	...	...	...	3·00
	– V194.	Spot by daffodil	...	...	...	3·00

B. Spanish Currency

1954–55. *Queen Elizabeth II.* Wmk Tudor Crown.   [S. G. 187/8]

188	10c. on 1d. (516) – V32. Flaw on shamrock		...	4·00

1956. *Queen Elizabeth II.* Wmk St. Edward's Crown. [S. G. 189/90]

190	40c. on 4d. (546) – V92. Dotted "R"	...	...	6·50

C. Tangier International Zone

1952–54. *Queen Elizabeth II.* Wmk Tudor Crown.   [S. G. 289/305]

295	4d. (521) – V92.	Dotted "R"	...	...	10·00
296	5d. (522) – V195.	Neck retouch	...	...	3·50
300	9d. (526) – V5.	Frame break at upper right	...	15·00
304	1s.3d. (530) – V200.	White flaw in Queen's hair	...	5·00
305	1s.6d. (531) – V201.	White flaw in Queen's head below diadem	...	...	14·00
	– V202.	White flaw in Queen's head opposite "N"	...	...	14·00

1953 (3 June). *Coronation.*   [S. G. 306/9]

307	4d. (533) – V137. Daffodil leaf flaw	...	...	6·00
308	1s.3d. (534) – V138. Clover leaf flaw	...	...	7·50

1955 (23 Sept). *Castles.* Waterlow ptgs.   [S. G. 310/12]

312	10s. (538) – V8. Weak entry	...	...	...	70·00

1956. *Queen Elizabeth II.* Wmk St. Edward's Crown. [S. G. 313/22]

315	1½d. (542) – V9.	Spot between rose and shamrock			2·00
317	2d. (543Eb) – V46.	Dot on shamrock	...	...	2·00
320	4d. (546) – V92.	Dotted "R"	...	...	4·00

1957 (1 Apr). *Centenary of British Post Office in Tangier.*
[S. G. 323/42]

1857·1957

V3

Short " 7 " in " 1957 " (R. 9/3). This was later corrected on the 2s.6d. value only.

324	1d. (541) – V32.	Flaw on shamrock	...	...	2·75
325	1½d. (542) – V9.	Spot between rose and shamrock			3·00
326	2d. (543Eb) – V46.	Dot on shamrock	...	...	3·00
	– V187.	"Double trumpet" flaw	...	3·00
328	3d. (545) – V279.	White eye	...	...	10·00
329	4d. (546) – V92.	Dotted "R"	...	...	3·50
330	5d. (547) – V193.	Spot by "E"	...	...	4·00
	– V194.	Spot on daffodil	...	...	4·00
334	9d. (551) – V5.	Frame break at upper right ...		10·00
340E	2s.6d. (536) – V3.	Short "7"	...	...	7·00
341	5s. (537) – V3.	Short "7"	...	...	10·00
	– V206.	Major re-entry	...	...	12·00
342	10s. (538) – V8.	Weak entry	...	...	30·00
	– V3.	Short "7"	...	...	20·00

Nauru

1975 (23 July). *Phosphate Mining Anniversaries.*   [S. G. 129/32]

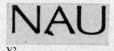

V1
5c. "Q" for "O" in
   date (R. 1/1).

V2
15c. Flaw on "A" of "NAURU"
   resembles a serif (R. 10/3).

129   5c. – V1. "Q" for "O"   ...   .   1·60
131   15c. – V2. Serif on "A"   ...   .   2·50

Negri Sembilan

1965 (15 Nov). *Flowers.* Wmk PTM (upright).   [S. G. 81/87E]

V2 and V4/15. See corresponding varieties on Johore.

81	1c.	– V2.	Caterpillar flaw	...	... ...	1·60
		– V4.	Line through petal	...	... ...	1·60
		– V5.	Dot under "A" ...	...	... ...	1·60
		– V9.	Spot above "VANDA"	...	... ...	1·60
		– V10.	Dot on flower	...	... ...	1·60
		– V11.	Dot in top petal	...	... ...	1·60
83E	5c.	– V6.	Short stroke	...	... ...	1·60
		– V12.	"A" and "P" joined	...	... ...	1·60
		– V13.	Dot under "H" ...	...	... ...	1·60
		– V14.	Dot under "5c."	...	... ...	1·60
		– V15.	Flaws on country name	...	...	2·00
85	10c.	– V7.	Short stroke	...	... ...	1·60
87Ea	20c.	– V8.	Brown blotches	...	... ...	1·50

1970 (27 May). As No. 81 but wmk PTM (sideways).   [S. G. 90]

90	1c	– V2.	Caterpillar flaw	...	... ...	1·75
		– V4.	Line through petal	...	... ...	1·75
		– V5.	Dot under "A"	...	... ...	1·75
		– V9.	Spot above "VANDA"	...	... ...	1·75
		– V10.	Dot on flower	...	... ...	1·75
		– V11.	Dot on top petal	...	... ...	1·75

New Hebrides

1956 (20 Oct). *Fiftieth Anniv. of Condominium.*   [S. G. 80/83]

V1

V2

10c. Small flaw between " F "   50c. Fasces above " RF "
and fasces (R. 1/3).   damaged (R. 2/5).

81	10c. – V1. "F" flaw	...	...	...	...	...	3·25
83	50c. – V2. Damaged fasces	...	...	...	...	5·00

1965 (24 Oct). *International Co-operation Year.*   [S. G. 112/13]

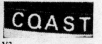

V7

5c. Spot in ' c " of " CONDOMINIUM "
makes it appear as " o " (R. 8/1).

112	5c. – V7. Closed "c"	...	...	...	...	...	4·00

1967 (26 Sept). *25th Anniv. of the Pacific War.*   [S. G. 125/8]

V3

15c. White spot by " o "
of " COAST " resem-
bling " Q " (R. 7/2).

25c. Retouch by shoulder of
Australian soldier
(R. 10/4).

V6

25c. Blue   line   runs
through " L " of
" CORAL " to top of
map (R. 6/4).

V5

25c. Vertical blue line after
" A " of " SEA " (R. 2/2).

125	15c. – V3. "CQAST" flaw	...	...	...	...	3·00
126	25c. – V4. Retouch	...	...	...	...	4·00
	– V5. Blue line after "SEA"		...	...	...	4·00
	– V6. Line through "CORAL"		...	...	...	4·00

1972 (20 Nov). *Royal Silver Wedding.*   [S. G. 172E/3]

V8. Dot on curtain. See V4 of Anguilla

172E	35c. – V8. Dot on curtain	...	...	...	...	3·50

New Zealand

1953 (7 Oct). *Health.* [S. G. 719/20E]

1½d. White flaw at top of right leg (R. 2/10).

V18

719 1½d. + ½d. – V18. Leg flaw   ...   .   1·50

1955–60. *Queen Elizabeth II.* [S. G. 745E/51E]

1d. Collar retouched, the shading being heavier (Pl. 11, R. 10/22)

V44

745E 1d. – V44. Collar retouch   ...   .   6·00

1957 (15 Feb). *75th Anniv. of First Export of N.Z. Lamb.* [S. G. 758E/59]

4d. A white flaw occurs after " 1957 " (R.12/4).

V1

V19
4d. White dot on " A " of " TRADE " (R. 1/5).

V20
4d. Right frame notched by " PO " of " EXPORT " (R. 1/6).

8d. A white flaw occurs between the " 1 " and the " 8 " of " 1882 " (R. 10/1).

V2

758E 4d. – V1. Flaw after "1957"   ...   .   5·00
      – V19. Dot on "A" of "TRADE"   ...   .   3·00
      – V20. Frame notched* ...   .   3·50
759   8d. – V2. Date flaw ...   .   7·00

* *Price for positional block of four of* V19 *and* V20, £10.

1957 (25 Sept). *Health.* [S. G. 761/2c]

2d. + 1d. Missing toes from life-guard's left foot (R. 3/3).

V21

761   2d. + 1d. – V21. Missing toes   ...   .   2·50

1958 (20 Aug). *Health.* [S. G. 764/5a]

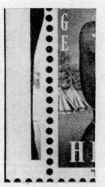

3d. An incomplete Jubilee line reveals a " Tent " (R. 4/1 (margin)).

V3

765   3d. + 1d. – V3. Phantom "Tent"   ...   .   5·00

1958 (27 Aug). *30th Anniv. of First Air Crossing of the Tasman Sea.* [S. G. 766]

Re-entry consists of partial doubling within the large star to the right of airman's head. The one illustrated is (R. 7/7), a similar re-entry occurs on (R. 9/5).

V4

766   6d. – V4. Re-entry   ...   .   5·0

1958 (3 Nov). *Centenary of Hawke's Bay Province.* [S. G. 768/70]

V5

3d. White flaw in sea above second A of " ZEALAND " (Cylinder 7 (stop), R. 10/2).

769   3d. – V5. White flaw in sea   ...   .   3·25

1959 (2 Mar). *Centenary of Marlborough Province.* [S. G. 772/4]

V17

2d. Extensive retouching in arc of bow and bow-sprit (R. 14/3).

772   2d. – V17. Retouch   ...   .   4·00

1959 (16 Sept). *Health.* [S. G. 776/7c]

/6

2d. A retouch occurs on the lower part of the bird's left wing (R. 5/6).

776   2d. + 1d. – V6. Wing retouch   ...   .   4·50

1960 (11 July–1 Sept)–66. *Pictorials.* [S. G. 781E/802]

ZFAL

/7

2d. " F " for " E " in " ZEALAND ". Occurs on (R. 3/1, black Pl. 2).

KOWHAI-NGUT'-KAKA

KOWHAI-NGUTU-KAKA

V22 2d. Damaged second " U " in " NGUTU ", later retouched (R. 9/12 black Pl. 3).
V23

V24
2d. White spur on " 2 " (R. 16/11 green Pl. 5).

V30
4d. White spot below " D " of " ZEALAND " (R. 9/9 blue Pl. 3). Later retouched.

V25   V26

8d. Lower left-hand leaf damaged at right, later retouched (R. 1/9 green Pl. 1).

V31
8d. White spot of third lower leaf from left, later retouched (R. 1/1 green Pl. ?).

V14
3s. Retouch in sky appearing as a dark cloud (R. 1/6).

783E	2d. – V7. "ZFALAND"	...	...	...	25·00
	– V22. Damaged "U"	...	...	...	5·00
	– V23. Retouched "U"	...	...	...	4·50
	– V24. Spur on "2"	...	...	...	4·00
786E	4d. – V30. Spot below "D"	...	...	...	1·75
789E	8d. – V25. Damaged leaf	...	...	...	3·50
	– V26. Retouched leaf	...	...	...	3·50
	– V31. Spot on leaf	...	...	...	3·50
799E	3s. – V14. Sky retouch	...	...	...	18·00

1962 (1 June). *Centenary of New Zealand Telegraph System.* [S. G. 810/11]

V8

3d. A damaged plate caused a green dotted line to appear below the hand (R. 14/1).

V13

3d. Damage to the plate also caused a large green spot to appear on the back of the hand (R. 11/2).

810   3d. – V8. Dotted line variety   ...   .   2·50
      – V13. Spot on hand variety   ...   .   3·00

1962 (15 Oct). *Christmas.* [S. G. 814]

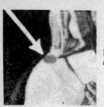

Blob on Virgin's right shoulder appears as stain (Pl. 1A, R. 7/1).

V36

814   2½d. – V36. Stain on shoulder   ...   .   1·25

1963 (7 Aug). *Health.* [S. G. 815E/16a]

V27

V28

2½d. Weak entry at bottom occurs on Pl. 1B, R. 10/10 which was re-entered in the later ultramarine shade.

3d. A prominent flaw (*see illustration*) exists between the index and middle fingers of Prince Andrew's right hand. Later attempts to remove the flaw met with only partial success (Pl. 1B, R. 3/5).

V9

815E   2½d. + 1d. – V27. Weak entry   ...   .   3·50
                    – V28. Re-entry   ...   .   3·00
816   3d. + 1d. – V9. Flaw on hand. *From*   ...   ...   12·00

1963 (14 Oct). *Christmas.* [S. G. 817E]

2½d. An orange-coloured flaw occurs above the donkey's nose (Pl. 1B. R. 3/8).

V10

817E   2½d. – V10. Nose flaw   ...   .   1·50

1963 (3 Dec). *Opening of COMPAC.* [S. G. 820]

A break in the cable joining the " E " occurs on (R. 10/4).

V11

820   8d. – V11. Broken cable   ...   .   6·50

1964 (1 May). *Road Safety Campaign.* [S. G. 821]

A yellow-coloured flaw exists between the " w " and " z " of " NEW ZEALAND " resembling an apostrophe (R. 3/2).

V12

821   3d. – V12. Apostrophe flaw   ...   .   3·00

1965 (14 Apr). *50th Anniv. of Gallipoli Landing.* [S. G. 826/7]

V15

V16

4d. White dot in sea over " A " of " ZEAL " (R. 9/4).

Disturbance under left leg of " A " of " ZAC " (R. 10/7).
    This exists in a number of states (eight have been reported) probably due to progressive plate damage over a long run. The illustration shows the first state, being a fleck of colour like a bird, and later states have from two to five brown spots.

826   4d. – V15. Flaw in sea   ...   .   2·50
              – V16. Disturbance   ...   .   2·50

1965 (28 Sept). *International Co-operation Year.* [S. G. 833E]

4d. Extra coloured dot below emblem (R. 4/1).

V29

833E   4d. – V29. Dot flaw   ...   .   2·50

1967 (10 July)–69. *Decimal Currency.* [S. G. 845/62]

V37

V32

2c. A flaw on the right-hand green branch, at tip of red flower, is seen as a white leaf (Pl. 1A, R. 18/3).

2½c. Large blue flaw on left flower (R. 8/5 blue Pl. 2A).

V33

V40

2½c. White projection on foot of large " 2 " (R. 10/6 blue Pl. 2A).

3c. Retouch showing as blue line flanked by an area of " washed-out " colouring (R. 19/1 blue Pl. 1A).

V34

25c. White spot under "G" of " MAKING " (R. 8/6 brown Pl. 1A).

847	2c. – V37. White leaf	...	...	...	...	1·00
848E	2½c. – V32. Blue flaw on flower	...	...	...	1·50
	– V33. Serif to large "2"	...	...	...	1·50
849E	3c. – V40. Retouch below "3"	...	...	...	1·50
858	25c. – V34. Spot under "G"	...	...	...	3·25

1967–69. *New Values.* [S. G. 870/9]

V46

7½c. "Cut" on trout's belly, beneath the top fin (Pl. 1A, R. 9/2).

871	7½c.	Wmk sideways inverted				
		– V46. Cut fish	...	...	...	1·75
	a.	Wmk upright				
		– V46. Cut fish	...	...	...	1·75

1967 (10 Oct). *Centenary of Royal Society of New Zealand.* [S. G. 881E/2]

4c. Large white flaw to right of fern. Multipositive flaw affecting all plates (R. 1/10).

V35

There are numerous other varieties on both values and some may not be fully constant.

881E	4c. – V35. Fern flaw	...	...	...	...	2·50

1969 (8 Apr). *Centenary of New Zealand Law Society.* [S. G. 894/6]

10c. Red blotch on shoulder of Maori figure. (Pl. 1 (×4), R. 7/5).

V41

895	10c. – V41. Red blotch on shoulder	...	...	...	3·00

1969 (3 June). *Centenary of Otago University.* [S. G. 897/8]

3c. Black spot over roof appears as chimney pot (Pl. 1 and 1a, R. 2/9).

V42

897	3c. – V42. "Chimney pot"	...	...	...	1·50

STAMP VARIETIES EXPLAINED

In this *Stanley Gibbons Guide* James Watson presents the knowledge essential to every philatelist—the various processes that are used to print stamps. By demonstrating just how varieties occur, he enables collectors to assess their relative importance and shows what contribution, if any, they can make to philatelic study. See the preliminary pages of this Catalogue for details of the current edition.

1969 (9 Oct). *Bicentenary of Capt. Cook's Landing in New Zealand.* [S. G. 906/10]

V38

V39

18c. Purple-brown flaw below first "o" of "COOK" appears as "Q" (R. 6/6).

18c. Circular retouch above "RH" to right of lowest flower (R. 9/7).

908 18c. – V38. "CQOK" ... ... 10·00
          – V39. Retouch ... ... 10·00

1972 (2 Feb). *International Vintage Car Rally.* (S. G. 972/7)

4c. Broken "O" in "INTERNATIONAL" (Pl. 1A, R. 9/4).

V43

973 4c. – V43. Broken "o" ... ... 2·50

1975 (6 Aug). *Health.* [S. G. 1079/81]

5c.+1c. White patch beneath boy's pocket (Pl. 1B, R. 3/6).

V45

1081 5c. + 1c. – V45. White patch ... ... 2·00

1977 (23 Feb). *Silver Jubilee.* [S. G. 1137E]

Retouch behind Queen's head. Occurs only on right-hand stamp in the sheet.

V47

MS 1137E 8c. × 5 – V47. Retouch behind head ... 2·00

1977 (19–21 Apr). *Surcharges.* [S. G. 1143/4E]

V48

V49

7c. on 3c. White ring on the obliterating square resembles a "Rivet Head".

8c. on 4c. Extra dot to right of "8c".

1143 7c. on 3c. – V48. "Rivet head" ... ... 1·00
1144 8c. on 4c. – V49. Extra dot ... ... 1·00

1977 (3 Aug). *Health.* [S. G. 1149/52]

7c.+2c. Flaw on girl's right wrist resembles a bracelet (Pl. 1A, R. 10/5).

V50

1149 7c. + 2c. – V50. Bracelet on girl's wrist ... ... 2·00

1978 (8 Mar). *Centenaries.* [S. G. 1160/3]

CENTENARY

12c. Serif on "E" of "CENTENARY" (Pl. 1A, R. 1/8).

V51

1162 12c. – V51. Serif on "E" ... ... 2·00

1978 (26 Apr). *Land Resources and Centenary of Lincoln College of Agriculture.* [S. G. 1164/9]

30c. Broken "r" in "Dairy" (Pl. 1A, R. 9/1).

V52

1169 30c. – V52. Broken "r" ... ... 3·00

Nigeria

1953 (1 Sept)–58. *Views.* [S. G. 69/80]

V6

1d. Die Ia. Black line from lance to neck of horse at left (R. 8/3).

2d. Major re-entry showing duplication of steps of the terraces (Pl. 3, R. 1/5).

V1

V2

Partial doubling of the 2d. and dot (R. 5/2 and 3). Also known on booklet panes.

V3

Flaw resembling an extra figure of a man (R. 5/4).

70Ea	1d. (Die Ia)		
	– V6. Line from lance to horse's neck	...	1·75
69e	2d. – V1. Re-entry	...	35·00
72a	2d. slate-violet (Type A)		
	– V2. Partial double 2d.	...	2·50
	– V3. Extra figure	...	3·00
	b. Slate-blue (shades) (Type A) (Col.)		
	– V2. Partial double 2d.	...	2·50
	– V3. Extra figure	...	3·25

1959 (14 Mar). *Attainment of Self-Government, Northern Region of Nigeria.* [S. G. 83/84]

V4

3d. Partial doubling of " 15TH MARCH. 1959." (R. 1/6).

83	3d. – V4. Re-entry			...	3·00

1962 (27 Oct). *International Trade Fair, Lagos.* [S. G. 122/5]

V7   V8

2s.6d. Yellow flaw on right of centre left oil derrick (R. 7/2). | Very similar flaw on left of same oil derrick (R. 5/4).

125	2s.6d. – V7. Derrick flaw at right			4·00
	– V8. Derrick flaw at left			4·00

1963 (21 June). *"Peaceful Use of Outer Space".* [S. G. 131/2]

V11   V12

6d. & 1s.3d. White blobs in the background appear as " extra stars " (6d. Pl. 1A, R. 1/2; 1s.3d. Pl. 1B, R. 1/1). A similar variety occurs on R. 1/2 (Pl. 1B) of the 1s.3d.

131	6d. – V11. Extra star	...			2·50
132	1s.3d. – V12. Extra star	...			2·75

1965 (1 Nov)–66. *Wild Life.* [S. G. 172/85]

FIEVET £1 Designers name at foot, " FIEVET ", is broken (R.4/2).

V 15

185	£1 – V15. Broken imprint			14·00

1966 (11 Jan). *Commonwealth Prime Ministers' Meeting, Lagos.*
[S. G. 186]

Flaw on the bank's roof resembles a man
(R. 8/5)

V16

186   2s.6d. – V16. Man on roof   ...   .   2·50

1968 (1 Oct). *5th Anniv. of Federal Republic.*   [S. G. 211/2]

4d. and 1s.6d. Green stroke on white dove's
tail (Pl. 1B, R. 5/3).

V9

1s.6d. White dot below " N " of
" NIGERIA " (R. 5/8).

V10

211   4d. – V9. Green tail feather   ...   .   1·60
212   1s.6d. – V9. Green tail feather   ...   .   2·75
            – V10. Dot below "N"   ...   .   2·75

1969–72. *Wild Life as Nos. 173 etc.*   [S. G. 220/30]

V13
3d. White patch on
    cheetah's chest
    (Pl. 1A, R. 9/1).

V14
9d. In the imprint the
    " td ' of " Ltd "
    is omitted (Pl. 1B,
    R. 10/2).

223   3d. – V13. Patch on Cheetah   ...   .   5·00
226   9d. – V14. "td" omitted   ...   .   2·75

THE ELIZABETHAN

Uniform with this volume, the *Elizabethan Specialised
Stamp Catalogue* covers all other aspects of the stamps
of the present reign, from both Great Britain and the
British Commonwealth, in considerable detail. See the
preliminary pages of this Catalogue for details of this
annual publication.

POSTAGE DUE STAMPS

1959 (4 Jan). Wmk Script CA.   [S. G. D1/5]

V5   V5a

6d. Complete break in lower outer frame line surrounding value
    (R. 8/4). In its second stage it was repaired with a thin line
    on No. D9.

D4   6d. – V5. Frame break   ...   .   5·00

1961 (1 Aug). Wmk Multiple FN.   [S. G. D6/10E]

D9   6d. – V5a. Frame repair   ...   .   5·00

Niue

1967 (10 July) *Decimal Currency.*   [S. G. 135E/8E]

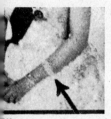

NIUE
V1

| | $1 and $2 | The bottom half of the left leg of " N " of " NIUE " is missing entirely (R. 8/9 and 10). |

| 137E | $1 – V1. Short "N" | ... | ... | ... | ... | ... | 7·00 |
| 138E | $2 – V1. Short "N" | ... | ... | ... | ... | ... | 10·00 |

1969 (27 Nov). *Flowers.*   [S. G. 141/150]

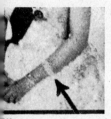

20c. Yellow band across arm appears as bandage (R. 9/5)

V2

| 49 | 20c. – V2. Bandaged arm | ... | ... | ... | ... | 3·50 |

Norfolk Island

1958 (1 July). *Surcharges.*   [S. G. 21/22]

7ᵈ   7d. Sliced "d" on right side of down-
V1   stroke (R. 3/2).

            Broken bottom bar of overprint
            near left end, later corrected (R. 8/1).
V2

21   7d. on 7½d. – V1. Sliced "d"   ...   .   14·00
         – V2. Bottom bar broken ...   .   15·00

1959 (7 Dec). *150th Anniv. of Australian Post Office.*   [S. G. 23]

            5d. Slight vertical scratches between inner
            and outer frame lines at left (R. 2/4).

V4

23   5d. on 4d. – V4. Frame scratch   ...   .   4·00

1964 (24 Feb–28 Sept). *Views.*   [S. G. 51/54]

Normal   V3

8d. The "extra craft" flaw consists of black spots over the sea
to the right of the ship (R. 6/6).

52   8d. – V3. "Extra craft"   ...   .   5·00

1966 (14 Feb). *Decimal Currency.*   [S. G. 60/71]

V6   V12
$1 Retouch in top frame $1 Broken top to figure
above "R" of   "1". (R. 1/5, early
"NORFOLK" (R. 5/4).   examples are not so
                            marked).

---

71   $1 on 10s. – V6. Retouched frame   ...   .   17·00
     a.   Value tablet smaller, 6½ × 4 mm.
          – V6. Retouched frame   ...   .   17·00
          – V12. "l" broken at top   ...   .   17·00

1967–68. *Ships.*   [S. G. 77/90]

V5   V7

1c. Slanting black line   5c. Black flaw in front of
in sail to upper left   man before the mast
of flag on bowsprit   appears as an extra crew
appears as a spar   member (R. 1/4).
(R.5/4).

            7c. White flaw in hull (R.1/1).

V11

77   1c. – V5.   Spar to sail   90
81   5c. – V7.   Third man in boat ...   .   1·60
82   7c. – V11. Flaw in hull   ...   .   2·00

1969 (29 Sept). *125th Anniv. of the Annexation of Norfolk Island to
Van Diemen's Land.*   [S. G. 100/1]

            30c. "F" for first "E" in
                "DIEMEN'S" (Pl. 1A, R. 8/5).

V8

101   30c. – V8. "DIFMEN'S"   ...   .   8·5

1970–71. *Birds.* [S. G. 103/117]

1c. Grey line appears as extra branch (R.1 Nos. 2/3).

V9

103 1c. – V9. Extra branch flaw (pair) ... ... 1·10

1970 (29 Apr). *Capt. Cook Bicentenary (2nd issue).* [S. G. 118/19]

5c. White spot in " N " of " Norfolk " (R. 5/2).

V10

118 5c. – V10. White spot on "N" ... ... 2·00

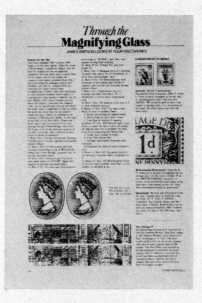

North Borneo

1954–60. *Views.*   [S. G. 372/86]

V1 5c. Strong retouch on the Queen's face from the neck to the
       forehead where the normal background of lines of dots
       appears as an irregular pattern of dots. Different printings
       disclose two states of this retouch which are difficult to
       distinguish (Pl. 1, R. 4/3).

376   5c. – V1. Retouch on face. *From*   ...   .   2·10

Northern Rhodesia

1953 (30 May). *Centenary of Birth of Cecil Rhodes.*   [S. G. 54/58]

V1

½d. Re-entry consists of doubling of
" CECIL " (Pl. 1B, R. 10/6). *Price
is for Plate No. block of four.*

54   ½d. – V1. Re-entry   ...   .   3·50

Nyasaland

1953 (1 Sept)–54. *Queen Elizabeth II.* [S. G. 173/87]

½d. Re-entry at top left corner chocolate Pl. 1, R. 1/7).

Normal   V1

173a ½d. – V1. Re-entry ...   .   4·00

1964 (1 Jan). *Pictorials.* [S. G. 199/210]

6d. White flaw resembling extra brim to hat (Cyl 1A, R. 8/2). This was corrected on the issue inscribed " MALAWI ".

V2

TIMBER

V3

1s. Broken " B " in " TIMBER " (Cyl 1A, R. 4/2). This was corrected on the issue inscribed " MALAWI ".

5s. Cloud reflection is elongated (R. 5/3).

V5

204 6d. – V2. Extra brim to hat ...   .   3·00
205 1s. – V3. Broken "B" in "TIMBER" ...   .   3·00
208 5s. – V5. Cloud reflection elongated   ...   ...   3·75

Pahang

1965 (15 Nov). *Flowers.* Wmk PTM (Upright). [S. G. 87E/93]

2c. Retouch below Sultan's chin almost looks like a grey beard (Pl. 1B, R. 7/7).

V1

V2 and V4/15. See corresponding varieties on Johore Nos. 166/72.

87E	1c. – V2.	Caterpillar flaw	...	...	...	90
	– V4.	Line through petal	...	...	...	1·60
	– V5.	Dot under "A" ...	...	...	...	1·60
	– V9.	Spot above 'VANDA"	...	...	...	1·60
	– V10.	Dot on flower ...	...	...	...	1·60
	– V11.	Dot on top flower	...	...	...	1·60
88	2c. – V1.	Retouch	...	...	...	90
89	5c. – V6.	Short stroke	...	...	...	1·60
	– V12.	"A" and "P"	...	...	...	1·60
	– V13.	Dot under "H" ...	...	...	...	1·60
	– V14.	Dot under "5c"	...	...	...	1·60
	– V15.	Flaws on country name	...	...	1·90
91E	10c. – V7.	Short stroke	...	...	...	2·00
93	20c. – V8.	Brown blotches	...	...	...	2·00

1970 (27 May). As Nos. 87 and 91 but wmk PTM (sideways). [S. G. 94/95]

94	1c. – V2.	Caterpillar flaw	...	...	...	1·00
	– V4.	Line through petal	...	...	...	1·60
	– V5.	Dot under "A"	...	...	...	1·60
	– V9.	Spot above "VANDA"	...	...	...	1·60
	– V10.	Dot on flower	...	...	...	1·60
	– V11.	Dot on top flower	...	...	...	1·60
95	10c. – V7.	Short stroke	...	...	...	2·50

Pakistan

1958 (10 Dec). *Tenth Anniv. of Declaration of Human Rights.* [S. G. 99/100]

1½a. Dot over "h" of "Rights" (R. 7/1).

V1

99   1½a. – V1. Dot over "h"   ...   .   2·40

1958 (28 Dec). *Second Pakistan Boy Scouts National Jamboree, Chittagong.* [S. G. 101/2]

2nd NATIONAL JAMBOREE

V2

6p. Dropped "R" in "JAMBOREE" (R. 1/10).

PAKISTA N

V3

8a. Spaced "N" in "PAKISTAN" (R. 7/8).

Dec. 58—Jan·59

V4

8a. Hyphen for stop after "Jan" (R. 1/4 and R. 3/4).

Other minor varieties in this overprint exist owing to defective type.

101   6p. – V2. Dropped "R"   ...   .   1·25
102   8a. – V3. Spaced "N"   ...   .   2·00
      – V4. Hyphen for stop   ...   .   1·50

1960 (23 Mar). *Map.* [S. G. 108/111E]

V8 6p. Re-entry. Practically the whole of the lettering is doubled (Pl. 1, R. 5/3).

8a. The Bengali inscription only, top right word, is doubled (Pl. 3 R. 15/1).

V11

V20

8a. Weak entry on bottom frame line (Pl. 3, R. 1/5).

108   6p. – V8. Re-entry   ...   .   2·40
110   8a. – V11. "Bengali" re-entry   ...   .   2·00
      – V20. Weak entry   ...   .   2·00

1960 (27 Oct). *Revolution Day.* [S. G. 116E/17]

Normal   V5

2a. Four instead of three dots under lower inscription (R. 6/1). This was later retouched but the extra dot was not completely removed and is listed as V6.

116E   2a. – V5. Extra dot   ...   .   1·25
       – V6. Dot retouched   ...   .   1·10

1960 (16 Nov). *Centenary of King Edward Medical College, Lahore.* [S. G. 118/19]

Normal   Retouch
V7 2a. Retouch in panel between "18" and "60" (R. 1/3).

118   2a. – V7. Retouch   ...   .   1·75

1961 (1 Jan). *Surharges.* [S. G. 122/7]

124   3p. on 6p. (108) – V8. Re-entry   ...   .   1·25

1962 (14 Aug). *Sports.* [S. G. 159/62]

PAKISTAN

V9

7p. The first "A" of "PAKISTAN" is much thicker than normal (R. 6/5).

159   7p. – V9. Thick "A"   ...   .   1·90

1966 (25 Dec). *90th Birth Anniv. of Mahomed Ali Jinnah.*
[S. G. 237/8]

15p. Break in the middle of " s " in " POSTAGE " (R. 2/2).

V12

237   15p. – V12. Sliced "s"   ...   .   1·10

1967 (1 Jan). *International Tourist Year.*   [S. G. 239]

Left-hand character of Urdu inscription has malformed right upright (R. 10/2).

V13

239   15p. – V13. Broken letter   ...   .   1·10

1967 (29 Jan). *4th National Scout Jamboree.*   [S. G. 241]

Malformed " P " appears as " F " in " PAISA " (R. 6/3).

V14

241   15p. – V14. "FAISA" for "PAISA"   ...   .   1·75

1967 (26 Sept). *Pakistan Exports.*   [S. G. 247/9]

10p. The left-hand character of the Bengali inscription, bottom left, is severed from the rest (R. 1/5).

V16

247   10p. – V16. Broken inscription   ...   ...   1·10

1967 (26 Dec). *The Fight Against Cancer.*   [S. G. 254]

Central orbit has a break to right of sword, below crab's leg (R. 2/4).

V15

254   15p. – V15. Broken orbit   ...   .   1·10

1968 (31 Jan). *Human Rights Year.*   [S. G. 255/6]

15p. " 5 " of value sliced at top right (R. 6/5).

V17

255   15p. – V17. Sliced "5"   90

1968 (7 April). *20th Anniv. of World Health Organization.*
[S. G. 258/9]

V10. Second "A" of "PAISA" omitted (R. 4/5).

258   15p. – V10. "PAIS" for "PAISA"   ...   .   1·00

1972 (7 Apr). *World Health Day.*   [S. G. 325]

LTH

Quotation mark after " HEALTH " is missing, only a small trace remaining (R.1/6).

V18

325   20p. – V18. Missing quotation mark   ...   ...   1·50

1972 (6 Sept). *National Blood Transfusion Service.*   [S. G. 336]

Cross on bottle is broken (R.5/10).

V19

336   20p. – V19. Broken cross   ...   .   1·40

OFFICIAL STAMPS

1961. *Surcharges.*   [S. G. Q68/73]

O70   3p. on 6p. – V8. Re-entry   ...   .   1·25

Papua New Guinea

POSTAGE DUE STAMPS

1957 (29 Jan). *Surcharges.*   [S. G. 16/17]

4ᵈ   4d. The left-hand end of the horizontal
V1   bar to the " 4 " is rounded (R. 4/6).

7ᵈ   **7ᵈ**   **7ᵈ**

V3   **V4**   Normal

7d. V3. Broken serif at bottom of " d " (R. 6 Nos. 1 and 4).
  V4. Elongated serif to " d " and blunted serif to " 7 " (R. 6
  Nos. 2 and 5).

(Price for strip of three comprising V3, V4 and normal £8).

These interesting varieties demonstrate that the surcharge was
done in a setting of 18 (3 × 6) repeated on each half of the sheets

16	4d. on 2½d. – V1. Rounded "4"	...	...	...	2·75
17	7d. on 1s. – V3. Broken serif to "d" ...	...	...	3·00
	– V4. Elongated serif to "d"	...	...	3·00

1959 (1 Dec). *Surcharge.*   [S. G. 25]

5d. on ½d. Strong retouch in top left
corner (R. 5/1). The unsurcharged
stamp was badly worn but the
retouch only occurs in the special
printing made for surcharging.

V5

25	5d. on ½d. – V5. Corner retouch	...	...	...	3·25

1964 (5 Aug). *Health Services.*   [S. G. 57/60]

V6   **V7**

1s.2d. Retouch appears as   Major retouch to left of
  shadow behind second   top corner of bench (R.
  " A " in " PAPUA " (R.   5/2).
  5/2).

60	1s.2d. – V6. Retouch behind "A"	...	...	...	3·00
	– V7. Major retouch by bench ...	...	...	4·50

POSTAGE DUE STAMPS

1960 (1 Mar). *Surcharges.*   [S. G. D1/6]

POSTAL   The " c " of " CHARGES " is badly
CHARGES   damaged (R. 3/5). Believed to have been
V2   later corrected.

D3	3d. on ½d. – V2. Damaged "c"	...	...	...	19·00
D5	1s.3d. on 3½d. – V2. Damaged "c"	...	...	...	30·00
D6	3s. on 2½d. – V2. Damaged "c"	...	...	...	75·00

Penang

1954 (9 June)–57. *Queen Elizabeth II.* [S. G. 28/43]

V1

1c. Black flaw by Queen's mouth resembling cigarette end (R. 2/3).

| 28 | 1c. – V1. "Cigarette" flaw ... | ... | ... | ... | 2·50 |

1965 (15 Nov). *Flowers.* Wmk PTM (upright). [S. G. 66/72]

V2 and V4/15. See corresponding varieties on Johore Nos. 166/72.

66	1c. – V2.	Caterpillar flaw ...	...	...	...	1·00
	– V4.	Line through petal	...	...	...	1·40
	– V5.	Dot under "A" ...	...	...	...	1·40
	– V9.	Spot above "VANDA"	...	...	...	1·60
	– V10.	Dot on flower ...	...	...	...	1·60
	– V11.	Dot on top petal ...	...	...	...	1·60
68E	5c. – V6.	Short stroke	...	...	...	1·40
	– V12.	"A" and "P" joined	...	...	...	1·60
	– V13.	Dot under "H" ...	...	...	...	1·60
	– V14.	Dot under "5c" ...	...	...	...	1·60
	– V15.	Flaws on country name ...	...	...	1·90
70E	10c.	*grey and multicoloured*				
	– V7.	Short stroke	...	...	...	1·40
	Ea.	*Jet-black and multicoloured*				
	– V7.	Short stroke	...	...	...	1·40
72	20c. – V8.	Brown blotches ...				1·60

1970. As Nos. 66 and 70 but wmk PTM (sideways). [S. G. 73/74]

73	1c. – V2.	Caterpillar flaw ...	...	...	...	1·10
	– V4.	Line through petal	...	...	...	1·60
	– V5.	Dot under "A" ...	...	...	...	1·60
	– V9.	Spot above "VANDA"	...	...	...	1·60
	– V10.	Dot on flower ...	...	...	...	1·60
	– V11.	Dot on top petal ...	...	...	...	1·60
74	10c. – V7.	Short stroke	...	...	...	2·50

Penrhyn Island

1973 (24 Oct–14 Nov). *Overprints.* [S. G. 41/52]

V1	V2	V3
1c. to 50c. Bottom cross-stroke of the " E " of " NORTHERN " has broken away, the " E " now looking like an " F " (R. 4/4).	1c. to 50c. Gaps appear in the " o " of " NORTHERN " and the " o " now resembles a pair of brackets (R. 2/2, 3/2, 4/2).	$1, $2. The right up-stroke of the " N " of " PENRHYN " has been shortened (R. 5/4).

V4

$1, $2. The " E " of " PENRHYN " is shortened at the foot (R. 3/2, 4/2).

A. *Without fluorescent security marking. Gum arabic.*
B. *With fluorescent security marking. PVA gum.*

						A	B
41	1c. – V1.	Broken "E"	...	...	...	4·50	80
	– V2.	Brackets for "o"	...	...	...	3·50	60
42	2c. – V1.	Broken "E"	...	...	...	8·50	80
	– V2.	Brackets for "o"	...	...	...	6·50	60
43	3c. – V1.	Broken "E"	...	...	...	12·00	1·00
	– V2.	Brackets for "o"	...	...	...	8·50	70
44	4c. – V1.	Broken "E"	...	...	...	12·00	1·10
	– V2.	Brackets for "o"	...	...	...	8·50	80
45	5c. – V1.	Broken "E"	...	...	...	14·00	1·25
	– V2.	Brackets for "o"	...	...	...	10·00	90
46	6c. – V1.	Broken "E"	...	...	...	14·00	1·60
	– V2.	Brackets for "o"	...	...	...	10·00	1·10
47	8c. – V1.	Broken "E"	...	...	...	15·00	2·10
	– V2.	Brackets for "o"	...	...	...	12·00	1·50
48	15c. – V1.	Broken "E"	...	...	...	19·00	3·75
	– V2.	Brackets for "o"	...	...	...	15·00	2·40
49	20c. – V1.	Broken "E"	...	...	...	†	6·00
	– V2.	Brackets for "o"	...	...	...	†	3·75
50	50c. – V1.	Broken "E"	...	...	...	27·00	9·50
	– V2.	Brackets for "o"	...	...	...	22·00	6·50
51	$1 – V3.	Short "N"	...	...	...	45·00	9·00
	– V4.	Short "E"	...	...	...	40·00	9·00
52	$2 – V3.	Short "N"	...	...	...	80·00	11·00
	– V4.	Short "E"	...	...	...	65·00	11·00

† Does not exist in this state

Perak

1965 (15 Nov). *Flowers.* Wmk PTM (upright).   [S. G. 159E/65]

V2, V4/7 and V9/15. See corresponding varieties on Johore Nos. 166/72.

V16

V17

All values except 6c. and 15c. stud on top of crest missing (Pl. 1A, R. 5/10).

All values except 6c. and 15c. Top of crest missing (Pl. 1A, R. 6/10).

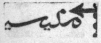

V18

All values except 6c. and 15c. Large dot to right of right-hand upright character of Malay word for "Malaysia" (Pl. 1A, R. 8/5).

V19

6c. and 15c. As V18 but flaw partly removed by retouching (Pl. 1A, R. 8/5). Subsequently removed on 15c.

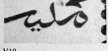

V20

6c. and 15c. Sultan's collar rounded at back (Pl. 1A, R. 3/2).

V21

6c. and 15c. Sultan's right eye missing (Pl. 1B, R. 5/7).

159E	1c. – V2.	Caterpillar flaw ...	...	...	...	...	1·10
	– V4.	Line through petal	...	...	...	...	1·40
	– V5.	Dot under "A" ...	...	...	...	...	1·40
	– V9.	Spot above "VANDA"	...	...	...	...	1·75
	– V10.	Dot on flower	...	...	...	...	1·75
	– V11.	Dot on top petal ...	...	...	...	...	1·75
	– V16.	Missing stud	...	...	...	...	1·75
	– V17.	Top of crest missing	...	...	...	...	1·75
	– V18.	Large dot ...	...	...	...	...	1·40
160E	2c. – V16.	Missing stud	...	...	...	...	1·75
	– V17.	Top of crest missing	...	...	...	...	1·75
	– V18.	Large dot ...	...	...	...	...	1·40
161E	5c. – V6.	Short stroke	...	...	...	...	1·40
	– V12.	"A" and "P" joined	...	...	...	...	1·75
	– V13.	Dot under "H"	...	...	...	...	1·75
	– V14.	Dot under "5c" ...	...	...	...	...	1·75
	– V15.	Flaw on country name	...	...	...	...	1·90
	– V16.	Missing stud	...	...	...	...	1·75
	– V17.	Top of crest missing	...	...	...	...	1·75
	– V18.	Large dot ...	...	...	...	...	1·40
	Eb.	*Grey-black*					
	– V6.	Short stroke	...	...	...	...	1·40
	– V12.	"A" and "P" joined	...	...	...	...	1·75
	– V13.	Dot under "H"	...	...	...	...	1·75
	– V14.	Dot under "5c" ...	...	...	...	...	1·75
	– V15.	Flaws on country name ...		...	...	...	1·90
	– V16.	Missing stud	...	...	...	...	1·75
	– V17.	Top of crest missing	...	...	...	...	1·75
	– V18.	Large dot ...	...	...	...	...	1·40
162	6c. – V19.	Large dot retouched	...	...	...	...	1·25
	– V20.	Sultan's collar rounded at neck ...			...	...	1·50
	– V21.	Sultan's eye is missing	...		...	...	1·50
163	10c. – V7.	Short stroke	...	...	...	...	1·75
	– V16.	Missing stud	...	...	...	...	1·75
	– V17.	Top of crest missing	...	...	...	...	1·75
	– V18.	Large dot ...	...	...	...	...	1·75
164	15c. – V19.	Large dot retouched	...	...	...	...	1·25
	– V20.	Sultan's collar rounded at neck ...			...	...	1·50
	– V21.	Sultan's eye missing	...		...	...	1·50
165	20c. – V16.	Stud missing	...	...	...	...	1·75
	– V17.	Top of crest missing	...	...	...	...	1·75
	– V18.	Large dot ...	...	...	...	...	1·50

In No. 161 *Eb* the contrast is between grey-black and the original pale black panel etc.

1970. As Nos. 159 and 163 but wmk PTM (sideways).
   [S. G. 166/7]

166	1c. – V2.	Caterpillar flaw ...	...	...	...	...	1·10
	– V4.	Line through petal	...	...	...	...	1·40
	– V5.	Dot under "A" ...	...	...	...	...	1·25
	– V9.	Spot above "VANDA"	...	...	...	...	1·75
	– V10.	Dot on flower	...	...	...	...	1·75
	– V11.	Dot on top petal ...	...	...	...	...	1·75
	– V16.	Stud missing	...	...	...	...	1·75
	– V17.	Top of crest missing	...	...	...	...	1·75
	– V18.	Large dot ...	...	...	...	...	1·50
167	10c. – V7.	Short stroke	...	...	...	...	1·75
	– V18.	Large dot ...	...	...	...	...	1·75

Perlis

1965 (15 Nov). *Flowers.* Wmk PTM (upright).　　　[S. G. 41/47]

Varieties: V2 and V4/15. See corresponding varieties on Johore Nos. 166/72.

V3

V16

All values except 6 and 15c. Small black dot beside top of left-hand character of Malay inscription at top (Pl. 1A, R. 2/3).

1c. and 2c. Break occurs in the left-hand character of Malay inscription at top (Pl. 1A, R. 10/10).

15c. Black line flaw next to the 1 of 15 (Pl. 1B, R. 10/1).

V17

41	1c. – V2.	Caterpillar flaw	...	...	...	1·40
	– V3.	Dot by character	...	...	...	1·40
	– V4.	Line through petal	...	...	...	1·40
	– V5.	Dot under "A"	...	...	...	1·40
	– V9.	Spot above "VANDA"	...	...	...	1·60
	– V10.	Dot on flower	...	...	...	1·60
	– V11.	Dot on top petal	...	...	...	1·60
	– V16.	Broken character	...	...	...	1·40
42	2c. – V3.	Dot by character	...	...	...	1·40
	– V16.	Broken character	...	...	...	1·40
43	5c. – V3.	Dot by character	...	...	...	1·40
	– V6.	Short stroke	...	...	...	1·40
	– V12.	"A" and "P" joined	...	...	...	1·60
	– V13.	Dot under "H"	...	...	...	1·60
	– V14.	Dot under "5c"	...	...	...	1·60
	– V15.	Flaws by country name	...	...	...	1·90
45	10c. – V3.	Dot by character	...	...	...	1·40
	– V7.	Short stroke	...	...	...	1·40
46	15c. – V17.	Black line flaw	...	...	...	1·40
47	20c. – V3.	Dot by character	...	...	...	1·60
	– V8.	Brown blotches	...	...	...	1·60

Pitcairn Islands

1961 (15 Nov). *Centenary of Return of Pitcairn Islanders from Norfolk Island.*   [S. G. 29/31]

6d. Right-angled line over top right of crown (R. 4/2).

V1

30   6d. – V1. Right-angle over crown   ...   .   6·50

1964 (5 Aug). *Pictorials.*   [S. G. 36/47]

V2   V8   V9

½d. V2. Large blue spot between eye-brows (Pl. 1A, R. 1/5). This was corrected for the decimal currency overprinted issue. This stamp also has an area of retouching to the right of the boat's mast.

½d. V8. Straight black line extends from upper right of diadem to edge of medallion (Pl. 1A, R. 2/5).

½d. V9. Curved black line extends from top of diadem to edge of medallion (Pl. 1A, R. 2/6).

Varieties V2, 8/9 are progressive flaws.   V8/9 are more pronounced on No. 69.

V13   V18

½d. Black flaw appears as grave accent over " A " of small " PITCAIRN " (R. 4/3).

½d. Patch over " G " of " LONGBOAT " (Pl. 1A R. 4/5).

1s.6d. Large spot on fork of branch (Pl. 1A, R. 6/1).

V3

V4   V10

2s.6d. White spots around Queen's forehead (Pl. 1A, R. 4/1). This was corrected for the decimal currency over-printed issue.

2s.6d. Grey scar on Queen's neck just above necklace (Pl. 1A, R. 3/6).

36   ½d. – V2.   Spot between eye-brows   ...   ...   2·10
       – V8.   Straight diadem flaw   ...   ...   2·10
       – V9.   Curved diadem flaw   ...   ...   2·10
       – V13. Accent over "A"   ...   ...   2·10
       – V18. Patch over "G"   ...   ...   2·10
45   1s.6d. – V3.   Spot on fork of branch   ...   ...   15·00
46   2s.6d. – V4.   Spots on forehead   ...   ...   16·00
       – V10. Mole on neck   ...   ...   16·00

1965 (24 Oct). *International Co-operation Year.*   [S. G. 51E/52E]

V6. Broken leaves. See V6 of Antigua.

1s.6d. Spot below Queen's lip (Pl. A1–A1, R. 12/4).

V21

51E   1d. – V6.   Broken leaves ...   .   5·50
52E   1s.6d. – V6.   Broken leaves ...   .   40·0
          – V21. Spot below lip ...   .   35·00

1966 (24 Jan). *Churchill Commemoration.*   [S. G. 53/56]

V7. Dot by St. Paul's. See V2 of Ascension.

53   2d. – V7. Dot by St. Paul's   ...   .   3·50
54   3d. – V7. Dot by St. Paul's   ...   .   8·00
55   6d. – V7. Dot by St. Paul's   ...   .   19·00
56   1s. – V7. Dot by St. Paul's   ...   .   30·00

1966 (20 Sept). *Inauguration of W.H.O. Headquarters, Geneva.*   [S. G. 59/60]

V5. Dotted "r" in "Headquarters". See V5 of Dominica.
59   8d. – V5. Dotted "r"   ...   .   10·0

1967 (1 Mar). *Bicentenary of Pitcairn Islands' Discovery.*
[S. G. 64/68]

½d. Top left corner of yellow panel shaved off (R. 2/2).

V11

64 ½d. – V11. Damaged panel ... ... 1·60

1967 (10 July). *Decimal Currency.* [S. G. 69E/81]

69E ½c. on ½d. – V8. Straight diadem flaw ... ... 1·75
– V9. Curved diadem flaw ... ... 1·75
– V13. Accent over "A" ... ... 1·75
– V18. Patch over "G" ... ... 1·75
78 25c. on 1s.6d. – V3. Spot on fork of branch ... ... 8·00
79 30c. on 2s.6d. – V10. Mole on neck ... ... 10·00

1967 (7 Dec). *150th Death Anniv. of Admiral Bligh.* [S. G. 82E/4]

1c. Flaw on "H" of "BLIGH" appears as serif (Pl. 1B, R. 2/2).

V14

V22

1c. Broken "h" in "150th" (R. 1/2).

V23

1c. Line from sail points into sea (Pl. 1A, R. 3/1).

8c. Nick in frame at upper left (Pl. 1B, R. 1/3).

V12

82E 1c. – V14. Serif on "H" ... ... 1·75
– V22. Broken "h" ... ... 1·75
– V23. Line flaw ... ... 2·00
83 – V12. Damaged frame ... ... 3·25

1969 (17 Sept)–75. *Views.* [S. G. 94E/106b]

1c. Spot below " LA " of " ISLAND " in top inscription (R. 9/10).

V15

94E 1c. – V15. Spot below "LA" ... ... 1·50

1973 (14 Nov). *Royal Wedding.* [S. G. 131/2]

V16. Weak spot in background. See V2 of Belize.
V17. Cotton on dress. See V8 of Ascension.
131 10c. – V16. Weak spot in background ... ... 3·00
132 25c. – V17. Cotton on dress ... ... 3·75

1977 (6 Feb). *Silver Jubilee.* [S. G. 171/3]

8c. Fibre on top left of ships wheel surrounding face-value (Pl. 1B, R. 5/1).

V19

171 8c. – V19. Fibre on wheel ... ... 3·75

1977 (12 Sept). [S. G. 174/84]

20c. Diagonal line above woman grating bananas (Pl. 1A and 1D, R. 4/2).

V20

180 20c. – V20. Diagonal line ... ... 2·00

Qatar

All V numbers are those of Great Britain where the varieties are
illustrated. G.B. numbers in brackets.

1957 (1 Apr)–59. *Queen Elizabeth II.* Wmk St. Edward's Crown.
[S. G. 1/12]

4	9np. on 1½d. (542) – V9. Spot between rose and shamrock	2·00
5	12np. on 2d. (543b) – V10. Flaw between shamrock and diadem	2·00
	– V46. Dot on shamrock ...	2·00
8	25np. on 4d. (546) – V92. Dotted "R"	2·50
10	50np. on 9d. (551) – V5. Frame break at upper right	5·50

1957 (18 Sept). *Castles.* Waterlow ptgs.   [S. G. 13I/15I]

15I	10r. on 10s. (538) – V8. Weak entry	40·00
	Type II – V8. Weak entry	95·00

1957 (1 Aug). *World Scout Jubilee Jamboree.*   [S. G. 16E/18]

16E	15np. on 2½d. (557) – V147. Retouch	7·50
17	25np. on 4d. (558) – V35. Solid pearl at right	6·50

Rhodesia

1965 (16 Aug). *Churchill Commemoration.* [S. G. 357]

Diagonal white scratch through sword (R. 2/1).

V1

357 1s.3d.—V1. Scratch through sword ... ... 8·50

1966 (17 Jan). *Independence overprints.* [S. G. 359/73]

V2. Dot after "LILY". See V3 of Southern Rhodesia.
V3. Dot over "IA". See V2 of Southern Rhodesia.
V4. Extra feather. See V1 of Southern Rhodesia.

364	6d. – V2. Dot after "LILY" ...	...	...	6·00
368	2s. – V3. Dot over "IA" ...	...	...	10·00
371	10s. – V4. Extra feather ...	...	...	32·00
373	5s. on 1s.3d. – V1. Scratch through sword ...		...	£140

1966 (2 May). *28th Congress of Southern Africa Philatelic Federation ("Rhopex").* [S. G. 388/92]

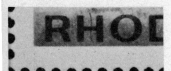

V5

3d. Hair on "H" in "RHODESIA" (1st printing, sheet "A").

MS392 – V5. Hair on "H" (*complete sheet with variety*) ... 60·00

1967 (12 July). *Tenth Anniv. of Opening of Rhodes National Gallery.* [S. G. 414/17]

9d. Dot flaw below hyphen between "CALAIS" and "RODIN" (Pl. 1A, R. 2/3, 2/8, 5/3, 5/8).

V6

9d. Dot flaw on "R" of "RODIN", which reads "BODIN" (Pl. 1A, R. 1/2, 1/7, 4/2, 4/7).

V7

415 9d. – V6. Dot flaw below hyphen ... ... 3·00
    – V7. Dot flaw on "R" ... ... 3·00

1967 (6 Sept). *Nature Conservation.* [S. G. 418/21]

RHODESIA

V8

Serif on "E" of "RHODESIA" (Pl. 1A, R. 1/1).

420 4d. – V8. Serif on "E" ... ... 3·00

Rhodesia and Nyasaland

1955 (15 June). *Centenary of Discovery of Victoria Falls.*
[S. G. 16/17]

V1

3d. A large green-coloured flaw occurs between the port wing of the aircraft and the date " 1955 " (R. 3/3).

16   3d. – V1. Wing flaw   ...   .   5·00

1960 (17 May). *Opening of Kariba Hydro-Electric Scheme.*
[S. G. 32/37]

V2

3d. A short white flaw occurs in the middle of the water just above " THE GORGE " (R. 4/6).

V3

1s.3d. A small white flaw just below the Queen's left ear on her ear-ring occurs on (R. 1/14). This flaw comes on the first shade only.

32   3d. – V2. Gorge flaw   ...   .   7·50
35E 1s.3d. – V3. Ear-ring flaw   ...   .   8·00

1963 (18 Feb). *World Tobacco Congress, Salisbury.*   [S. G. 43/46]

V4

3d. White flaw to top curve of " 3 " appears as a serif (R. 2/2).

43   3d. – V4. Serif to "3"   ...   .   2·50

Sabah

1965 (15 Nov)–68. *Flowers.* Wmk PTM (upright).   [S. G. 424/30]

V2 and V4/15. See corresponding varieties in Johore Nos. 166/72.

424	1c. – V2.	Caterpillar flaw	...	...	...	1·60
	– V4.	Line through petal	...	...	...	1·60
	– V5.	Dot under "A"	...		...	1·60
	– V9.	Spot above "VANDA"		...	...	1·60
	– V10.	Dot on flower	...	...	...	1·60
	– V11.	Dot on top petal	...		...	1·60
426	5c. – V6.	Short stroke	...	...	...	1·75
	– V12.	"A" and "P" joined	...	...	...	1·75
	– V13.	Dot under "H"	...	...	...	1·75
	– V14.	Dot under "5c"	...	...	...	1·75
	– V15.	Flaws on country name		...	...	1·90
428	10c. – V7.	Short stroke	...	...	...	2·10
430	20c. – V8.	Brown blotches	...	...	...	2·10

1970 (20 Nov). As No. 428 but wmk PTM (sideways).   [S. G. 431]

431   10c. – V7. Short stroke   ...   .   3·00

St. Christopher, Nevis and Anguilla

1954 (1 Mar)–63. Views. [S. G. 106a/118]

5c. Additional curly line at lower left of medallion (R. 9/5).

V1

111 5c. – V1. Curly line ... ... 2·75

1963 (20 Nov). Views. Wmk Block CA (upright). [S. G. 129E/44]

6c. Broken serif at top right of "N" of "Nevis" (R. 9/3).

Normal V4.

135E 6c. – V4. Broken serif to "N" ... ... 1·90
  Ei. Wmk inverted
   – V4. Broken serif to "N" ... ... 1·60

1964 (14 Sept). Arts Festival. [S. G. 145/6E]

FESTIVAI 25c. "FESTIVAI" for "FESTIVAL" and
ST KITTS "s" of "KITTS" shaved at right (R. 1/10).
V2

146E 25c. – V2. "FESTIVAI" ... ... 65·00

1965 (17 May). I.T.U. Centenary. [S. G. 147/8]

V3. Broken "U" in "TELECOMMUNICATIONS". See V1 of Antigua.
147 2c. – V3. Broken "U" ... ... 2·75
148 50c. – V3. Broken "U" ... ... 4·00

1965 (15 Oct). International Co-operation Year. [S. G. 149/50]

V5. Broken "Y" in "YEAR". See V3 of Antigua.
V7. Broken leaves. See V6 of Antigua.
149 2c. – V7. Broken leaves ... ... 2·75
150 25c. – V5. Broken "Y" ... ... 8·50
   – V7. Broken leaves ... ... 3·50

1966 (20 Sept). Inauguration of W.H.O. Headquarters, Geneva. [S. G. 161/2]

V6. Dotted "r" in "Headquarters". See V5 of Dominica.
161 3c. – V6. Dotted "r" ... ... 2·10

1970 (2 Feb)–74. Naval History. Wmk Block CA. [S. G. 206E/21E]

V8 V9
6c. Red patch to right of hat appears as a cloud (Pl. 1B. R. 4/5). 15c. Additional short red line on map to right of coin between it and "NEVIS" (Pl. 1B, R. 2/3).

212E 6c. – V8. Red Cloud ... ... 1·00
214 15c. – V9. Extra red line ... ... 1·90

1972 (20 Nov). Royal Silver Wedding. [S. G. 256E/7]

V10. Dot on curtain. See V4 of Anguilla.
256E 20c. – V10. Dot on curtain ... ... 2·75
257 25c. – V10. Dot on curtain ... ... 3·25

1973 (1 Oct). 70th Anniv. of First St. Kitts–Nevis Stamps. [S. G. 285/9]

4c. Dot in frame has increased to resemble a comma (R. 8/1).

V12

285 4c. – V12. "Comma" flaw ... ... 1·10

1973 (14 Nov). Royal Wedding. [S. G. 290/1]

V11. Weak spot in background. See V2 of Belize.
291 40c. – V11. Weak spot in background ... ... 2·75

THE ELIZABETHAN

All other aspects of the stamps of the present reign are fully covered by the *Elizabethan Specialised Stamp Catalogue*, published annually.

1975–77. *Naval History.* Wmk CA Diagonal.   [S. G. 322/31]

V13   V14

6c. Hole in hat (Pl. 3A,   6c. Green "mole" between
     R. 6/3).   eyebrows (Pl. 3A, R. 9/3).

328E   6c. – V13. Hole in hat   ...   .   1·25
       – V14. Mole between eyebrows   ...   ...   1·25

1977 (7 Feb). *Silver Jubilee.*   [S. G. 367/9]

          50c. Black apostrophe above
                "50c" (Pl. 1D, R. 3/2).

V15

367   50c. – V15. Black apostrophe   ...   .   4·50

St. Helena

1961 (12 Dec)–65. *Queen Elizabeth II.*   [S. G. 176/89]

1d. Lower fin and background behind it damaged (R. 3/3).

V1

7d. Two white dots appear half way along head of fish (R. 5/2).

V9

V2   V3

1s.6d. Small white spot on dark lines of shading on tail (R. 2/5).

1s.6d. Large white spot on blue background behind tail (R. 3/10).

176	1d. – V1. Damaged lower fin	...	...	...		2·10
	a. Chalky paper					
	– V1. Damaged lower fin	...	...	...		2·10
182	7d. – V9. Dots on head	...	...	...		2·50
185	1s.6d. – V2. Spot on tail	...	...	...		4·00
	– V3. Large spot behind tail	...	...	...		4·00

1965 (4 Jan). *First Local Post.*   [S. G. 193/6]

V4. 1d. Damaged " UA " of " JANUARY " (R. 5/4).
V5. 3d. Broken " h " of " 4th " (R. 5/7).
V6 3d., 6d., 1s.6d. Broken " N " in " JANUARY " (3d. R. 2/2 only 6d. R. 2/2 and R. 3/5; 1s.6d. R. 2/2 only).

193	1d. – V1. Damaged lower fin	...	...	...	3·25
	– V4. Damaged "UA"	...	...	...	3·25
194	3d. – V5. Broken "h"	...	...	...	2·25
	– V6. Broken "N"	...	...	...	2·25
195	6d. – V6. Broken "N"	...	...	...	2·25
196	1s.6d. – V2. Spot on tail	...	...	...	3·25
	– V3. Large spot behind tail	...	...	...	3·25
	– V6. Broken "N"	...	...	...	3·75

1965 (15 Oct). *International Co-operation Year.*   [S. G. 199/200E]

V7. Broken leaves. See V6 of Antigua.

199	1d. – V7. Broken leaves	...	...	...	...	3·00
200E	6d. – V7. Broken leaves	...	...	...	...	3·75

1966 (24 Jan). *Churchill Commemoration.*   [S. G. 201/4]

V8. Dot by St. Paul's. See V2 of Ascension.

202	3d. – V8. Dot by St. Paul's	...	...	...	2·50
204	1s.6d. – V8. Dot by St. Paul's	...	...	...	5·00

1966 (1 July). *World Cup Football Championship.*   [S. G. 205/6]

6d. Broken " N " in " HELENA " (R. 3/2).

V16

206	6d. – V16. Broken "N"	...	...	...	...	3·00

1966 (20 Sept). *Inauguration of W.H.O. Headquarters.* [S. G. 207/8]

V13. Dotted "r" in "Headquarters". See V5 of Dominica.

207	3d. – V13. Dotted "r"	...	...	...	...	2·50

1968 (4 Nov). *Pictorials.*   [S. G. 226E/40]

V10

¼d. Thin white curved line from cement mixer to " St. Helena " (Pl. 2A, R. 5/2).

V11   V12

Thin white patch at base of portrait (Pl. 2A, R. 5/1).

Black oblique line to right of road (Pl. 1B, R. 12/3).

226E	¼d. – V10. White line flaw	...	...	...	...	85
	– V11. Neck flaw	...	...	...	...	85
	– V12. Line right of road	...	...	...	85

1972 (20 Nov). *Royal Silver Wedding.*   [S. G. 289E/90E]

  V17. Dot on curtain. See V4 of Anguilla.
290E   16p. – V17. Dot on curtain ...   .   6·00

1973 (14 Nov). *Royal Wedding.*   [S. G. 295/6]

  V14. Cotton on dress. See V8 of Ascension.
  V15. Weak spot in background. See V2 of Belize.
295   2p. – V14. Cotton on dress ...   .   2·10
296   18p. – V15. Weak spot in background   ...   ...   2·10

St. Lucia

1964 (1 Mar). *Views.* [S. G. 197E/210]

1c. White flaw at foot of "L" of "St. LUCIA" (Pl. 1A, R. 4/6).

V1

197E   1c. – V1. "L" flaw   ...   .   1·10

1964 (23 Apr). *400th Anniv. of Birth of William Shakespeare.*
[S. G. 211]

White spot on lower left of crown (Pl. 1A, R. 4/4).

V2

211   10c. – V2. Flaw on crown   ...   .   2·50

1965 (17 May). *I.T.U. Centenary.* [S. G. 212/13]

V3. Broken "U" in "TELECOMMUNICATIONS". See V1 of Antigua.

212   2c. – V3. Broken "U"   ...   .   2·50
213   50c. – V3. Broken "U"   ...   .   4·50

1965 (25 Oct). *International Co-operation Year.* [S. G. 214/5]

V4. Broken "Y" in "YEAR". See V3 of Antigua.
V5. Broken leaves. See V6 of Antigua.

214   1c. – V5. Broken leaves   ...   .   2·50
215   25c. – V4. Broken "Y"   ...   .   11·00
        – V5. Broken leaves   ...   .   3·50

1966 (20 Sept). *Inauguration of W.H.O. Headquarters, Geneva.*
[S. G. 224/5]

V6. Dotted "r" in "Headquarters". See V5 of Dominica.
224   4c. – V6. Dotted "r"   ...   .   2·10

1967 (16 Oct). *Christmas.* [S. G. 241/2]

4c. Broken gold scroll under first "a" of "Madonna" (R. 2/8).

V7

25c. Broken gold scroll under hyphen (R. 5/7).

V8

241   4c. – V7. Broken scroll   ...   .   2·10
242   25c. – V8. Broken scroll   ...   .   2·10

1970 (2 Feb)–73. *Pictorials.* [S. G. 276/89a]

25c. Break in frameline above "C" of "LUCIA" (Pl. 1A, R. 1/5).

V9

284E   25c. – V9. Frameline break   ...   .   2·00

1972 (20 Nov). *Royal Silver Wedding.* [S. G. 343E/4E]

V10. Dot on curtain. See V4 of Anguilla.

35c. Spot on Parrot's tail (Pl. 2C–3C–3C–4C–2C–1B, R. 3/5).

V11

343E   15c. – V10. Dot on curtain ...   .   1·10
344E   35c. – V10. Dot on curtain ...   .   2·25
        – V11. Spot on Parrot's tail   ...   .   2·25

1973 (24 May). *Old Ships.* [S. G. 352/6]

15c. "t" of "St. Lucia" has a red bar descending from the cross-stroke (Pl. 1B, R. 1/4).

V13

352   15c. – V13. Extra bar   ...   .   2·00

1973 (17 Oct). *Christmas.*   [S. G. 361/4E]

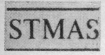

5c. Second " s " of " CHRISTMAS "
is broken (Pl. 1D, R. 1/5).

V14

361   5c. – V14. Broken "s"   ...   .   1·25

1973 (14 Nov). *Royal Wedding.*   [S. G. 365/6]

V12. Weak spot in background. See V2 of Belize.
366   50c. – V12. Weak spot in background   ...   ...   1·90

1977 (7 Feb). *Silver Jubilee.*   [S. G. 443/7]

$2 White flaw by
scroll at right
(R. 2/3).

V15

446   $2 – V15. White flaw ...   .   3·00

St. Vincent

1965 (17 May). *I.T.U. Centenary.* [S. G. 229/30]

V1. Broken "U" in "TELECOMMUNICATIONS". See V1 of Antigua.

229	4c. – V1. Broken "U"	...	...	...	...	4·00
230	48c. – V1. Broken "U"	...	...	...	...	8·50

1965 (16 Aug)–67. *Pictorials.* Wmk Block CA (upright).
[S. G. 231/45]

V3

4c. Strong retouch just below feet and extending to the " s " (Pl. 1A, R. 5/9).

234E 4c. – V3. Retouch ... ... 3·00

1966 (20 Sept). *Inauguration of W.H.O. Headquarters, Geneva.*
[S. G. 252/3]

V2. Dotted "r" in "Headquarters". See V5 of Dominica.

252 4c. – V2. Dotted "r" ... ... 3·00

1968 (20 Feb). As No. 234, but wmk Block CA sideways.
[S. G. 261]

261 4c. – V3. Retouch ... ... 3·00

1970 (12 Jan)–71. *Birds.* Wmk Block CA (upright). Chalk-surfaced paper.
[S. G. 285/300]

V9

1c. Heron's claw appears broken (Pl. 1A, R. 8/5).

V4

3c. Break in frame line over " P " of " Parrot " (Pl. 1A, R. 10/3).

V5

Normal

V10

4c. Spur on " u " of " Soufriere " (Pl. 1A, R. 3/3).

6c. Much of the shading of the bird's belly is missing (Pl. 1B, R. 3/5).

286E	1c.	(wmk sideways)					
		– V9. Broken claw	...	...	...	...	1·25
	a.	Glazed, ordinary paper					
		– V9. Broken claw	...	...	...	...	1·25
288	3c.	(wmk sideways)					
		– V4. Broken frame		...	...	...	1·50
289	4c. – V5. Spur on "u"			...	...	...	1·50
291	6c.	(wmk sideways)					
		– V10. Missing shading ...		...	...	...	2·00

1973. As No. 285 etc. Wmk Block CA. White, glazed paper.
[S. G. 361/8]

V8

5c. " B " for " R " in " Ramier " (Pl. 1B, R. 4/9).

362	3c. – V4. Broken frame		...	...	...	...	1·25
363	4c.	(wmk sideways)					
		– V5. Spur on "u"	...	...	...	...	1·50
364E	5c.	(wmk sideways)					
		– V8. "B" for "R"	...	...	...	...	2·00
365	6c. – V10. Missing shading ...		...	...	...	2·00

1973 (14 Nov). *Royal Wedding.* [S. G. 374/5]

THE St.

V6

50c. Broken " E " in " THE " (Pl. 1D, R. 1/2).

V7. Cotton on dress. See V8 of Ascension.

374	50c. – V6. Broken "E"	...	...	...	...	3·25
375	70c. – V7. Cotton on dress	...	...	...	...	3·25

1976 (8 Apr). *Surcharges.* [S. G. 485/6]

ENT,

V11

No. 486. " Comma " flaw after " ST. VINCENT " (Pl. 1D, R. 3/3).

486 90c. on 50c. – V11. "Comma" flaw ... ... 3·25

1977 (7 Feb). *Silver Jubilee.*   [S. G. 502/13]

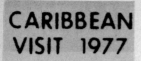

$2. Short "9" in overprint
(Pl. 9H, R. 2/1).

V14

513   $2 – V14. Short "9"   ...   .   3·00

1977 (2 June). *Carnival '77.*   [S. G. 531/5]

1977
All values. Missing serif on "1" in "1977" and
hyphen before "JULY" (Lower pane, R. 4/4).

V12

531   5c. – V12. Missing serif and hyphen   ...   ...   1·25
532   10c. – V12. Missing serif and hyphen   ...   ...   1·50
533   15c. – V12. Missing serif and hyphen   ...   ...   2·00
534   20c. – V12. Missing serif and hyphen   ...   ...   2·25
535    $1 – V12. Missing serif and hyphen   ...   ...   3·25

1977 (1 Sept). *50th Anniv. of St. Vincent Girl Guides.*   [S. G. 536/9]

30 – 19 $2. Broken hyphen in date above Lady Baden-
Powell's head (Pl. 1D, R. 2/4).

V13

539   $2 – V13. Broken hyphen   ...   .   3·75

Samoa

Sarawak

1967 (16 Jan). *Fifth Anniv. of Independence.*   [S. G. 274/7]

All values. Marked retouch above "SA" of "SAMOA" (R. 12/2).

V1

274	3d. – V1. Retouch	...	...	...	...	...	1·60
275	8d. – V1. Retouch	...	...	...	...	...	1·60
276	2s. – V1. Retouch	...	...	...	...	...	2·75
277	3s. – V1. Retouch	...	...	...	...	...	3·00

1967 (16 May). *Centenary of Mulinu'u as Seat of Government.*
    [S. G. 278/9]

8d. Blue spot over tree at right (R. 10/1).

V2

278	8d. – V2. Blue spot	...	...	...	...	1·60

1977 (11 Feb). *Silver Jubilee and Royal Visit.*   [S. G. 479E/82]

V3   **V4**

26s. Hair in   32s. White flaw in
"SPURS" (Pl.   "E" (Pl. 1A, R. 3/3).
1A, R. 5/3).

480	26s. – V3. Hair in "Spurs"	...	...	...	...	2·50
481E	32s. – V4. Flaw in "E"	...	...	...	...	2·75

1965 (15 Nov). *Flowers.*   [S. G. 212E/18]

Normal V1

1c., 5c., 10c., 20c. Left stroke of "M" in "MALAYSIA" is broken off at foot (Pl. 1B, R. 10/1).

V2 and V4, V6/15. See corresponding varieties of Johore Nos. 166/72.

V3

2c., 5c., 10c. Nick in cross (Pl. 1A, R. 2/10). This developed during printing.

212	1c. – V1.	Short "M"	...	...	...	...	1·60
	– V2.	Caterpillar flaw	...	...	...		1·60
	– V4.	Line through petal	...	...	...		1·60
	– V9.	Spot above "VANDA"	...	...	...		1·60
	– V10.	Dot on flower	...	...	...		1·60
	– V11.	Dot on top petal	...	...	...		1·60
213	2c. – V3.	Nick in cross	...	...	...		1·60
214	5c. – V1.	Short "M"	...	...	...		2·25
	– V3.	Nick in cross	...	...	...		2·25
	– V6.	Short stroke	...	...	...		2·25
	– V12.	"A" and "P" joined	...	...	...		2·25
	– V13.	Dot under "H"	...	...	...		2·25
	– V14.	Dot under "5c"	...	...	...		2·25
	– V15.	Flaws on country name	...	...		2·50
216E	10c. – V1.	Short "M"	...	...	...		2·25
	– V3.	Nick in cross	...	...	...		2·25
	– V7.	Short stroke	...	...	...		2·25
218	20c. – V1.	Short "M"	...	...	...		3·00
	– V8.	Brown blotches	...	...	...		2·25

Selangor

1965 (15 Nov). *Flowers.* Wmk PTM (upright).   [S. G. 136E/42E]

V2 and V4/15. See corresponding varieties on Johore Nos. 166/72.

6c. and 10c. Large black dot below right-hand upright character of Malay word for "Malaysia" (Pl. 1B. R. 4/1).

V1

V16

V17

6c. and 10c. V1 retouched but still visible as a pale lilac dot (Pl. 1B, R. 4/1).

10c. Red blob over " L " of " SELANGOR " below green leaf (Pl. ?, R. 7/3).

136E	1c. – V2.	Caterpillar flaw	...	...	...	1·60
	– V4.	Line through petal	...	...	...	1·60
	– V5.	Dot under "A"	...	...	...	1·60
	– V9.	Spot above "VANDA"	...		...	1·60
	– V10.	Dot on flower	...	...	...	1·60
138E	5c. – V6.	Short stroke	...	...	...	2·10
	– V12.	"A" and "P" joined	...	...	...	1·60
	– V13.	Dot under "H"	...	...	...	1·60
	– V14.	Dot under "5c"	...	...	...	1·60
	– V15.	Flaws on country name		...	...	1·90
139	6c. – V1.	Dot below Malay letter		...	...	2·60
	– V16.	Dot retouched	...	...	...	2·10
140E	10c. – V1.	Dot below Malay letter		...	...	2·10
	– V7.	Short stroke	...	...	...	2·10
	– V16.	Dot retouched	...	...	...	2·10
	– V17.	Blob over "L"	...	...	...	2·10
142E	20c. – V8.	Brown blotches	...	...	...	2·75

1970 (20 Nov). As Nos. 136 etc. but wmk PTM (sideways).
[S. G. 143/5]

143	1c. – V2.	Caterpillar flaw	...	...	...	1·60
	– V4.	Line through petal	...	...	...	1·60
	– V5.	Dot under "A"	...	...	...	1·60
	– V9.	Spot above "VANDA"	...	...	...	1·60
	– V10.	Dot on flower	...	...	...	1·60
	– V11.	Dot on top petal	...	...	...	1·60
144	10c. – V16.	Retouched	...	...	...	1·90
	– V17.	Blob over "L"	...	...	...	1·90
	– V7.	Short stroke	...	...	...	1·90
145	20c. – V8.	Brown blotches	...	...	...	3·00

Seychelles

1954 (1 Feb.)–61. *Pictorials.* [S. G. 174/88]

10c. Coloured flaw below lower left branch and background on either side very faint (R. 3/2).

V1

176E*a*	10c. *chalky blue*	– VI. Flaw on branch	...	...	1·90
	Eb Blue	– VI. Flaw on branch	...	...	2·10

1956 (15 Nov.). *Bicentenary of "La Pierre de Possession".* [S. G. 189/90]

40c. " Worm " flaw consists of curly line on stone (R. 1/8).

V2

Retouch extends diagonally downwards across pedestal and affects Queen's head and background between head and balustrade (R. 5/3).

V3

189	40c. – V2. "Worm" flaw	...	...	...	4·00
	– V3. Retouch on pedestal	...	...	4·00

1962 (21 Feb.)–68. *Pictorials.* [S. G. 196/212]

10r. Major retouch appears as dark cloud in top left-hand corner (Pl. 1B, R. 8/4).

V4

212	10r. – V4. Retouch	...	...	...	22·00

1965 (1 June). *I.T.U. Centenary.* [S. G. 218/19]

V5. Broken "u" in "TELECOMMUNICATIONS". See V1 of Antigua.

218	5c. – V5. Broken "u"	...	...	...	2·75
219	1r. 50 – V5. Broken "u"	...	...	...	5·00

1965 (25 Oct). *International Co-operation Year.* [S. G. 220/1]

V7. Broken leaves. See V6 of Antigua.

220	5c. – V7. Broken leaves	...	...	...	2·75
221	40c. – V7. Broken leaves	...	...	...	3·25

1966 (20 Sept). *Inauguration of W.H.O. Headquarters, Geneva.* [S. G. 228/9]

V6. Dotted "r" in "Headquarters". See V5 of Dominica.

228	20c. – V6. Dotted "r"	...	...	...	1·50

1967 (19 Sept). *Universal Adult Suffrage.* [S. G. 238/41]

UNIVERSAL

V8

15c. Black line from frame to " u " of " UNIVERSAL " (R. 7/3).

238	15c. – V8. Line variety	...	...	...	2·10

1969 (3 Nov)–75. *Views.* [S. G. 262E/79]

V10. "DE" omitted from "PIERRE DE POSSESSION" (R. 3/1). Occurs on 40c. surcharge (No. 303), but has not been seen on 30c. (No. 267).

268	40c. – V10. "DE" omitted	...	...	...	1·75

1971 (21 Dec). *Surcharge.* [S. G. 303/5]

303	40c. on 30c. – V10. "DE" omitted	...	...	2·40

1973 (14 Nov). *Royal Wedding.* [S. G. 321/2]

V9. Cotton on dress. See V8 of Ascension.

321	95c. – V9. Cotton on dress	...	...	...	2·50

Sierra Leone

1963 (1 Jan). *Flowers.*   [S. G. 242/54]

3d. Double dot variety consists of a dot over the " n " as well as the " i " of " Beniseed " (Cyl. 1A, R. 3/5).

V1

246   3d. – V1. Double dot ...   .   5·00

1963 (27 Apr). *Second Anniv. of Independence.*   [S. G. 257/69]

2ND YEAR OF INDEPENDENCE 19 PROGRESS 63 DEVELOPMENT
3d.
V2

Narrow setting
" 19 PROGRESS 63 " normally measures between 19 and 21 mm. but in the narrow setting it measures 17½ to 18 mm. with the " 19 " coming under the " IN ". Occurs on R. 5 Nos. 1, 2, 4, 5 and R. 10/4.

2nd Year
V3

10d. Printer's " quad " after " 2nd " (R. 4/11).

AIR MAIL 3/-
V4

3s. Printer's " quad " before " 3/– " (R. 3/7).

257   3d. on ½d. – V2. Narrow setting   60
258   4d. on 1½d. – V2. Narrow setting   60
259   6d. on ½d. – V2. Narrow setting   60
260   10d. on 3d. – V3. Quad after "2nd"   ...   ...   7·00
263   7d. on 1½d. – V2. Narrow setting   70
264   1s.3d. on 1½d. – V2. Narrow setting   ...   ...   1·25
266   3s. on 3d. – V4. Quad before "3/-"   ...   ...   4·50
268   11s. on 10s. – V2. Narrow setting   ...   ...   10·00
269   11s. on £1 – V2. Narrow setting £600

1963 (4 Nov). *Postal Commemorations.*   [S. G. 273/84]

* During the overprinting some of the errors were corrected and these only occur on part of the printing. The sheet positions (which vary in different values) are given in the list and semi-constant positions are indicated by an asterisk.

1853-1895-1963
V5

" 1895 "
This was an error for " 1859 ".

1853/1859/1963
V6

Obliques
Oblique strokes in place of hyphens between dates.

1853*1859*1963
V7

Asterisks
Asterisks in place of hyphens between dates.

1853 1859*1963
V8

Blank and asterisk
One place blank and asterisk in place of hyphens between dates. This has also been seen with two asterisks in both values. The 1s.6d. on ½d. has also been seen with asterisk and blank in this position.

1853·1859·1963
V9

Stops
Stops in place of hyphens between dates.

Newest G.P.O in West Africa
V10

Missing stop
The stop after " o " of " G.P.O." is omitted.

Newest G.P.O in West Africa.
V11

Dropped stop
The stop after " o " of " G.P.O." is omitted but now appears after " a " of " Africa ".

There are numerous other varieties in this issue.

(a) Postage.
273   3d. – V5. "1895" (R. 3/3) ...   .   2·50
             – V6. Obliques (R. 2/3)   ...   ...   2·50
274   4d. on 1½d. – V5. "1895" (R. 1/2) ...   .   3·50
             – V7. Asterisks (R. 3/2)   ...   ...   2·10
             – V8. Blank and asterisk (R. 11/4)* ...   3·00
             – V11. Dropped stop (R. 10/1)   ...   2·50
275   9d. on 1½d. – V7. Asterisks (R. 3/2) and (R. 11/4)   2·40
             – V11. Dropped stop (R. 10/1)   ...   2·50
276   1s. on 1s.3d. – V7. Asterisks (R. 3/4) and (R. 10/2)   3·00
277   1s.6d. on ½d. – V7. Asterisks (R. 11/1)   ...   3·75
             – V8. Blank and asterisk (R. 4/5)*   ...   5·00
278   2s. on 3d. – V5. "1895" (R. 4/10)   ...   8·00
             – V6. Obliques (R. 2/3)   ...   ...   5·00

(b) Air
279   7d. on 3d. – V5. "1895" (R. 3/6)* or (R. 4/4)   3·00
             – V9. Stops (R. 2/3) and (R. 4/10)   ...   2·10
             – V10. Missing stop (R. 1/2)   ...   2·50
280   1s.3d. – V5. "1895" (R. 7/3)*   ...   12·00
             – V7. Asterisks (R. 3/2) and (R. 10/4)   2·40
             – V10. Missing stop (R. 8/3)   ...   2·50
281   2s.6d. on 4d. – V5. "1895" (R. 7/3)*   ...   35·00
             – V7. Asterisks (R. 3/2) and (R. 10/4)   4·50
             – V10. Missing stop (R. 8/3)   ...   6·00
282   3s. on 3d. – V5. "1895" (R. 3/3)*   ...   £180
             – V9. Stops (R. 2/3) and (R. 4/10)   6·00
             – V10. Missing stop (R. 1/2)   ...   6·00
283   6s. on 6d. – V5. "1895" (R. 1/1)*   ...   40·00
             – V7. Asterisks (R. 3/2) and (R. 10/4)   5·
             – V10. Missing stop (R. 8/3)   ...   7·
284   £1 – V5. "1895" (R. 11/4)* £16
             – V7. Asterisks (R. 4/5) and (R. 11/1)   25·00

STAMP VARIETIES EXPLAINED

In this *Stanley Gibbons Guide* James Watson presents the knowledge essential to every philatelist—the various processes that are used to print stamps. By demonstrating just how varieties occur, he enables collectors to assess their relative importance and shows what contribution, if any, they can make to philatelic study. See the preliminary pages of this Catalogue for details of the current edition.

1964 (10 Feb). *World's Fair, New York.*   [S. G. 285/98]

V12. " Ghost " town.

On certain values of the air stamps with the initials " NS " the town of " Kailahun " has been inserted just North of Pendembu and then partially erased, leaving traces of the word. It appears as normal on all values of the postage set, but not on the air stamps.
In No. 295 the variety has been confirmed as existing on the stamp with initials " BE ".

Europe coast omitted

European coast line from Spain to Denmark is omitted on all values of the air stamps with initials " AA "

V13 Also shows initials

(b) Air

292	7d. – V12. "Ghost" town ...	...	...	...	3·50
	– V13. Europe coast omitted ...	...	...	90
293	9d. – V12. "Ghost" town ...	...	...	3·00
	– V13. Europe coast omitted ...	...	...	90
294	1s.3d. – V12. "Ghost" town ...	...	...	5·00
	– V13. Europe coast omitted ...	...	...	1·40
295	2s.6d. – V12. "Ghost" town ...	...	...	6·00
	– V13. Europe coast omitted ...	...	...	1·40
296	3s.6d. – V12. "Ghost" town ...	...	...	6·00
	– V13. Europe coast omitted ...	...	...	2·00
297	6s. – V12. "Ghost" town ...	...	...	6·00
	– V13. Europe coast omitted ...	...	...	2·00
298	11s. – V12. "Ghost" town ...	...	...	4·00
	– V13. Europe coast omitted ...	...	...	2·75

1964 (11 May). *President Kennedy Memorial Issue.* [S. G. 299/312]

V12. " Ghost " town.

The town " Kailahun " appears as normal on the 2s. and 5s. postage stamps but also exists on all values of the air stamps in the position with the initials " VU ". However it only comes on about one sheet in four because these stamps were printed in sheets of 120 and then cut up into four panes of 30.

(b) Air

306	7d. – V12. "Ghost" town ...	...	...	...	1·50
307	9d. – V12. "Ghost" town ...	...	...	...	1·50
308	1s.3d. – V12. "Ghost" town ...	...	...	...	1·60
309	2s.6d. – V12. "Ghost" town ...	...	...	...	1·75
310	3s.6d. – V12. "Ghost" town ...	...	...	...	1·90
311	6s. – V12. "Ghost" town ...	...	...	...	2·50
312	11s. – V12. "Ghost" town ...	...	...	...	3·50

1964–66. *New Currency.*   [S. G. 313/64]

(i) First issue (4.8.64).

2c   2c

Normal   **V14**

2c. Dropped " c " in the surcharge (R. 3/2).

V15. 1c. Small "c" in the surcharge (R. 3/3).

(a) Postage

314	2c. on 3d. – V14. Dropped "c"	...	...	...	5·00
315	3c. on 3d. – V1. Double dot	...	...	...	4·50

(b) Air

326	1l. on 1s.3d. – V12. "Ghost" town	...	...	...	4·00
327	2l. on 11s. – V12. "Ghost" town	...	...	...	5·50

(iii) Third issue (4.65).

(a) Postage

336	1c. on 1½d. – V15. Small "c" ...	...	...	...	4·00

(b) Air

350	7c. on 9d. – V12. "Ghost" town	...	...	...	2·50
	– V13. Europe coast omitted	...	...	2·75

1965 (19 May). *Sir Milton Margai and Sir Winston Churchill Commemoration.*   [S. G. 366/76]

(a) Postage

367	3c. on 3d. – V1. Double dot ...	...	...	...	3·00

Singapore

1955 (4 Sept)–61. *Views.*   [S. G. 38/52]

V1
1c. A flaw between the two Sampans resembles a reflection in the water of one of the figures (Pl. 1B, R. 9/1) (MG 6.56, 1.57).

V2
In the next printing an attempt was made to retouch the flaw but it is still visible as a disturbed background.

V4
1c. Extra white dot in bow of sampan (Pl. 1D, R. 9/2). Later touched out.

V7
1c. Black flaw on Queen's neck. Also retouch to right of head (Pl. 1A, R. 3/3).

1c. White flaw on the rear of the small sampan (Pl. 1B, R. 10/1).

V8

38	1c. – V1. Reflection in water ...	...	...	...	2·75
	– V2. Reflection retouched	...	...	...	1·10
	– V4. Extra dot in bow	...	...	...	1·10
	– V7. Neck flaw and background retouch	...	1·00
	– V8. White flaw on sampan	...	...	1·00

1960 (3 June). *National Day.*   [S. G. 59E/60E]

4c. The "o" and "f" at foot of stamp are joined together (R. 7/2).

V3

59E	4c. – V3. Joined "of"	...	...	...	...	1·75

1962 (31 Mar)–66. *Orchids and birds.* Wmk Block CA (upright).   [S. G. 63/77E]

V9
1c. Green blotch over yellow and red flower, immediately below green leaf extending to left (Pl. 1A, R. 5/3).

V6
4c. White spot on pectoral fin (Pl. 1A, R. 6/10).

V10
6c. White vertical line cuts across fish's tail (Pl. 1A, R. 10/2).

V11
8c. Bottom of "N" in "CENTS" broken (Pl. 1A, R. 8/2).

V13
8c. Retouches occur on the red of the petals at left (Pl. 1A, R. 7/4).

V5
20c. Nick in fin (R. 1/1)

63	1c. – V9. Leaf flaw ...	...	...	...	...	1·6
65	4c. – V6. Spot on fin	...	...	...	...	1·7
67	6c. – V10. Tail flaw ...	...	...	...	...	2·1
68	8c. – V11. Broken "N"	...	...	...	...	2·5
	– V13. Petal retouches	...	...	...	...	2·5
71	20c. – V5. Nick in fin	...	...	...	...	1·5

1966 (1 Mar)–67. As No. 63 but wmk Block CA (sideways).
                                                           [S. G. 83/88]

83   1c. – V9. Leaf flaw   ...   .   1·10

1970 (15 Mar). *World Fair, Osaka.*   [S. G. 128/32]

15c. Large black gash on middle Japanese
character (R. 2/2).

V12

128   15c – V12. Gash in character   ...   .   2·50

1974 (7 July). *Centenary of Universal Postal Union.*   [S. G. 235/7]

10c. Brown flaw above border
shaped like hook (R. 10/10).
V14

235   10c. – V14. Brown hook   ...   .   2·10

1975 (29 June). *"Science and Industry".*   [S. G. 253/5]

V15   V16

10c. Yellow dot by base   10c. Blue dot on rim of
of telescope at   left-hand dish
right resembles a   aerial (R. 4/4).
window (R. 3/4).

253   10c. – V15. Yellow window ...   .   2·00
       – V16. Blue dot ...   .   2·00

1975 (9 Aug). *Tenth National Day.*   [S. G. 256/9]

10c. Squiggle on "D" of "DAY"
(R. 10/8).
V17

256   10c. – V17. Squiggle on "D" ...   .   1·90

Solomon Islands

1961 (19 Jan). *New Constitution, 1960.* Wmk Block CA (sideways).   [S. G. 97E/9E]

Damaged "9". Consists of the tail-end of the "9" being rounded with a fine line leading off to the left. The loop of the "9" is also damaged at the base (R. 10/3).

V1

99E	9d. – V1. Damaged "9"	...	...	...	...	2·75
	Ea. Wmk Crown to right					
	– V1. Damaged "9"	...	...	...	...	2·75

1965 (24 May). *Pictorials.*   [S. G. 112/26]

V2
½d. White spot on tiara (Pls 1A and 1B, R. 3/4).

V3
1½d. Large flaw in central upper prong, later retouched (Pl 1A, R. 8/1).

V4
6d. The fifth line below "D" of "6D" is shortened by flaw (Pl 1B, R. 1/1).

V5
£1 Violet flaw above right eyebrow (Pl 1B, R. 2/2).

112	½d. – V2. White spot	...	...	...	...	1·40
114	1½d. – V3. Chipped prong	...	...	...	...	1·60
118	6d. – V4. Short line	...	...	...	...	2·10
126	£1 – V5. Extra eyebrow	...	...	...	...	17·00

1965 (25 Oct). *International Co-operation Year.*   [S. G. 129/30]

V8. Broken leaves. See V6 of Antigua.

129	1d. – V8. Broken leaves	...	...	...	...	2·25
130	2s.6d. – V8. Broken leaves	...	...	...	...	3·00

1966 (24 Jan). *Churchill Commemoration.*   [S. G. 131/4]

V9. Dot by St. Paul's. See V2 of Ascension.

2d., 1s.3d. and 2s.6d. White flaw by Queen's ear (Pl 2B) (R. 7/2).

V11

131	2d. – V9. Dot by St. Paul's	...	...	...	1·50
	– V11. Flaw by Queen's ear	...	...	...	1·50
132	9d. – V9. Dot by St. Paul's	...	...	...	2·10
133	1s.3d. – V9. Dot by St. Paul's	...	...	...	2·50
	– V11. Flaw by Queen's ear	...	...	...	2·50
134	2s.6d. – V9. Dot by St. Paul's	...	...	...	3·25
	– V11. Flaw by Queen's ear	...	...	...	3·25

1966 (14 Feb)–67. *Decimal Currency.*   [S. G. 135A/52B]

A. *Wmk upright*

135A	1c. on ½d. – V2. White spot	...	...	...	1·25
139A	5c. on 6d. – V4. Short line	...	...	...	2·00
152A	$2 on £1 – V5. Extra eyebrow	...	...	...	10·50

B. *Wmk sideways*

135B	1c. on ½d. – V2. White spot	...	...	...	1·10
139B	5c. on 6d. – V4. Short line	...	...	...	1·75
152B	$2 on £1 – V5. Extra eyebrow	...	...	...	11·00

1968 (7 Feb). *Quatercentenary of the Discovery of the Solomon Islands.*   [S. G. 162/5]

8c. Scratch on Queen's face resembling scar (R. 5/2).

V7

163	8c. – V7. Scratch on face	...	...	...	...	2·50

STAMP VARIETIES EXPLAINED

In this *Stanley Gibbons Guide* James Watson presents the knowledge essential to every philatelist—the various processes that are used to print stamps. By demonstrating just how varieties occur, he enables collectors to assess their relative importance and shows what contribution, if any, they can make to philatelic study. See the preliminary pages of this Catalogue for details of the current edition.

1968 (20 May)–71. *Views.*   [S. G. 166E/80E]

V10   V12

6c. Yellow flaw between "P" and "s" appears as an extra air bubble (Pl 1A, R. 10/5).

45c. White spot over hills appears as rising Sun (R.2/3).

170	6c. – V10. Extra air bubble ...	...	...	... 1·90
178	45c. – V12. Rising sun	...	...	... 3·75

1969 (13 Aug). *Third South Pacific Games, Port Moresby.*
     [S. G. 184E/88]

3c. Red spot between "G" and "A" of "GAMES" (R. 5/2).

V13

184E   3c. – V13. Spot between "G" and "A"   ...   ...   1·75

1970 (17 Aug). *Centenary of British Red Cross.*   [S. G. 197/8]

35c. Diagonal line between "T" and "I" of "BRITISH" (Pl. 1A, R. 3/2).

V14

198   35c. – V14. Diagonal line between "T" and "I"   ...   3·50

South Africa

1952 (14 Mar). *Tercentenary of Landing of Van Riebeeck.*
[S. G. 136/40]

1d. " Pennon " over first " A "
of " AFRICA " (R. 6/6).

V1

V41
1d. Wrinkle on forehead
(R. 2/14).

V2
2d. " Full Moon " flaw
under " R " of "AFRIKA"
(R. 6/3).

V3

V62
4½d. Apostrophe in date:
" 195'2 " (Rt. pane,
R. 4/4).

Line through sails consists
of a vertical line from near
the top of the stamp extending to the stamp below (Pair
comprising R. 11/2 and R.
12/2).

Normal   V4

1s. Missing shadow behind
foot of seated figure
(R. 19/2).

137	1d.	– V1. "Pennon" over "A"	...	...	...	1·90
		– V41. Wrinkle on forehead	...	...		1·90
138	2d.	– V2. "Full Moon"	...	...	...	1·90
		– V3. Line through sails (vert pair)	...	...	1·90
139	4½d.	– V62. "195'2" variety	...	...		2·25
140	1s.	– V4. Shadow missing	...	...	...	7·00

1952 (26 Mar). *South African Tercentenary International Stamp
Exhibition.*   [S. G. 141/2]

141	1d.	– V1. "Pennon" over "A"	...	...	...	2·10
		– V41. Wrinkle on forehead	...	...	...	2·10
142	2d.	– V2. "Full Moon"	...	...	...	3·75
		– V3. Line through sails (vert pair)	...	...	4·25

1953 (2 June). *Coronation.*   [S. G. 143]

Scar on neck (Cyls. 66 and 98,
R. 4/7).

V5

| 143 | 2d. *deep violet-blue* | – V5. Scar on neck | ... | 2·10 |
| | a. *Ultramarine* | – V5. Scar on neck | ... | 2·10 |

1953 (1 Sept). *Cape of Good Hope Stamp Centenary.*   [S. G. 144/5]

V48   V49
1d. Large brown dot   Smaller brown dot in
appears below the   similar position to V48
design under " 53 "   (R. 9/6 or 19/6).
of " 1953 " (R. 8/4
or 18/4).

Separate pairs of cylinders were used for each pane and during
the course of printing one of the pairs of cylinders became trans-
posed. Consequently when V48 occurs on R. 8/4, V49 comes on
R. 19/6 and when V48 occurs on R. 18/4, V49 comes on R. 9/6.

V55   V63
Large brown dot over " PO "   Damaged " 5 " in " 1953 "
of " POSTAGE " (R. 5/2 or   (R. 1/6 or 11/6).
15/2).

144	1d.	– V48. Large dot below "53"	...	...	...	1·40
		– V49. Smaller dot below "53"	...	...	...	1·40
		– V55. Large dot over "PO"	...	...	...	1·40
		– V63. Damaged "5" in "1953"	...	...	2·10

1954 (23 Feb). *Centenary of Orange Free State.*   [S. G. 149/50]

Diagonal flaw near top left-hand corner
over " O " of " O.V.S." in 2d. and of
" O.F.S." in 4½d. (Upper pane R. 1/4).

V29

| 149 | 2d. | – V29. Diagonal flaw | ... | ... | ... | 1·40 |
| 150 | 4½d. | – V29. Diagonal flaw | ... | ... | ... | 1·40 |

1954 (14 Oct). *Animals.* Wmk Multiple Springbok. [S. G. 151/64]

4d. Broken " A " in " Afrika " (R. 1/6).

V7

4½d. Short " u " in " Suid " (R. 2/9).

V8

156	4d. – V7. Broken "A"	...	...	...	...	2·40
157	4½d. – V8. Short "u"	...	...	...	...	3·00

1955 (21 Oct). *Centenary of Pretoria.* [S. G. 165/6]

6d. Scar on chin (R. 1/7).

V9

166	6d. – V9. Scar on chin	...	...	...	...	2·50

1958 (1 July). *Centenary of Arrival of German Settlers in South Africa.* [S. G. 168]

Upper part of "d" in " Suid " damaged (R. 6/1).

V10

168	2d. – V10. Damaged "d"	...	...	...	...	1·90

1959 (1 May). *Fiftieth Anniv. of the South African Academy of Science and Art, Pretoria.* [S. G. 169]

Normal   V11   V12

Normally there are two diagonal lines in the cogwheel at the base of the shield. In 47 stamps in the sheet one or other of the diagonal lines is missing. See MG 8.59

Extra spur to wheat sprig at bottom right extending towards shield, also coloured flaw under " 3d." (R. 20/1).

13

69	3d. – V11. Lower line missing	...	...	...	50
	– V12. Upper line missing	...	...	...	50
	– V13. Extra spur	...	...	...	1·60

1959–61. As Nos. 156, etc., but wmk. Union Coat-of-Arms. [S.G. 170/77]

73	4d. – V7. Broken "A"	...	...	...	3·00

1960 (2 May). *Fiftieth Anniv. of Union of South Africa.* [S. G. 179/82]

1s. Curved line over " UT " of " SOUTH " resembling a bracket (R. 20/4).

V14

181	1s. – V14. "Bracket" flaw	...	...	...	...	2.50

1960 (31 May). *Union Day.* [S. G. 184]

Flaw resembling split across head of Verwoerd (R. 19/3).

V15

184	3d. – V15. Split head ...	...	...	...	...	2·10

1961 (31 May)–63. *Pictorials.* Wmk Union Coat-of-Arms. [S. G. 198E/210]

REPUBLIEK VAN SUID-AFRIKA

½c. Flaw resembling large " J " in front of " VAN " (Cyls. 104-66-45, R. 10/20).

V16

½c. Dotted line between and below " HE " of " KINGFISHER " (Cyls. 104–66–45, R. 6/17).

V30

5c. Stop after " BAOBAB " (Cyl. 31-S1, R. 5/15).

V17

V31

5c. White spot on " F "
of " OF " (Cyl. 31-S1,
R. 5/14).

V39

5c. White flaw left of tree
resembling a comet
(Cyl. 31-S1, R. 5/16).

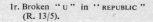

V18

1r. Broken " U " in " REPUBLIC "
(R. 13/5).

198Ea	½c. – V16. "J" before "VAN"	...	...	...	1·40
	– V30. Dotted line	...	...	...	1·25
204	5c. – V17. Stop after "BAOBAB"	...	...	...	1·90
	– V31. Spot on "F"	...	...	...	1·50
	– V39. Comet flaw	...	...	...	1·50
210	1r. – V18. Broken "U"	...	...	...	15·00

1961–63. *Pictorials.* No wmk.   [S. G. 211/219]

V19

2½c. Damaged door (Cyl. 3D-5D, R. 1/15).

V20

2½c. Broken arch (Cyl. 3D-5D, R. 3/15).

V44

2½c. Broken line under first " A " of " CON-
STANTIA " and " A " damaged (Cyl. 3A–5A,
R. 4/14).

V21

3c. Flaw resembling inverted
" v " under " SHRIKE " (Cyl.
S8–S35, R 2/4).

V22

10c. Falling leaves to
right of tree (Cyl.
51A–121A, R. 5/17).

V40

10c. Brown spot on
" ST " of " KAAFSTAD "
(Cyl. 51B–121B, R. 5/20).

213Ea	2½c. – V19. Damaged door	...	...	...	2·00
	– V20. Broken arch	...	...	...	2·00
	– V44. Broken line	...	...	...	1·60
214	3c. – V21. Inverted "v"	...	...	...	2·00
215	5c. – V17. Stop after "BAOBAB"	...	...	...	1·50
	– V31. Spot on "F"	...	...	...	1·50
	– V39. Comet flaw	...	...	...	1·50
217Ea	10c. – V22. Falling leaves	...	...	...	2·75
	– V40. Spot on "ST"	...	...	...	2·50

1961 (1 Dec). *Fiftieth Anniv. of First South African Aerial
Post.*   [S. G. 220]

Red spot in cloud over first " 1 " of
" 1961 " (R. 1/11).

V64

220   3c. – V64. Spot in cloud   ...   .   2·75

1962 (20 Aug). *Unveiling of Precinct Stone. British Settlers Monument,
Grahamstown.*   [S. G. 222/3]

V36

2½c. " tt " of " Settlers "
joined as if by a hyphen
(R. 14/1).

V23

12½c. The " buoy " flaw consists
of a brown spot on the
surface of the water above
" H " of " CHAPMAN "
(R. 10/5).

222	2½c. – V36. "tt" joined by "hyphen"	...	...	1·75
223	12½c. – V23. "Buoy" flaw	...	...	8·00

STAMP VARIETIES EXPLAINED

In this *Stanley Gibbons Guide* James Watson presents
the knowledge essential to every philatelist—the various
processes that are used to print stamps. By demonstrating just how varieties occur, he enables collectors to
assess their relative importance and shows what contribution, if any, they can make to philatelic study. See the
preliminary pages of this Catalogue for details of the
current edition.

1963–67. *Pictorials.* Wmk Multiple RSA in triangle.

[S. G. 227E/36]

V38
1c. Grey flaw on top of right hand flower (Cyl. S25–23A R. 15/2).

V75
1c. White spot beneath first "A" of "AFRICA" (Cyl. S33A–S13A, R. 17/4).

V56
Red flaw after "C" of value appears as a hyphen (Cyl 261–260A, R. 5/2). The illustration is taken from the original printing of July 1968. In the Nov 1968 printing the colour is not so solid and the outline at top is missing and in the printing of Dec 1968 the outline is clear but the colour is solid only in the centre.

V85
White "berry" at the top of the left-hand flower (Cyl. 241–240D, R. 9/9).

V37
2c. Flaw at top centre appearing as "Moon" (Cyl. G2–G1A, R. 9/4).

V76
2c. Flaw on Cradle resembling a bolt (Cyl. G2–G1B, R. 20/4).

V47
2½c. Large flaw on right-hand of roof of building (Cyl 17D–23, R. 2/20).

V65
2½c. Dark patch to right of roof (Cyl 17D–23, R 1/18).

2½c. Violet smudge over right edge of roof appearing as a flag (Cyl. 60–S27, R. 1/7).

'50

V32
12½c. Prominent white dot on tip of left large leaf (Cyl 3–1–6B, R. 4/14).

V51
15c. White flaw on upper left of cooling tower (Cyl 208–207–206B, R. 2/18).

227E	1c. – V38. Grey flaw	...	...	...	1·00
	– V75. White spot	...	...	...	1·75
229	2c. – V37. "Moon"	...	...	...	1·25
	– V76. Bolt on Cradle	...	...	...	1·75
230a	2½c. – V50. "Flag" on roof	...	...	1·40
231	5c. – V17. Stop after "BAOBAB"	...		2·00
	– V31. Spot on "F"	...	...	...	2·00
	– V39. Comet flaw	...	...	...	2·00
233E	10c. *sepia-brown and light emerald*			
	– V22. Falling leaves	...	...	...	2·00
	– V40. Spot on "ST"	...	...	...	2·00
	Ea. *Sepia-brown and green*			
	– V22. Falling leaves	...	...	...	2·00
	– V40. Spot on "ST"	...	...	...	2·00
236	1r. – V18. Broken "U"	...	...	...	55·00

1964–72. *Pictorials.* As 1961–63 but designs redrawn.

[S. G. 237E/50E]

V52
15c. Two black smudges over chimney stack (Cyl 281–280–279B R. 5/1).

V57
1r. Retouch to background inside top frame towards centre (Cyl G11–4–6B, R. 12/2).

1c. Broken "C" in "AFRICA" (Cyl 219–218C, 241–240C, 261–260C, R. 4/4).

46

238	1c. (perf 15 × 14)	– V46. Broken "C" ...	1·00
		– V85. White berry ...	1·25
	a. Perf 13½ × 14	– V56. "Hyphen" flaw	1·50
241E	2½c. *Violet and green*	– V47. Roof flaw ...	1·50
		– V65. Patch by roof ...	1·90

241*Ea.* 2½c.   *Reddish violet and green*
              – V47. Roof flaw   ...   .   1·40
              – V65. Patch by roof ...   .   1·90
246   12½c. – V32. Dot on leaf   ...   .   3·00
247   15c. – V51. Cooling tower bulge ... ...   4·50
              – V52. Smoking chimney ...   .   4·50
250E   1r.   – V57. Retouch   ...   .   11·50

1963 (11 Dec). *First Meeting of Transkei Legislative Assembly.*
                                            [S. G. 251E]

Brown smudge by second window
(Cyl. S31B, R. 20/1).

V42

251E   2½c. – V42. Window flaw   ...   .   2·40

1964 (10 July). *400th Anniv. of Death of Calvin (Protestant Reformer).*
                                            [S. G. 254]

" Feather in cap "
(All panes, R. 2/1
and 2/11).

V24

" Mole " (All panes,
R. 5/10 and 5/20).

V25

White spot under " AF " of " AFRICA " (Pane D,
R. 3/13).

V33

Brown patch on white part of beard
(All panes, R. 3/1 and 3/11).

V43

Numerous other varieties of a minor nature occur on this stamp.

254   2½c. – V24. "Feather in cap"   ...   .   1·25
              – V25. "Mole"   ...   .   1·25
              – V33. Spot under "AF"   ...   .   1·25
              – V43. Patch on beard ...   .   1·25

1964 (12 Oct). *Fiftieth Anniv. of South African Nursing Association.*
                                            [S. G. 255/7]

V26

12½c. Screened background extends into upper margins extending
from R. 11 Nos. 2 to 4.

12½c. White spot over " U " of
" SOUTH " (R. 11/5).

V27

257   12½c. – V26/7. Screened background in gutter and
                spot over "U". *Block of* 10   24·00

1966 (6 Dec). *Verwoerd Commemoration.*   [S. G. 266/8]

2½c. Line rising from roof of
Union Buildings resembles
a radio mast (Cyl. 201A–200A,
R. 19/3).

V77

V45

3c. White flaw below " 3c "
(Pane B, R. 4/12).

V53

12½c. A series of blue
diagonal lines on map
above the head (Pane
B, R. 18/5).

266   2½c. – V77. Radio mast   ...   .   1·6⁰
267   3c. – V45. Flaw below "3c"   ...   .   1·7⁵
268   12½c. – V53. Extra map markings ...   .   3·75

1968 (21 Sept). *Inauguration of General Hertzog Monument, Bloemfontein.* [S. G. 273/5]

12½c. A line of orange dots across cheek appears as a gash (Pane A, R. 4/15).

V54

275 12½c. – V54. Gash on cheek ...   .   3·25

1969 (Jan–May). *Natal Kingfisher.* [S. G. 276/7]

V59
½c. Red diagonal streak to right of beak (Pane A, R. 4/3).

V60
½c. Red dash to left of " ½ " (Pane C, R. 3/3).

276 ½c. – V59. Streak by beak   ...   .   1·40
     – V60. Dash left of "½"   ...   .   1·40

1969 (15 Mar). *South African Games, Bloemfontein.* [S. G. 278/9]

2½c. and 12½c. Large spot and halo left of value (Cyl 275B, R. 3/4).

'66

78 2½c. – V66. Spot by value   ...   .   2·10
79 12½c. – V66. Spot by value   ...   .   3·75

---

9 (7 July). *World's First Heart Transplant and 47th South African Medical Association Congress.* [S. G. 280/1]

12½c. Two white dots centrally over " SA " of " RSA " (R. 18/4).

58

31 12½c. – V58. Dots over "SA" ...   .   4·50

1969 (6 Oct). *Centenary of First Stamps of South African Republic (Transvaal).* [S. G. 282/3]

V61
2½c. Ring-shaped flaw beneath mountain peak on right (Pane B. R. 15/5).

V67
2½c. Large white spot left of value (B and D panes, R. 10/3).

282 2½c. – V61. Ring beneath mountain peak   ...   ...   1·25
     – V67. Spot left of value   ...   .   1·75

1969–72. *Pictorials.* Phosphor issue. [S. G. 284E/98]

12½c. White spot by bottom left leaf (Pane B, R. 2/11).

V68

284E ½c. – V59. Streak by beak **   ...   .   1·40
      – V60. Dash left of "½" **   ...   .   1·40
      Er. Wmk reversed
      – V59. Streak by beak **   ...   .   5·50
      – V60. Dash left of "½" **   ...   .   5·50
288E 2½c. – V47. Roof flaw   ...   .   1·40
      – V65. Patch by roof   ...   .   , 1·75
296 12½c. – V68. Leaf spot ...   .   3·50

** Due to the transposition of A and B panes with C and D panes, varieties which originated on panes A and B now occur on panes C and D respectively.

1970 (14 Feb). *Water 70 Campaign.* [S. G. 299/300]

2½c. Large chocolate spot in top right margin (Pane B, R. 5/6).

V69

299 2½c. – V69. Spot in margin   ...   .   1·25

1972–74. As Nos. 284 etc., but no wmk.   [S. G. 313/25]

V 70

4c. Extra imprint appears above " RSA " (R. 1/5, Cyl. 546–545–544B–543).

V78   V86   V71

4c. Blue blob beneath sheep's horn (Cyl. 546–545–544A–543, R. 5/7).

9c. White patch around " PROTEA " (Cyl. 595–596–597, R. 4/18).

20c. Spot by bird's leg (R 5/1, Cyl. 515–514–513B).

317	4c. – V70. Extra imprint	...	...	...	...	2·40
	– V78. Blue blob	...	...	...	...	1·75
320Ea	9c. – V86. Patch around "PROTEA"			...	...	3·00
323	20c. – V71. Spot by leg	...	...	...	...	2·50

1973 (1 Aug). *Birth Centenary of C.J. Langenhoven (politician and composer of national anthem).*   [S. G. 335/7]

V72
4c. White flaw over " L " of " Langenhoven " (B pane, R. 5/3).

V73
Black line extending from left eye to ear appears as a " scar " (B pane, R. 5/4).

V74

5c. Cylinder scratch extends diagonally across two stamps (R. 5, Stamps 7 and 8).

335	4c. – V72. Flaw over "L"	...	...	...	...	1·75
	– V73. "Scarred face" flaw	...	...	∴	...	1·75
336	5c. – V74. Cylinder scratch ...		...	...	...	1·75

1974 (20 Nov)–76. *Flowers, birds and fish.*   [S. G. 348/63]

V79   V91

                                               Normal

4c. White spot beneath face-value (Cyl. 660–661–662–663B–S12, R. 10/2).

5c. Weak shading on bird's wing to right of head (A and B panes, R. 8/1).

V80   V81

9c. Scratch through face-value (Cyl. 637–638–639–640B–S9, R. 4/1).

9c. " A " of " RSA " has a comma-shaped flaw at its foot (Cyl. 637–638–639–640B–S9, R. 10/10).

V82

10c. Blue line extending across the stamp gives the fish the appearance of being speared (Cyl. 633–634–635–636B–S8, R. 3/9).

15c. Pale blob behind bird's tail resembles a sunburst (Cyl. 625–626–627–628B–S7, R. 10/10).

V83

351a	4c. – V79. White spot	...	...	...	...	1·7
352	5c. – V91. Weak wing flaw	...		...	...	1·7
355	9c. – V80. Vertical scratch	...		...	...	1·7
	– V81. Comma on "A"	...		...	...	1·7
356	10c. – V82. "Speared fish"	...		...	...	1·9
358	15c. – V83. Sun flaw	...	...	...	...	2·5

1975 (14 Aug). *Centenary of Genootskap van Regte Afrikaners (Afrikaner Language Movement).* [S. G. 384]

Brown dot to right of year date (Cyl. 692–693–694B–S17, R. 9/9).

V 84

384 4c. – V84. Brown dot ... ... 1·60

1975 (10 Oct). *Inauguration of the Language Monument, Paarl.* [S. G. 386/7]

5c. Black dot under "A" of "Afrikaanse" (Pane A, R. 5/19).

V87

387 5c. – V87. Dot under "A" ... ... 1·75

1976 (5 June). *World Environmental Day.* [S. G. 404E/7]

4c. Orange flaw in front of cheetah resembles a "burning bush" (R. 16/1).

V89

404E 3c. – V89. Burning bush ... ... 2·10
Ea. Toned yellow paper
– V89. Burning bush ... ... 3·25

1976 (6 Nov). *Family Planning and Child Welfare.* [S. G. 410]

Accent over "S" of "RSA" (Pane B, R. 10/7).

'88

10 4c. – V88. Accent over "s" ... ... 1·75

977 (14 Feb). *International Wine Symposium, Cape Town.* [S. G. 411]

First "die" in Afrikaans inscription at left is missing (Every third sheet, R. 1/3).

90

11 15c. – V90. "Die" missing ... ... 9·00

1977 (27 May). *Proteas or Succulents.* [S. G. 414/34]

2c. Latin name at foot of stamp is broken (Pane B, R. 1/8).

V92

V93 V94
4c. Magenta blobs across "4" (Pane B, R. 4/7). 4c. Magenta blobs under "4" (Pane B, R. 7/10).

415 2c. – V92. Broken latin name ... ... 1·00
417 4c. – V93. Blobs across "4" ... ... 1·10
– V94. Blobs under "4" ... ... 1·10

POSTAGE DUE STAMPS

1950–58. [S. G. D39/44]

Dotted diagonal line below value in the colour of the frame (R. 18/7).

V34

4d. Crude retouch to flaw on "4" (R. 1/1).

V35

D39 1d. – V34. Diagonal line ... ... 1·25
D40E 2d. *black and violet*
– V34. Diagonal line ... ... 1·25
Eb. *Black and reddish violet*
– V34. Diagonal line ... ... 1·40
D41 3d. – V34. Diagonal line ... ... 1·75
D42 4d. – V34. Diagonal line ... ... 2·75
– V35. Retouch ... ... 2·75
D43 6d. – V34. Diagonal line ... ... 3·00
D44 1s. – V34. Diagonal line ... ... 7·00

1961 (14 Feb). Value in cents.   [S. G. D45/50]

5c. Spur projects upwards from ball of "5" (R. 3/8).

V28

D48   5c. – V28. Spur to "5"   ...   .   3·75

1961 (31 May)–69.   [S. G. D51/58]

D55   5c. *deep blue and grey-blue* – V28. Spur to "5"   ...   3·50
D56   5c. *black and grey-blue*   – V28. Spur to "5"   ...   3·00

South Georgia

1971 (15 Feb)–76. *Decimal Currency.* Wmk Block CA (upright). [S. G. 18/31]

V1

No. 20. Various dots and blotches on the bottom margin (Pl. 1B, R. 8/4).

V2

No. 20a. Retouch above seal's tail flipper (Pl. 2A, R. 9/6).

V5

2p. on 2d. Short centre bar in surcharge (Both Plates, R.6/2).

20	1½p. on 5½d. – V1. Marginal marks				3·00
	a. Larger surcharge (wmk sideways).				
	– V2. Retouch				2·75
21	2p. on 2d. – V5. Short centre bar				2·75

1973 (1 Dec*). *Royal Wedding.* [S. G. 38/39]

V8. Cotton on dress. See V8 of Ascension

39 15p. – V8. Cotton on dress ... ... 3·00

*This is the local date of issue; the Crown Agents in London released the stamps on 14th November.

1976 (21 Dec). *75th Anniv. of "Discovery" Investigations.* [S. G. 46/49]

8p. White flaw on the top of the ship's fore-mast resembles a flag (Pl. 1B, R. 1/3).

V3

47 8p. – V3. White flag ... ... 2·50

THE ELIZABETHAN

Uniform with this volume, the *Elizabethan Specialised Stamp Catalogue* covers all other aspects of the stamps of the present reign, from both Great Britain and the British Commonwealth, in considerable detail. See the preliminary pages of this Catalogue for details of this annual publication.

1977 (7 Feb). *Silver Jubilee.* [S. G. 50/52]

V4

6p. Blob on " H " of " SOUTH " (Pl. 1D, R. 5/1).

V6

6p. Serif on foot of " I " in " Jubilee " (Pl. 1C, R. 4/2).

V7

11p. Black " button " on Queen's dress above arm (Pl. 1C, R. 5/4).

11p. Magenta bow tie on Queen's gown (Pl. 1C, R. 5/2)

V9

50	6p. – V4. Blob on "H"					3·50
	– V6. Serif on "I"					3·50
51E	11p. – V7. Black button					5·00
	– V9. Flaw on gown					4·00

1977 (17 May)–78. As Nos. 20 etc., but Wmk CA Diagonal. [S. G. 53/66]

55 1½p. on 5½d. – V2. Retouch ... ... 2·50

South West Africa

1952 (14 Mar). *Tercentenary of Landing of Van Riebeeck.*
[S. G. 144/8]

V1/4, V7. See corresponding varieties on South Africa Nos. 136/40.

145	1d. – V1.	"Pennon" over "A"	...	...	...	1·90
	– V7.	Wrinkle flaw	...	...	...	1·90
146	2d. – V2.	"Full Moon"	...	...	...	2·25
	– V3.	Line through sails (vert pair)	...	...	3·25
148	1s. – V4.	Shadow missing ...	...	...	...	15·00

1963 (16 Mar). *Opening of Hardap Dam.*
[S. G. 192]

V5   V6

Line through " WEST " and   White flaws over " T A " of
bottom frame line (R. 2/2).   " WEST AFRICA " (R. 1/7).

192	3c. – V5.	Line through "WEST"	...	...	...	2·25
	– V6.	"TA" flaw ...	...	...	...	2·25

1964 (1 Oct). *400th Anniv. of Death of Calvin (Protestant Reformer).*
[S. G. 196/7]

V10   V11

2½c. Brown-purple flaw   2½c. Brown-purple gash above
below ear (R. 1/1).   eye (R. 4/3).

196	2½c. – V10.	Earring flaw	...	...	...	2·00
	– V11.	Gash in forehead	...	...	...	2·00

1966–72. *Pictorials.*
[S. G. 202/16]

4c. " s " of " SOUTH " is broken
and largely missing (Cyls
319–318B, R. 16/5).

V12

209	4c. – V12.	Broken "s" in "SOUTH"	...	...	...	2·10

1967 (6 Jan). *Verwoerd Commemoration.*
[S. G. 217/19]

V8   V9

3c. White patch at left   15c. Brown spot on forehead
margin above value   (R. 2/4).
(Pane A, R, 1/12).

218	3c. – V8.	White patch	...	...	...	1·90
219	15c. – V9.	Spot on forehead ...	...	...	...	3·50

1970 (24 Aug). *150th Anniv. of Bible Society of South Africa.*
[S. G. 228/9]

12½c. Letters " SWA " shaved at
bottom (Pane A, R. 10/4).

V13

229	12½c. – V13. "SWA" shaved	...	...	...	5.50

1971 (31 May). *"Interstex" Stamp Exhibition, Cape Town.*
[S. G. 231]

5c. Black line at back of head appearing as a feather (R.1/4).

V14

230	5c. – V14. "Feather" in hair ...	...	...	...	2·50

1973 (1 Sept). *Succulents.*
[S. G. 241/56]

V15   V17

20c. Vertical dash at
left appears as an
" extra cactus " (Cyl.   4c. "Cucumber" flaw on stone (Cyl
620 to 624, R. 10/9).   208/11, P212, B pane R. 9/6).

244	4c. – V17.	"Cucumber" flaw	...	...	...	1·5(
252	20c. – V15.	Extra cactus	...	...	...	1·6(

1973 (1 Sept)–78. Coil stamps   [S. G. 257/9]

1c. White flaw shaped like a berry on the
     topmost spine (every 22nd stamp).

V16

257a   1c. – V16. White berry   ...   .   1·60

Southern Cameroons

Southern Rhodesia

1960 (1 Oct)–61. *"CAMEROONS U.K.T.T." overprint.* [S. G. 1/12]

V6. Line flaw see No. S.G. 70Ea of Nigeria.

V1

6d. A major retouch occurs on left side of stamp immediately below and to left of " c " of " CAMEROONS " overprint. This appears as heavy diagonal shading (Pl. 2–1, R. 2/10).

V2

6d. The " Colon " variety consists of two small black dots near left-hand edge of stamp by " c " of " CAMEROONS " (Pl. 2–1, R. 3/10).
    Although V1 and V2 are constant on some sheets they have not yet been found together on the one sheet.

2	1d. (70 Ea)	– V6. Line flaw ...	...	...	...	1·75
7a	6d.	– V1. Major retouch	...	...	...	5·00
		– V2. "Colon" variety ...	...	...	7·00

1964 (19 Feb). *Pictorials.*   [S. G. 92/105]

V3

6d. White dot after " LILY " (R. 4/9).

V2

2s. Large white dot over " IA " of " RHODESIA " (R. 5/8).

V1

10s. A large coloured flaw on the small guineafowl gives the appearance of an extra feather (R. 2/2).

97	6d. – V3. Dot after "LILY"	...	...	...	...	2·40
101	2s. – V2. Dot over "IA"	...	...	...	...	6·50
104	10s. – V1. Extra feather	...	...	...	...	24·00

Sri Lanka

1972 (8 Sept). *International Book Year.* [S. G. 593]

V14
Arm of right-hand figure
is damaged at the
bottom (R. 8/5).

V15
Forehead of left-hand
figure has a notch
(R. 8/8).

593	20c. – V14. Damaged arm	...	...	...	...	1·75
	– V15. Notch in head	...	...	...	...	1·75

1973 (17 May). *Opening of Bandaranaike Memorial Hall.* [S. G. 598]

V16
Scratch above country-name, extending into the margin
(Cyl. 7A–7A, R. 8/1).

Dot on parapet (Pl. 1A–2A and
3A–2A, R. 5/4).

V17

598	15c. – V16. Blue scratch	...	...	...	...	1·60
	– V17. Dot on parapet	...	...	...	...	1·60

Swaziland

1962 (24 Apr). *Pictorials.*   [S. G. 90/105]

V2
½c. Flaw resembling figure " 2 " under shield and between sticks (Imprint at right, R. 4/6).

V11
Left-hand stick is damaged at its base (R. 10/2).

V6
2½c. Retouch between " s " and " w " of " SWAZILAND " appears as a red patch (Imprint at right. R. 1/6).

V7
12½c. White spot below right leg of " w " of " SWAZILAND " (Imprint at left, R. 4/10).

90	½c. – V2. "2" flaw	...	...	...	...	2·10
	– V11. Damaged stick	...	...	...	...	2·10
93E	2½c. *black and vermilion*					
	– V6. "sw" retouch	...	...	...	...	1·60
Ea.	*Black and dull red*					
	– V6. "sw" retouch	...	...	...	...	1·60
99	12½c. – V7. Spot below "w"	...	...	...	...	2·50

1965 (17 May). *I.T.U. Centenary.*   [S. G. 113/4]

V3. Broken "U" in "TELECOMMUNICATIONS". See V1 of Antigua.

113	2½c. – V3. Broken "U"	...	...	...	...	2·50
114	15c. – V3. Broken "U"	...	...	...	...	3·75

1965 (25 Oct). *International Co-operation Year.*   [S.G. 115/6]

V5. Broken leaves. See V6 of Antigua.
V4. Broken "Y" in "YEAR". See V3 of Antigua.

115	½c. – V5. Broken leaves	...	...	...	...	2·50
116	15c. – V4. Broken "Y"	...	...	...	...	8·00
	– V5. Broken leaves	...	...	...	...	3·75

PHILATELIC TERMS ILLUSTRATED

The essential philatelic dictionary. Terms covering printing methods, papers, errors, varieties, watermarks, perforations and much more are explained and illustrated, many in full colour. See the preliminary pages of this Catalogue for details of the current edition.

1968 (6 Sept). *"INDEPENDENCE 1968 overprint.*   [S. G. 142/60]

V8   **V9**

3½c. White spot below tail of " z " of " SWAZILAND " (Imprint at right, R. 2/7).

7½c. Large white flaw between " LA " of " SWAZILAND " R. 2/7).

20c. Mosquito's right wing tip missing (imprint at right, R. 4/3).

V10

145E	2½c.	*Black and vermilion*					
		– V6. "sw" retouch	...	...	...	...	1·25
	Ea.	*Black and dull red*					
		– V6. "sw" retouch	...	...	...	...	1·25
147E	3½c. – V8.	Spot below "z"	...	...	...	...	1·25
150	7½c. – V9.	Dot between "LA"	...	...	...	...	1·40
152E	12½c. – V7.	Spot below "w"	...	...	...	...	1·50
154	20c – Vi0.	Clipped wing	...	...	...	...	3·50

1974 (22 July). *75th Birthday of King Sobhuza II.*   [S. G. 212/14]

3c. "F" for second "E" in College (Pl. 1 (× 5) right pane, R. 1/5 stamp 5).

V13

212	3c. – 13 "F" for "E"	...	...	...	...	1·25

1977 (7 Feb). *Silver Jubilee.*   [S. G. 268/70]

50c. Black line on Coronation Coach, beneath " w " of " SWAZILAND " (Pl. 1D, R. 4/5).

V12

270	50c. – V12. Black line beneath "w"	...	...	3·25

POSTAGE DUE STAMPS

1933–57. Wmk Script CA. Ordinary paper.   [S. G. D1/2]

V1. Bolder "d". See Basutoland V3.

D2a	2d. – V1. Bolder "d"	...	...	...	...	2·50

Tanganyika

1961 (9 Dec)–64. *Independence.*   [S. G. 108/19]

Normal R. 10/9 R. 10/10
V1

10c. The shading on the nurse's skirt above and to the right of
" KA " of " TANGANYIKA " has been retouched on Pl. 1B,
R. 10, Nos. 9 and 10. The shading appears very rough and
uneven and extends over the edge on the right of stamp 9 and
below the right-hand corner of stamp 10. The general appearance is more solid looking, compared with the normal screen
of dots.

1s. " Wart " on finger of
right hand (R. 10/3).

V3

1s.30 White blob on " 6 " of " 1961 " (R. 9/8).

V5

1s.30 White flaw after " DEC." which resembles a
colon instead of a stop (R. 10/9). This was retouched on No. 115Ea but not entirely success-
fully as the area is darker than in the normal
stamps.

V6

20s. A large white flaw in the sky above
the mountain gives the appearance
of it being extra high (R. 8/8).

V2

109	10c. – V1.	Retouches *Each*	...	...	...	1·50
114	1s. – V3.	"Wart" on finger	...	...	...	2·00

115E	1s. 3d.	*red, yellow, black, brown and blue*				
		– V5. Blob on "6" ...	...	...	...	2·00
		– V6. Colon flaw ...	...	...	...	2·00
	Ea.	*Red, yellow, black, brown and dp. blue*				
		– V5. Blob on "6" ...	...	...	...	2·00
		– V6. Colon retouched	...	...	...	2·00
119	20s.	– V2. Mountain flaw	...	...	...	19·00

1962 (9 Dec). *Inauguration of Republic.*   [S. G. 120/3]

50c. White spot in front of goggles
right of flame (R. 5/8).

V7

121	50c. – V7. Spot above frame ...	...	...	...	1·60

OFFICIAL STAMPS

1961 (9 Dec). Postage stamps overprinted "OFFICIAL". [S. G. 01/8]

02	10c. (109) – V1. Retouches *Each*	...	...	...	1·75
07	1s. (114) – V3. "Wart" on finger	...	...	...	2·25

Tanzania

1965 (9 Dec). *Pictorials.*   [S. G. 128/41]

5c. White spot under " T " of
" TANZANIA " (Pl. 1B, R. 7/9).

V4

128   5c. – V4. Spot under "T"   ...   .   1·00

1975 (17 Nov). *Surcharges.*   [S. G. 173/6]

No. 174. The " 2/– " is
misplaced,   being
higher and closer to
the border (All Plates,
R. 4/5).

Normal   V8

174   2s. on 1s.50 – V8. Misplaced surcharge   ...   ...   7·00

1978 (1 July). *Road safety.*   [S. G. 238/41]

50c. Broken "0" later retouched (Pl. 1B,
R. 3/1).

V9

238   50c. – V4. Broken "0"   ...   .   2·00

OFFICIAL STAMPS

1965 (9 Dec). Postage stamps overprinted "OFFICIAL".
                                              [S. G. O9/16]

O9   5c. (128) – V4. Spot under "T"   ...   .   1·10

Tokelau

1966 (8 Nov). *Surcharges.* [S. G. 6/8]

V5

6d. Sliced loop of " 6 " (R.3/8, 5/7, 6/7 on printing (*a*); R. 2/5, 3/1, 3/7 on printing (*b*)).

6   6d. – V5. Sliced "6"   ...   .   2·50

1967 (10 July). *Decimal Currency.* Perf 14 line. [S. G. 9/15E]

The line perf measures 14 × 13·9 and the comb perf is 14 × 13·8

V1

3c. The lower loop is damaged (R. 1/6).

Normal   V2

5c. Indistinct impression of figure at left gives a white ghostlike appearance (R.7/9).

5c., 7c. Plate cracked at bottom of stamp (R. 10/3).

V8

V7

5c. Broken " o " in " TOKELAU " (R.5/6) (pig 5).

V9

7c. Broken " 7 " (R. 9/10).

TOKELAU ISLANDS
V3

All values. " TOKELAU ISLANDS " set closer together (R. 7/1).

V6

All values. Upper part of " A " of " ISLANDS " blocked out (R. 5/6).

12E	3c. – V1. Damaged "3"	...	...	...	...	2·00
	– V3. Narrow setting	...	...	...	...	2·25
	– V6. Blocked "A"	...	...	...	...	2·10
	Ea. Comb perf					
	– V1. Damaged "3"	...	...	...	...	2·00
	– V3. Narrow setting	...	...	...	...	2·40
	– V6. Blocked "A"	...	...	...	...	2·10
13E	5c. – V2. Ghost flaw	...	...	...	...	2·40
	– V3. Narrow setting	...	...	...	...	2·00
	– V6. Blocked "A"	...	...	...	...	2·00
	– V8. Cracked plate	...	...	...	...	2·25
	Ea. Comb perf					
	– V2. Ghost flaw	...	...	...	...	5·00
	– V3. Narrow setting	...	...	...	...	2·25
	– V6. Blocked "A"	...	...	...	...	2·00
	– V7. Broken "o"	...	...	...	...	2·25
	– V8. Cracked plate	...	...	...	...	2·25
14E	7c. – V3. Narrow setting	...	...	...	...	2·40
	– V6. Blocked "A"	...	...	...	...	2·40
	– V8. Cracked plate	...	...	...	...	2·50
	– V9. Broken "7"	...	...	...	...	2·40
	Ea. Comb perf					
	– V3. Narrow setting	...	...	...	...	2·25
	– V6. Blocked "A"	...	...	...	...	2·00
	– V8. Cracked plate	...	...	...	...	2·25
	– V9. Broken "7"	...	...	...	...	2·00
15E	20c. – V3. Narrow setting	...	...	...	...	4·00
	– V6. Blocked "A"	...	...	...	...	3·25
	Ea. Comb perf					
	– V3. Narrow setting	...	...	...	...	4·00
	– V6. Blocked "A"	...	...	...	...	3·25

1971 (20 Oct). *Handicrafts.* [S. G. 25/32]

V4

15c. Top of " c " of value is sliced off (Pl. 1A, R. 10/2). This developed during printing.

30   15c. – V4. Sliced "c"   ...   .   7·50

Tonga

Trengganu

1966 (18 June). *Centenary of Tupou College and Secondary Education.*   [S. G. 162/73]

OU COLLE
    &   Air. Misplaced ampersand (R. 5/5).
ARY EDUC

V2

168	5d. – V2. Misplaced "&"	...	...	...	1·00
169	10d. on 1d. – V2. Misplaced "&"	...	...	...	1·25
170	1s. – V2. Misplaced "&"	...	...	...	1·40
171	2s.9d. on 2d. – V2. Misplaced "&"	...	...	...	1·75
172	3s.6d. on 5d. – V2. Misplaced "&"	...	...	...	1·90
173	4s.6d. on 1s. – V2. Misplaced "&"	...	...	...	2·10

1969. *Emergency Provisionals.*   [S. G. 271/9]

277	1s. on 2s.9d. on 2d. – V2. Misplaced "&"	...	...	1·50
278	1s. on 3s.6d. on 5d. – V2. Misplaced "&"	...	...	2·75
279	1s. on 4s.6d. on 1s. – V2. Misplaced "&"	...	...	1·50

1972 (15 July). *Fifth Anniv. of Coronation.*   [S. G. 403/12]

All values. Missing " A " in " TAUFA'AHAU " (R. 2/1).

V3

(a) Postage

403	5s. – V3. Missing "A"	...	...	...	...	1·75
404	7s. – V3. Missing "A"	...	...	...	...	1·75
405	10s. – V3. Missing "A"	...	...	...	...	1·75
406	17s. – V3. Missing "A"	...	...	...	...	2·75
407	60s. – V3. Missing "A"	...	...	...	...	7·00

(b) Air

408	9s. – V3. Missing "A"	...	...	...	...	1·75
409	12s. – V3. Missing "A"	...	...	...	...	2·25
410	14s. – V3. Missing "A"	...	...	...	...	2·25
411	21s. – V3. Missing "A"	...	...	...	...	3·25
412	75s. – V3. Missing "A"	...	...	...	...	7·50

1965 (15 Nov). *Flowers*   [S. G. 100/6]

1c., 2c., 5c., 10c. and 20c. Bottom of collar is shortened (Pl. 1B, R. 10/10).

V1

V2, V4/6 and V8/15. See corresponding varieties on Johore Nos. 166/72.

V16   V17

All values except 6 and 15c. Malay script in the top right-hand corner has an extra diamond-shaped character (Pl. 1A, R. 8/3).

All values except 6 and 15c. Shaved diamond beneath Malay script (Pl. 1B, R. 9/2).

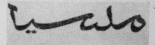

V18

All values except 6 and 15c. Diamond-shaped characters beneath Malay script at right are completely missing (Pl. 1B, R. 10/3).

100	1c. –	V1.	Short collar	...	...	...	1·40
		– V2.	Caterpillar flaw	...	...	...	1·60
		– V4.	Line through petal	...	...	...	1·40
		– V5.	Dot under "A"	...	...	...	1·40
		– V9.	Spot above "VANDA"	...	...	...	1·60
		– V10.	Dot on flower	...	...	...	1·60
		– V11.	Dot on top petal	...	...	...	1·60
		– V16.	Extra diamond	...	...	...	1·40
		– V17.	Shaved diamond	...	...	...	1·40
		– V18.	Missing diamonds	...	...	...	1·60
101	2c. –	V1.	Short collar	...	...	...	1·75
		– V16.	Extra diamond	...	...	...	1·40
		– V17.	Shaved diamond	...	...	...	1·40
		– V18.	Missing diamonds	...	...	...	1·60
102	5c. –	V1.	Short collar	...	...	...	1·40
		– V6.	Short stroke	...	...	...	1·40
		– V12.	"A" and "P" joined	...	...	...	1·60
		– V13.	Dot under "H"	...	...	...	1·60
		– V14.	Dot under "5c"	...	...	...	1·60
		– V15.	Flaws on country name	...	...	...	1·90
		– V16.	Extra diamond	...	...	...	1·40
		– V17.	Shaved diamond	...	...	...	1·40
		– V18.	Missing diamonds	...	...	...	1·60
104	10c. –	V1.	Short collar	...	...	...	1·40
		– V8.	Brown blotches	...	...	...	1·40
		– V16.	Extra diamond	...	...	...	1·40
		– V17.	Shaved diamond	...	...	...	1·40
		– V18.	Missing diamonds	...	...	...	1·60
106	20c. –	V1.	Short collar	...	...	...	1·40
		– V8.	Brown blotches	...	...	...	1·40
		– V16.	Extra diamond	...	...	...	1·60
		– V17.	Shaved diamond	...	...	...	1·60
		– V18.	Missing diamonds	...	...	...	1·75

Trinidad and Tobago

1956 (20 Dec). *Surcharge.* [S. G. 280]

V1. Sliced " C " in " CENT " (R. 11/1).
V1

V2. Broken " O " in " ONE " (R. 8/5).
V2

280	1c. on 2c. – V1. Sliced "C"	...	...	...	8·00
	– V2. Broken "O"	...	...	...	8·00

1960 (24 Sept)–65. *Views.* [S. G. 284/97]

V3

5c. White line after second " D " in " TRINIDAD " (Pl. 1C. R. 3/2).

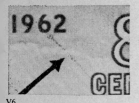

V7

5c. White flaw on " A " of " TOBAGO " (Pl. 2B, R. 4/8).

286E	5c. – V3. Line after "D"	...	...	...	1·00
	– V7. Flaw on "A"	...	...	...	1·00

1962 (31 Aug). *Independence.* [S. G. 300/4]

V4
8c. White line joins " & " and " T " of " TOBAGO " (R. 8/1).

V5
White flaw below "9" of " 1962 ". This has been partially retouched (R. 9/1).

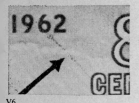

V6

Diagonal retouch from " 6 " of " 1962 " to " C " of " CENTS " (R. 10/1).

These three varieties are probably related due to cylinder damage.

301	8c. – V4. "&" and "T" joined	...	...	...	1·90
	– V5. "Extra cloud"	...	...	...	1·90
	– V6. Sky retouch ...	...	...	...	1·90

1965 (10 Dec). *Eleanor Roosevelt Memorial Foundation.* [S. G. 312]

V9

25c. Tip of central laurel leaf on right is extended to right (R. 1/5).

312	25c. – V9. Wilted leaf	...	...	...	2·10

1966 (8 Feb). *Royal Visit.* [S. G. 313/16]

V8
5c. Stop after " the " (R. 10/5).

V15a. Blocked " c " in " Scarborough " (R.4/1).
V15b. " c " retouched, the inside curve being irregular (R. 4/1).

8c.

313	5c. – V8. Stop after "the"	...	...	...	1·60
314	8c. – V15a. Blocked "c"	...	...	...	1·75
	– V15b. "c" retouched	...	...	...	1·75

1969–72. *Pictorials.* Wmk Block CA (sideways). [S. G. 339E/54E]

V19

3c. Broken scrollwork (Pl. 1A × 4, R. 4/4).

V 11
5c. Lower scrollwork broken at top (Pl. 2B, R. 9/4).

V 18
5c. Scrollwork broken at bottom right (Pl. 2A–3A–2A–2A, R. 10/2).

A. *Chalk-surfaced paper.*
B. *Glazed, ordinary paper.*

					A.	B.
340E	3c. – V19. Broken scrollwork	...	...	†	2·00
341E	5c. – V11. Broken scrollwork	...	...	2·50	1·75
	– V18. Broken scrollwork	...	...	†	2·00

1971 (25 Oct). *Christmas.*   [S. G. 399/402E]

3c. Left top " T " of " CTS " is missing (Pl. 1A, R. 1/1).

V10

399   3c. – V10. Broken "T" in "CTS"   ...   .   1·40

1973–74. As No. 341 but Wmk Block CA (upright).   [S. G. 432/3]

433   5c. – V18. Broken scrollwork   ...   .   5·50

1974 (18 Nov). *Centenary of Universal Postal Union.*   [S. G. 451/3]

40c. Dot on " H " of " THE " (Pl. 1A, R. 1/3).

V12

451   40c. – V12. Dot on "H"   ...   .   2·10

1974 (2 Dec). *First Anniv. of World Voyage by H. and K. La Borde.*   [S. G. 454/6E]

40c. Cylinder scratch extends from the top of the stamp to the " A " in " TOBAGO " (Pl. 1A, R. 7/1).

50c. Flaw between " 0 " and " c " of " 50c " appears as an apostrophe (Pl. 1A, R. 6/2).

V13   V14

454   40c. – V13. Cylinder scratch ...   .   2·50
455   50c. – V14. Apostrophe flaw ...   .   3·00

1975 (23 June). *International Women's Year.*   [S. G. 457/8]

30c. Male figure has a break in the arm at the wrist (R. 7/1).

V16

458   30c. – V16. Broken arm   ...   .   2·00

1975 (27 Nov). *35th Anniv. of British West Indian Airways.*
                                        [S. G. 461/4]

30c. Flaw on the tail-plane appears as a " shell-hole " (Pl. 1A, R. 3/1).

V17

462   30c. – V17. Shell-hole   ...   .   2·00

Tristan da Cunha

1963 (12 Apr). *Tristan Resettlement* [S. G. 55/67]

V1/3. See corresponding varieties on St. Helena Nos. 176 and 185

55	1d. (176) – V1. Damaged lower fin	...	...	1·50
64	1s.6d. (185) – V2. Spot on tail ...	...	...	3·75
	– V3. Large spot behind tail	...	...	3·75

1964 (1 Feb). *Red Cross Centenary.* [S. G. 69/70]

1s.6d. Break in front jewel of tiara occurs in all stamps in row 2, Pl. 1a–1a.

V4

70	1s.6d. – V4. Broken jewel	...	...	...	5·00

1965 (25 Oct). *International Co-operation Year.* [S. G. 87/88]

V6. broken leaves. See V6 of Antigua.

87	1d. – V6. Broken leaves	...	...	...	2·50
88	6d. – V6. Broken leaves	...	...	...	7·50

1966 (24 Jan). *Churchill Commemoration.* [S. G. 89E/92]

V7. Dot by St. Paul's. See V2 of Ascension.
V11. Flaw by Queen's ear. See V11 of Solomon Islands.

89E	1d. – V7. Dot by St. Paul's ...	...	...	3·00
90	3d. – V7. Dot by St. Paul's ...	...	...	4·00
91	6d. – V7. Dot by St. Paul's ...	...	...	6·50
92	1s.6d. – V7. Dot by St. Paul's ...	...	...	9·50
	– V11. Flaw by Queen's ear	...	...	9·50

1966 (1 Oct). *Inauguration of W.H.O. Headquarters, Geneva.* [S. G. 99/100]

V10 Dotted "r" in "Headquarters". See V5 of Dominica.

9	6d. – V10. Dotted "r" ...	...	...	...	3·00

1967 (10 July). *Centenary of First Duke of Edinburgh's Visit to Tristan.* [S. G. 109/12]

6d. Figure " 8 " of " 1867 " damaged (R. 3/2).

V8

10	6d. – V8. Damaged "8"	...	...	...	1·50

1977 (7 Feb). *Silver Jubilee.* [S. G. 212/14]

V12
10p. Comma under "1" of "TRISTAN" (Pl. 1B, R. 3/1).

V13
15p. Dot before "N" (Pl. 1A, R. 1/2).

V14
15p. Serif on "J" of "JUBILEE" (Pl. 1D, R. 2/1).

V15
25p. "Torn Carpet" in the background, right of the heraldic lion (Pl. 1A, R. 2/3).

212	10p. – V12. Comma under "1"	...	...	...	2·50
213	15p. – V13. Dot before "N"	...	...	...	2·50
	– V14. Serif on "J"	...	...	...	2·50
214	25p. – V15. Torn carpet	...	...	...	3·25

1978 (19 Jan*). *Surcharge.* [S. G. 232/33]

7½p. Straight top serif to "1" in surcharge (Pl. 1C, all stamps in row 5)

Normal V16

233	7½p. on 25p. – V16. Straight serif	...	...	...	21·00

*This is the local date of issue. Covers dated 26th November 1977 were philatelic mail forwarded to the island for cancellation, the stamps having been released in London on 31 October 1977. Supplies for the island population did not arrive until 19th January.

POSTAGE DUE STAMPS

1957 (1 Feb). *Wmk Script CA.* [S. G. D1/5]

V5. Bolder "d". See V3 of Basutoland.
V9. Broken and seriffed "d". As V25 of Gibraltar but more pronounced, being a later state.

D2	2d. – V5. Bolder "d" ...	...	...	...	6·00
D4	4d. – V9. Broken and seriffed "d"	...	...	9·50

Turks and Caicos Islands

1964 (23 Apr). *400th Anniv. of Birth of William Shakespeare.*
[S. G. 257]

V1

V2

The flaw consists of a short green coloured line through the " 64 " of " 1564 " (R. 10/1).

Light patch on wall of theatre (R. 7/2).

257   8d. – V1. Date flaw ... ... 1·90
        – V2. Patch on wall ... ... 1·90

1965 (25 Oct). *International Co-operation Year.* [S. G. 260E/1]

V3. Broken leaves. See V6 of Antigua.
260E   1d. – V3. Broken leaves ... ... 1·40
261   8d. – V3. Broken leaves ... ... 1·60

1966 (24 Jan). *Churchill Commemoration.* [S. G. 262/5]

V4. Dot by St. Paul's. See V2 of Ascension.
V8. Flaw by Queen's ear. See V11 of Solomon Islands.
262   1d. – V4. Dot by St. Paul's ... ... 1·75
263   2d. – V4. Dot by St. Paul's ... ... 1·75
        – V8. Flaw by Queen's ear ... ... 1·75
264   8d. – V4. Dot by St. Paul's ... ... 2·10

1966 (1 Oct). *Bicentenary of "Ties with Britain".* [S. G. 268/70]

8d. Top of second " c " of large " caicos " is broken (Pl. 1A, R. 7/1).

V6
269   8d. – V6. Broken "c" ... ... 3·75

1967 (1 Feb). *Pictorials.* [S. G. 274/87]

6d. White flaw on Queen's neck appearing as crack (R. 2/11).

V5
279   6d. – V5. Flaw on neck ... ... 1·60

1969 (8 Sept). *Decimal Currency.* Wmk Block CA (upright).
[S. G. 297E/311]

302   5c. on 6d. – V5. Flaw on neck ... ... 1·60
      a.   Wmk sideways
        – V5. Flaw on neck ... ... 1·60

1971 (2 Feb). *Decimal Currency.* [S. G. 333/46]

4c. Smudge on quay to left of " T " of " TURKS " (Pl. 1A, R. 3/3).

V7

336   4c. – V7. Smudge on quay ... ... 1·00

1972 (20 Nov). *Royal Silver Wedding.* [S. G. 372/3]

V9. Dot on curtain. See V4 of Anguilla.
373   20c. – V9. Dot on curtain ... ... 3·75

1977 (7 Feb–6 Dec). *Silver Jubilee.* [S. G. 472E/5]

25c. Silver dot behind Queen's head (Pl. 1C, R 4/4).

V10

473   25c. – V10. Silver dot ... ... 3·75

Tuvalu

1976 (1 Jan). *"TUVALU" overprints.*   [S. G. 4/25]

V1. Broken "A" see Gilbert Is.
23   20c.(18) – V1. Broken "A"   ...   .   3·75

Uganda

1962 (9 Oct)–64. Independence.   [S. G. 99/110]

V4

V1

10c. Flaw on stalk in front
of man's hand appears as
an extra flower (Pl. 1B,
R. 10/5).

1s.30 Dome flaw consists of a
large white flaw to left
of dome of Namirembe
Cathedral (Pl. 1A–1A,
R. 9/10).

100E 10c. *reddish brown*
     – V4. Extra flower   85
 Eb. Deep yellow-brown
     – V4. Extra flower   85

1965 (20 Feb). International Trade Fair, Kampala.   [S. G. 111/12]

Both values. Spherical flaw consisting
of disturbed screening-dots left of
the bird's wing (Pl. 1A, R. 10/10).

V5

111   30c. – V5. Background disturbance ...   .   1·50
112 1s.30 – V5. Background disturbance ...   .   1·90

1965 (9 Oct). Birds.   [S. G. 113/26]

50c. Large patch in lower right corner
(Pl. 1A–1A, R. 4/9).

V2

119   50c. – V2. Large patch   ...   .   1·50

1967 (26 Oct). *13th Commonwealth Parliamentary Association*
Conference.   [S. G. 127/30]

PARLIAMENTARY

30c. Second "R" in "PARLIA-
MENTARY" has short left foot
(R. 9/10).

V3

127   30c. – V3. Short "R" ...   .   1·10

1975 (9 Oct). *Ugandan Crops.*   [S. G. 149/62]

V6

V7

20c. Yellow blob on leaf
of sugar-cane
(Pl. 1H, R. 4/4).

30c. Retouched "C" in
face-value, the top
curve having a thick
end (Pl. 1A, R. 1/1).

150   20c. – V6. Yellow blob   ...   .   1·10
151   30c. – V7. Retouched "C"   ...   .   1·10

Zambia

1964 (24 Oct). *Views.* [S. G. 94/107]

V1

1d. White dot over X-ray machine (Pl. 1A, R. 3/6).

V4

3d. White diamond appears below " s " of " POSTAGE " (Pl. 1A, R. 9/1).

V2

5s. Third child has black line through head giving effect of a mortarboard (Pl. 1A, R. 6/9).

95	1d. – V1. White dot ...	...	...	...	1·10
97	3d. – V4. Diamond flaw	...	...	...	1·60
105	5s. – V2. "Mortar Board" ...	...	...	...	3·00

1965 (18 Oct). *First Anniversary of Independence.* [S. G. 112/15]

3d. White stop after " State " (Pl. 1B, R.7/1).

V3

112	3d. – V3. Stop after "State" ...	...	...	...	1·60

1966 (12 July). *Opening of Zambia University.* [S. G. 118/19]

3d. Distorted " M " in large " ZAMBIA " (Pl. 1B, R. 12/5).

V5

118	3d. – V5. Distorted "M"	...	...	...	2·50

1968 (16 Jan). *Decimal Currency.* [S. G. 129/40]

V6

1n. Projection to right of yellow window at top right appearing as an extra window (Pl. 1A, R. 2/3).

V7

1n. Black line through white window upper left of third column, also extending through yellow window below appearing as a rope (Pl. 1A, R. 9/9).

V8

10n. Large white patch below woman's left arm (Pl. 1A, R. 10/7).

V9

10n. Diagonal line of retouching between elbow and leaf (R. Pl. 1A, ?/10).

V10

10n. Dash of white by leaf edge (Pl. 1A, R. 7/2).

V12

White dot on woman's chest (Pl. 1A, R. 10/2).

V13

50n. White line on skirt (Pl. 1A, R. 1/7).

129	1n. – V6. "Extra window" ...	...	...	...	1·40
	– V7. "Rope from window"	...	...	...	1·40
134	10n. – V8. Patch under arm	...	...	...	1·75
	– V9. Retouch between elbow and leaf		...	...	1·75
	– V10. White dash by leaf edge		...	...	1·75
	– V12. Dot on chest	...	...	...	1·75
138	50n. – V13. Line flaw ...	...	...	...	3·00

1969 (18 June). *50th Anniv. of International Labour Organization.*   [S. G. 145/6]

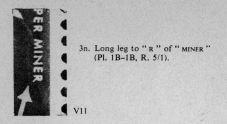

3n. Long leg to " R " of " MINER " (Pl. 1B–1B, R. 5/1).

V11

145   3n. – V11. Long leg to "R"   ...   .   1·75

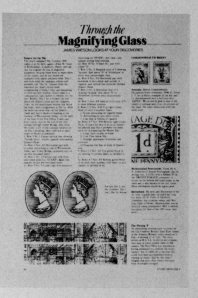